D1480462

ROOSEVELT
The Party Leader

ROOSEVELT

The Party Leader 1932-1945

SEAN J. SAVAGE

THE UNIVERSITY PRESS OF KENTUCKY

Editorial and Sales Offices: Lexington, Kentucky 40508-4008

Library of Congress Cataloging-in-Publication Data

Savage, Sean J., 1964-
  Roosevelt the party leader 1932-1945 / Sean J. Savage.
    p. cm.
  Includes bibliographical references and index.
  ISBN 0-8131-1755-0 (alk. paper)
  1. Roosevelt, Franklin D. (Franklin Delano), 1882-1945.
  2. Political leadership—United States—History—20th century.
  3. Democratic Party (U.S.)—History—20th century.   4. United
States—Politics and government—1933-1945.   I. Title.
E807.S28   1991
973.917'092—dc20

Contents

Acknowledgments

As with any scholarly endeavor, the writing of this book benefited from the intellectual inspiration, counsel, and assistance of many people. *Roosevelt The Party Leader, 1932-1945* is an expanded, revised version of my doctoral dissertation on Franklin D. Roosevelt's leadership of the Democratic party. I am greatly indebted to Professor Marc Landy of Boston College, my dissertation chairman, for his indispensable guidance during my research and writing. Professors Robert Faulkner of Boston College and Sidney Milkis of Brandeis University, two other members of my dissertation committee, provided valuable advice during my research and writing. I was greatly honored to have the page proofs reviewed by Arthur M. Schlesinger, Jr., William E. Leuchtenburg, Frank Freidel, Robert Kuttner, Frank Sorauf, Everett C. Ladd, Sidney Milkis, Doris Kearns Goodwin, and Charles D. Hadley.

The diligence of Nicole M. DeMatteis, my student assistant, enabled me to complete the index of this book. I would like to also thank my colleagues at Saint Mary's College for their patient understanding as I combined the preparation of this book for publication with a busy teaching schedule. During the entire process of creating this book, Joseph J. Dinneen, a great friend and political analyst, was always available for discussing ideas about the book's content.

Finally, but foremost, I would like to dedicate this book to my mother, Mrs. Irene M. Schollard.

INTRODUCTION
The Master
Party-Builder

Much has been written about the life and presidency of
Franklin D. Roosevelt. His biographers include such distinguished historians and political scientists as James
MacGregor Burns, Arthur M. Schlesinger, Jr., William E.
Leuchtenburg, and Frank Freidel. Roosevelt is generally
praised by scholars for his inspiring and successful leadership during the major crises of the Depression and World
War II. He is also widely perceived as the founder of the
modern presidency characterized by its elaborate bureaucracy devoted to serving presidential leadership, high public
expectations of presidential performance, and constant media
attention to presidential behavior.

Despite extensive research and publishing about Franklin
D. Roosevelt's life and presidency, no book has ever focused
exclusively on his leadership of the Democratic party. Major
biographies and histories of his presidency do provide discus-
sions of his relationship with the Party and prominent Democratic politicians. No book, however, entirely devotes its
content to explaining and analyzing Roosevelt's perception of,
plans for, and relationships within the Party. In order to
understand Roosevelt's political behavior, both before and
during his presidency, one must recognize two goals that he
wanted to achieve for the Party that extended beyond his own
political ambition for public office.

First, he wanted the Democratic party to become an electorally successful, enduring majority party in national politics and public policy. This was no small task. From 1860
until 1932, the Democrats had elected only two presidents
and usually held a minority of seats in both houses of Congress. Other than southern whites and Irish Catholics, few
voters felt a strong, visceral identification with the Party.

Second, Roosevelt wanted to transform the Party into a

distinctly liberal party in its ideology and policy agenda. His
own liberalism was a product of his mentor relationships with
Theodore Roosevelt, Woodrow Wilson, and Endicott Peabody,
his prep school headmaster, and his experiences in New York
state politics. Except for a brief period when progressive
legislation was promoted by the Wilson administration and
enacted by a Democratic Congress, the party was not widely
perceived as the liberal party within the American two-party
system—until Roosevelt's presidency. He hoped that liberalism would unite the conflicting northern and southern
wings of the Party behind an ideology and policy agenda that
would seek to address commonly-held economic grievances
through federal intervention. He also believed that transforming the Party into a distinctly liberal one would expand
its electoral base by attracting non-Irish urban ethnics and
liberally-inclined Republicans, independents, and third-
party members.

By assessing Roosevelt's actions and decisions in intraparty affairs according to his pursuit of these two goals, we
can understand why Roosevelt occasionally and consciously
threatened his own political career. For example, Roosevelt's
ideological commitment to the liberal transformation of the
Party motivated him to clash with John Raskob, the powerful,
conservative chairman of the Democratic National Committee from 1928 to 1932, who vindictively sought to deny
Roosevelt the Democratic presidential nomination in 1932.
Likewise, he launched a courageous yet quixotic attempt to
defeat well-entrenched southern conservative senators in the
Democratic primaries of 1938. This approach to studying
Roosevelt's party leadership enables us to understand that
Roosevelt did not merely intend to manipulate the Party as a
personal vehicle for his presidential candidacies. More importantly, this perspective helps to explain why the fulfillment of
his party-building objectives for the Party endured long after
his presidency.

Because existing biographies provide thorough explana-
tions of his pre-presidential life and his career in the New
York state senate and the Wilson administration, this book
begins with an explanation of the development of Roosevelt's

party-building strategy during the 1920s. Roosevelt's efforts to end the conservative domination of the Democratic National Committee and to make the New York state Democratic party more attractive to traditionally Republican upstate voters are significant as harbingers of his party-building tactics as president. If this book began with an analysis of Roosevelt's 1932 campaign, it would overlook the importance of the 1920s as a period in which Roosevelt formulated the party-building objectives that he wanted to achieve for the Democratic party.

Franklin D. Roosevelt was a masterful party leader having few, if any, equals among American presidents. He operated within the American political system in which the separation of powers, federalism, and primary nominations discourage the type of strong, centralized party leadership that a prime minister can exercise in a unitary, parliamentary system. Still, he emerges as an unusually successful presidential party leader. Several presidents, including Thomas Jefferson, Andrew Jackson, and Woodrow Wilson, were able to unite and mobilize the Democratic party enough to win federal elections and achieve major legislative victories during their administrations. Roosevelt not only accomplished these political goals during his presidency, but also developed an enduring coalition of voting blocs and interest groups, a vibrant party structure responsive to them, and an ideology and policy agenda which dominated electoral politics and public policy for over twenty years after his death. This book chronicles Franklin D. Roosevelt's unparalleled accomplishment of presidential party leadership.

1 The Development of a Party-Building Strategy

From 1921 until 1928, Franklin D. Roosevelt devoted most of his political efforts toward improving the ideology, structure, finances, and voter appeal of the Democratic party. Despite the Republican landslide of 1920, he was confident that the Democratic party could become the majority party in national politics if it developed a coherent ideology and specific policy proposals that addressed the economic problems confronted by ordinary Americans.[1] The Party, he believed, should clearly distinguish itself from the Republicans and offer the voters a clear choice. As the 1920s progressed, he became even more convinced that his party would chronically lose presidential elections and remain the minority party in national politics as long as it continued to express an ill-defined, vacillating conservatism as the only alternative to the Republican party's articulate, well-defined conservatism.[2]

During the 1920s, disunity and discord within the party intensified over the Prohibition issue. Opposing positions on this issue exacerbated the stark, antagonistic cultural differences between urban ethnic Democrats of the North and rural Protestant Democrats of the South and West.[3] Roosevelt was dismayed that leading Democrats, both "wets" like Al Smith and "drys" like William Gibbs McAdoo, focused on this implacably divisive issue, hampering his efforts to reorganize and reunite the Party.[4] Roosevelt avoided the issue by supporting Prohibition as a local option to be determined by a referendum.[5]

In October 1921, Roosevelt sent a letter to the Democratic National Committee proposing a full-time party bureaucracy at a national headquarters and periodic national conferences of rank-and-file Democratic activists. He suggested that discussing issues and party principles would facilitate the development of a common ideology and unite the fragmented Party.[6] The DNC ignored these proposals. Following the bitterly divisive Democratic National Convention of 1924 and the subsequent defeat of its nominee, John Davis, Roosevelt submitted similar proposals, hoping they would stimulate the Party's ideological development as a true party "of progress and liberal thought."[7] Once again, he was rebuffed by the DNC. Roosevelt enjoyed a rapport, though, with Cordell Hull, DNC chairman from 1921 to 1924.[8] He admired Hull's success in paying off the 1920 campaign debt of nearly $300,000, partially through his personal finances.[9] He also created Victory Clubs to raise party funds.[10] Clement Shaver, who succeeded Hull as chairman in 1924, lacked Hull's fiscal and organizational skills. To the dismay and protest of Roosevelt, Shaver reduced the party apparatus in order to cut costs.[11]

Roosevelt realized that organizational changes within the Party meant little if it remained so bitterly divided and dispirited that its members could not unite behind a presidential nominee and a common platform. Although he initially entered the nominating race of 1924 to prevent the nomination of William Gibbs McAdoo, Governor Al Smith soon became a viable candidate for the nomination. His candidacy inflamed anti-Catholic prejudice among Protestant Democrats, who rallied around McAdoo. McAdoo's refusal to repudiate the Ku Klux Klan's endorsement of his candidacy strengthened Smith's support among urban ethnics.[12] The Democratic State Committee of New York had met in April and pledged its delegates to Smith. Smith asked Roosevelt, a member of the state committee since 1921, to become chairman of his campaign committee. Roosevelt accepted the offer, thereby becoming the most prominent Protestant Democrat to support Smith.[13] He also agreed to deliver the nomination speech for Smith at the convention.[14] Roosevelt's "Happy Warrior" speech was the highlight of this tumultuous convention and endeared him to the growing number of urban ethnic Democrats. The convention itself was an egregiously raucous affair at which 103 ballots were required to nominate a compromise candidate, John Davis, for president.[15]

In an October 1924 letter to Eleanor, Roosevelt remarked
that "even if Coolidge is elected we shall be so darned sick of
conservatism . . . that we [will] get a real progressive landslide in 1928."[16] He already perceived the electorate's
conservatism to be crumbling as Robert La Follette, the presidential nominee of a progressive third party, received over 16
percent of the popular votes compared to 28.8 percent for
Davis.[17] La Follette's strident big business bashing populism
attracted the support of farmers and blue-collar workers.[18]
His appeal to low-income Americans, rural and urban, confirmed Roosevelt's earlier assumption that the party must
formulate an ideology and policy platform that would address
economic grievances being ignored by the Republican administration.

In December 1924, as he had done in 1921, Roosevelt proposed the creation of a permanent headquarters for the Party
and a more democratic, participatory decision-making process for determining positions on issues and public policy. He
circumvented the Democratic National Committee by sending a letter to over 3,000 Democrats, including delegates at
the recent convention.[19] He asked for suggestions on how to
strengthen and reform the party.

The respondents provided a myriad of proposals and opinions ranging from those of southern Bourbons like Carter
Glass and Albert Ritchie, who complained that the Democratic party was becoming too liberal, to those of western
progressives who asserted that their party was too conservative.[20] Despite this continuing internal discord over principles Roosevelt remained firm in his conviction that, in order
to transform itself into the majority party in national politics,
the Party must become "by definite policy, the Party of constructive progress, before we can attract a larger following."[21]
Addressing the New York Democratic State Convention in
1926, Roosevelt asserted that both national and state governments must be able and willing to become large enough and
active enough to solve social and economic problems.[22]

In his 1925 review of Claude Bowers's book *Jefferson and
Hamilton,* Roosevelt noted the ideological differences between these two founders and their relevance to the current

two-party system. Jefferson, founder of the Democratic party, expressed great faith in the wisdom of the common man's influence in public affairs. Hamilton rejected it.

Roosevelt admired Hamilton's success in establishing the fledgling government's finances on a sound basis. But he criticized the Federalist for his "fondness" for "Chambers of Commerce and his contempt for the opinion of the masses" which made him "wholly lacking in understanding . . . the rights of the poor, the uneducated, the average human being who, even then, made up the mass of his countrymen."[23] He concluded his review by stating that it was fortunate that the republic evolved according to Jeffersonian populism instead of Hamiltonian elitism.

This review illustrates Roosevelt's desire to apply the ideals of Jeffersonian populism to the party politics of the 1920s, and expresses his contempt for economic policies dominated by business interests. His admiration of Hamilton's administrative and fiscal skills implies that he believed a "modern Jefferson" may be required to use the Hamiltonian means of a strong, effective, interventionist national government to achieve Jeffersonian ends.

In September 1928, after Roosevelt had served as floor manager and nomination speaker at the national convention, Smith asked him to run for governor.[24] Smith and his advisers realized that, in order to carry New York's electoral votes in the presidential election, they needed an attractive vote-getter as a gubernatorial nominee. When Roosevelt refused, they enlisted Eleanor's aid in persuading her husband, and appeals to his sense of duty to the Party finally convinced him to run.[25]

With barely six weeks to campaign for governor, Roosevelt was pessimistic about victory. Louis Howe, his top political aide, considered his acceptance of the nomination a fatal mistake that could destroy his political career.[26] Roosevelt assumed that Hoover's probable victory would spearhead a Republican landslide that would elect his Republican opponent, Albert Ottinger. Smith, fearing that Ottinger, a Jew, would attract traditionally Democratic Jewish votes, had secured the nomination of Herbert Lehman, a liberal Jewish

businessman and philanthropist, for lieutenant governor.[27]
Despite his reformer image created by his crusade as attorney
general against corrupt stock brokers, Ottinger was conservative on economic and social welfare issues.

Facing an uphill battle, Roosevelt had public opinion on his
side on one prominent issue in particular—hydroelectric
power. While Ottinger supported private ownership of it,
Roosevelt supported public ownership so that low-cost electricity could be provided to isolated, rural areas often neglected by private utility companies.[28] He exploited this issue
to appeal to traditionally Republican rural New Yorkers, and
also hastily strengthened the Democratic organizations in
upstate areas. In performing this task, he relied heavily on
James Farley, secretary of the Democratic State Committee.[29] To attract women voters in upstate New York, Nancy
Cook and Caroline O'Day, members of the Women's Division
of the Democratic State Committee, joined Eleanor in establishing units of the Women's Division.[30]

Roosevelt conducted a whirlwind campaign in which he
occasionally addressed issues of the presidential campaign,
especially in his strident denunciation of religious bigotry.[31]
In general, though, his rhetoric promised a continuation and
further development of Smith's progressive policies.[32] Despite his dynamic campaigning, Roosevelt was convinced that
he had lost the election. He was stunned to learn that, while
Smith had lost New York by 103,481 votes, he had been
elected governor by a margin of 25,564 votes.[33]

Because of his upset, razor-thin victory, Roosevelt immediately became aware of the need to strengthen the state
party organizations, especially in upstate rural areas. He
realized that the votes of independents and progressive Republicans had been indispensable to his narrow victory margin. Smith's failure to attract these same votes explained why
he had lost his own state in the presidential election. Roosevelt was so attractive to independents that contributions
to the Independent Citizens Committee for Roosevelt and
Lehman totaled more than $300,000, while contributions to
the entire state party totaled only $134,000.[34]

Roosevelt realized that he could not rely on the votes of

independents and ticket-splitting Republicans to assure his re-election as governor and the election of Democratic majorities to the state legislature. According to Kenneth S. Davis, "Roosevelt strove mightily toward a consummation of his long effort, initiated in the aftermath of his 1920 defeat, to make the New York Democracy a smoothly functioning amalgam of city and country, in his public image, a symbol of the process and of its end."[35] By January 1929, he had established a permanent press bureau for the state party, with an annual budget of $100,000. Its primary purpose was to disseminate news to rural newspapers, especially news about agriculture and the voting records of local state legislators on agricultural issues.

Roosevelt chose James Farley, who would become chairman of the Democratic State Committee in 1930, to manage the effort to increase the number of Democratic voters and strengthen upstate Democratic organizations. Like Roosevelt, he understood that in order to make the New York Democracy more attractive to upstate voters it must distinguish itself from Tammany Hall and address issues that concerned rural voters, such as farm tax relief, road building, and electrification.[36] As state party chairman, and later as DNC chairman, however, Farley rarely asserted himself on matters of public policy and party ideology.[37]

In addition to his focus on rural interests, Farley recognized the importance of attracting women, not only as Democratic voters but also as party activists. He relied on the efforts of Eleanor Roosevelt, Caroline O'Day, and other leading members of the state party's Women's Division to accomplish this task.[38] Farley was confident that women in these heavily Republican areas would become active in the state Democratic party if it gave them a prominent, influential role in its organization and addressed issues that concerned them.[39] O'Day's prominence and success in attracting women into the state party later enabled her to be elected to Congress.[40]

Farley's primary partner was Edward Flynn, the newly-appointed secretary of state and Democratic boss of the Bronx. Farley and Flynn did not hesitate to secure the replacement of upstate Democratic county chairmen whom they found to be ineffective.[41] They also tried to field a Democratic candidate for every elective office in Republican-dominated areas. According to Flynn, approximately 90 percent of the people Roosevelt appointed to state positions were registered Democrats, making his patronage policy more partisan than Smith's had been.[42]

As the most prominent and powerful leaders of New York's Democratic party, Roosevelt recognized the need to project an attractive public image that would personify his party. His two primary methods for accomplishing this were his statewide radio broadcasts and his inspection cruises of the canals and rivers of New York. In January 1929, Roosevelt directed the Democratic State Committee to arrange for him to deliver a one-hour, statewide radio broadcast once a month.[43] Through these broadcasts, he delivered his political messages directly to New Yorkers, circumventing upstate newspapers, which were often Republican-oriented.

Roosevelt's inspection cruises most dramatically symbolized his cultivation of upstate political support. The official purpose of these cruises was to inspect state construction projects. According to Ed Flynn, these visits to remote parts of New York inspired the development of active Democratic organizations in these areas. Flynn stated, "Many men and women who had never before taken an active part in politics were attracted to party membership."[44]

As Samuel Rosenman, counsel to the governor, later recalled, Roosevelt recognized party-building and his advocacy of a liberal policy agenda as being complementary. "Roosevelt taught me how closely these two subjects were intertwined . . . a good affirmative liberal program and a good party organization."[45] The need to build a party organization able to elect a Democratic majority to the state legislature was evident as the Republican domination of both houses opposed much of Roosevelt's policy proposals, such as farm tax relief, a gasoline tax earmarked for rural road building, agricultural research, and state-sponsored development of hydroelectric power.[46] The Republican control of the state legislature forced Roosevelt to compromise his policy objectives so that many of his bills, when passed, were weak, diluted versions of his original proposals.[47]

The stock market crash of 1929 and the ensuing Depression made Roosevelt realize how crucial the state election of 1930 would be, not only to his own career but also to his party and the viability of his liberal policy agenda. Roosevelt and Howe had originally planned for Roosevelt to run for president in 1936 because they had assumed that Hoover would be re-elected in 1932.[48] Hoover's declining popularity and his inability to solve the problems of the Depression convinced Roosevelt and Howe that the governor's re-election in 1930 should be impressive enough to convince party leaders that Roosevelt, unlike Smith, could win the next presidential election by being equally attractive to both rural Protestants and urban ethnics throughout the nation.[49] Roosevelt's own analysis of the 1928 presidential election made him aware of the growing importance of the urban ethnic vote, which was confirmed by later analyses by Samuel Lubell and Kristi Andersen.[50] Therefore, during his re-election campaign, Roosevelt focused on winning upstate rural votes in order to strengthen the party leaders' assessment of his budding presidential campaign and to facilitate the election of upstate Democrats to the state legislature with the hope of ending its Republican control.

In a five-page report entitled "Summary of the Situation," Howe pessimistically analyzed for Roosevelt the condition of the state's party organization.[51] Despite the party-building efforts of the governor, Flynn, and Farley, Howe asserts that a "State consciousness" was lacking in many upstate Democratic organizations. "There is no feeling in these localities that they are members of a powerful and triumphant State Organization to which every vote they give contributes its share toward the general success."[52] Howe recommended the purging of ineffective Democratic county chairmen, the creation of local Democratic clubs coordinated by the state committee, and a major expansion of the state committee's publicity division.

Roosevelt agreed with this analysis and granted Howe, Farley, and Flynn discretion in removing county chairmen who were ineffective and even disloyal through their collaboration with local Republicans. These chairmen tried but failed to re-elect William Bray, the sluggish, lackluster state chairman, at the 1930 Democratic state convention. Roosevelt secured the removal of Bray and the appointment of Farley as state chairman. Farley then created the Union of Democratic Clubs, which would purge anti-Roosevelt local chairmen.[53]

Sharing a flair for the dramatic in campaigning, Roosevelt and Farley arranged to have talking movies, then a novelty, made of speeches given by Roosevelt, Smith, and Senator Robert Wagner. These movies were especially attractive and effective in remote rural counties in which many people had not yet seen "talkies." Mrs. Merritt Van de Bogart, the associate chairman of the Democratic Committee of Tioga County, confidently told Howe that, because of these movies, the "age old serenity of this rock ribbed Republican County seems to be broken. We Democrats must make the most of it."[54]

Despite the Roosevelt campaign's special attention to rural, upstate WASPs, the Democratic State Committee strengthened its Naturalized Citizens Bureau to cultivate the urban ethnic vote. It was divided into twenty-eight divisions, one for each major ethnic group. In a letter to James J. Hoey, vice chairman of the Democratic State Committee, Howe estimated that this bureau needed an additional $40,000 for increased activity and $140,000 for publicity.[55] Campaign literature was printed in Yiddish, Italian, and other foreign languages. Howe also revealed to Hoey that this bureau would be a model for organizing a nationwide effort to cultivate urban ethnic voters for the 1932 presidential campaign.

Roosevelt's re-election in 1930 was a massive landslide. He defeated his Republican opponent, Charles H. Tuttle, by over 725,000 votes. He carried 41 of the 57 counties outside of New York City and his upstate margin of victory exceeded 167,000 votes.[56] He had received 62 percent of the total votes.

Despite Roosevelt's impressive ability to attract traditionally Republican upstate voters to his own candidacy, his party failed to win a majority of seats in either house of the state legislature in the 1930 election. The Democrats' failure to gain control of the state legislature can be attributed to the highly-publicized Tammany corruption uncovered by Judge Samuel Seabury's investigation of Mayor Jimmy Walker's administration and New York City's court system. While Roosevelt's party-building efforts had expanded and revitalized Party organizations in upstate, rural counties, his personal popularity and party-building efforts could not overcome the resurgence of anti-Tammany (and thus anti-Democratic) sentiment among upstate voters.

In 1930, upstate voters expressed their approval of Roosevelt's leadership; he carried upstate counties by over 167,000 votes. They also expressed their antipathy toward Tammany Hall that year by re-electing Republican legislators. In 1932, however, Democrats won a majority of seats in the state senate. Party-building efforts in upstate New York finally came to fruition in 1934 when Democrats won majorities in both the Assembly and the Senate.[57]

Meanwhile, Howe and Farley were busy building a nationwide network of supporters and endorsements for Roosevelt for the 1932 presidential election.[58] Their party-building efforts within New York were suspended as they busied themselves with national party relations. Roosevelt himself oriented his policy initiatives and speeches toward attracting favorable national attention. Earlier, at the 1930 Governors' Conference, he had increased his national prominence by being the first governor to advocate unemployment insurance and old-age pensions.[59] He was careful, though, to balance this social welfare liberalism with the assertion that public works programs should be conducted only by state governments, not by the federal government.[60] His address of August 28, 1932, outlined his unemployment program and revealed the increasing welfare-state emphasis of his liberalism. The more abstract passages of this speech illustrate what would become the ideological foundation of the New Deal. "One of these duties of the State is that of caring for those of its citizens who find themselves the victims of such adverse circumstances as makes them unable to obtain even the necessities for mere existence without the aid of others."[61]

Exploratory, pre-campaign communications by Howe and Farley indicated that there would be widespread party support for Roosevelt's presidential candidacy, especially in the South and West.[62] The governor, however, faced opposition from the leadership of the Democratic National Committee. John Raskob, DNC chairman, attempted to embarrass Roosevelt and damage his appeal among "dry" Democrats by holding a DNC meeting on March 5, 1931, to propose that the party's 1932 platform advocate the repeal of Prohibition.[63] Farley sought to undermine the impact of the DNC resolution by holding a Democratic State Committee meeting in Albany whose resolution asserted that "the national committee had no authority to pledge or advise the party on controversial political questions."[64]

Despite Roosevelt's personal dislike and ideological antipathy toward Raskob, the former Republican had proven to be an effective party chairman. As Roosevelt had long advocated, Raskob created a permanent Publicity Division for the DNC in 1929 and appointed Charles Michelson as its director.[65] Michelson "fed statements to Senators and Congressmen, circulated cartoons unfavorable to the Republican cause, . . . sent clip-sheets of news items and editorial suggestions to newspapers, and generally made and interpreted news to hurt Hoover."[66] During the 1928 campaign, Raskob led the Democratic fund-raising effort, which exceeded the Republican effort.[67] He then managed the successful liquidation of the approximately $1.5 million campaign debt.[68] Raskob also created a permanent Executive Committee and selected Jouett Shouse as its chairman.[69]

Meanwhile, Smith's animosity toward Roosevelt first became public in 1931 when he criticized Roosevelt's forest conservation proposal as being "Socialistic."[70] Although Smith would not announce his presidential candidacy until February 1932, it was apparent that Raskob would use his position as DNC chairman to promote Smith's candidacy and obstruct Roosevelt's. This maneuvering clearly violated the long-held DNC principle that its chairman remain neutral toward candidates competing for the nomination.[71]

Despite problems during the 1932 campaign, Roosevelt succeeded in winning his party's nomination and the election. His platform and rhetoric were criticized, not only by the

Republicans but also by some Democrats, as being ambiguous, contradictory, and even deceitful. It is certainly true that, combined, Roosevelt's campaign promises were perplexing for their inconsistency and dichotomy. While accusing Hoover of not doing enough to address the problems of the Depression, he also criticized him for higher taxes, deficit spending, and a bloated federal bureaucracy. He promised to balance the budget and streamline the bureaucracy, but also to use more federal action to combat the Depression.[72]

The most famous indictment of Roosevelt's inconsistent promises was given by columnist Walter Lippmann, who described Roosevelt as "a pleasant man who, without any important qualifications for the office, would very much like to be President."[73] Roosevelt's rhetoric, which sometimes reflected the conservatism of states' rights, balanced budgets, and bureaucracy bashing, might be perceived as a retreat from his liberalism. We must recognize, however, that during his campaigns Roosevelt had always been careful to subordinate his idealism about the ends of government (i.e., his liberal policy objectives) to his pragmatism about the means necessary to achieve them (i.e., winning nominations and elections by appealing to a diverse coalition of supporters). As he once bluntly told Samuel Rosenman, "You have to get the votes first—then you can do the good work."[74] To appeal to all conflicting factions and elements of his party, Roosevelt knew that he had to harmonize and unite the Democratic party by being all things to all Democrats—urban ethnics and rural Protestants, southern conservatives and western populists, machine bosses and reformers.

Long before his first presidential campaign, Roosevelt recognized the importance of making the Party more attractive to the voters by developing a consensus-building, liberal policy agenda. He simultaneously built party organizations that could be effective in recruiting candidates and activists committed to a liberal identity and policy agenda and in mobilizing the voters necessary for electoral victories. As a party-builder in New York, Roosevelt expanded the voter appeal of the state party beyond New York City by addressing the specific interests of traditionally Republican upstate New

Yorkers through his policy agenda and expanding the party structure in upstate New York. He would now apply these methods to the national Democratic party so that it would become not only an electorally successful majority party but more coherently, consistently liberal in its ideology and policy agenda. The New Deal would alter not only the role of the federal government in American society but also the ideology, voter appeal, coalition, electoral strength, and organization of the Democratic party.

2 The New Deal: A Foundation for Party-Building

Development of a Democratic Policy Agenda

As part of his party-building strategy, Franklin D. Roosevelt hoped that by addressing the diverse economic interests and grievances of both rural and urban voters, the New Deal policy agenda would expand and unite the Democratic party, transforming it into the enduring majority party in national politics. His assumption that the New Deal would be a consensual, inclusive means for party-building appeared to be correct during his first term and first re-election campaign. After 1936, however, additional New Deal policy initiatives divided the Party, especially in Congress, as northern urban Democrats proved to be more supportive of a liberal, interventionist federal government than rural southern Democrats.

The economic crisis of the Depression and Roosevelt's overwhelming victory in 1932 made most Democrats, despite their intraparty differences, receptive to strong presidential leadership in policy-making and party-building. If Roosevelt and the Democratic-controlled Congress failed to induce economic recovery, the credibility of the Party as a source of effective leadership and public policy might very well disintegrate. Nevertheless, even in the aftermath of the stock market crash, it was not evident that the Party would sharply distinguish itself from the pro-big-business, anti-big-government orientation of the Republican party and the Hoover administration. In 1931, University of Chicago economist Paul Douglas asserted that "both the Republican and Democratic parties are now primarily business parties, operating consciously or unconsciously through their policies and ideas to protect the interests of the owners of industrial and

commercial capital, and they do not represent the interests of
. . . the urban and town wage-workers and the farmers."[1]

On May 19, 1932, Raymond Moley, a Columbia University
professor and head of the Brains Trust, Roosevelt's inner
circle of economic advisors, sent the governor a memo in
which he first suggested the term "new deal."[2] Moley intended these words to signify a major change not only in the
relationship between government and the economy but also
in the policy agenda, ideology, and coalition of the Party. In
his memo, Moley expressed his belief that a policy agenda of
economic planning and redistributive social welfare, agricultural, and public works programs could effect a realignment of the party system by attracting the bulk of middle-
and low-income Americans into the Party, transforming it
into the enduring majority party in national politics. In short,
Moley proposed in 1932 that the Democratic party adopt an
economic policy agenda that would be more responsive to
modern economic problems as well as the economic needs and
grievances of lower-income Americans.[3]

The policy ideas which Roosevelt and the Brains Trust
sought to instill in the Party were contained in the National
Industrial Recovery Act of 1933. Passed on June 16, 1933, the
NIRA sought to stimulate economic recovery by promoting
cooperation among government, business, and labor.[4] Despite the NIRA's apparently impartial approach toward
business and labor by granting concessions to both, its empowerment of labor through Section 7a and the creation of the
National Labor Board in August 1933 greatly strengthened
the position of labor in the event of a conflict between business and labor.[5] This reflected Herbert Croly's earlier assertion that labor's right to organize and engage in collective
bargaining must be protected so that unions could not only
protect the economic interests of their members but also
serve as a powerful force to check and balance the power of
business.[6] Croly's vision of labor becoming an effective coun-
terorganization against business seemed plausible as union
membership grew rapidly from 2.8 million in 1933 to 3.7
million in 1935.[7] According to Donald Brand, "New Dealers
insisted that the abstract legal rights of individuals could not

protect real choices unless those choices were legitimated and upheld by the power of organization." [8]

The Works Progress Administration, created on May 6, 1935, was originally intended to serve only the limited function of supervising and inspecting the existing public works programs, namely the projects conducted by Federal Emergency Relief Administration's Work Division, which had absorbed the activities of the dismantled Civil Works Administration. The FERA administrator, Harry Hopkins, was appointed administrator of the WPA as well. Although it was originally intended merely to monitor existing public works programs, the WPA soon became the largest and most prominent public works and relief program because of an obscure clause in Executive Order 7034. This clause stated that the WPA had the authority to suggest "and carry on small useful projects designed to assure a maximum of employment in all localities." [9]

With the creation of the WPA, Hopkins, never previously active in Democratic politics, was determined not to have the WPA publicly discredited and rendered ineffective by being exploited and manipulated for partisan purposes. [10] By centralizing the approval of work projects proposed by state and local governments in the WPA's Washington headquarters, Hopkins hoped close scrutiny of these proposals would minimize the possibility of WPA projects becoming boondoggles for Democratic partisans. Therefore, the main function of the WPA's Division of Investigation was to investigate charges that particular WPA projects were being used for patronage by local politicians. [11]

The rapidity with which Hopkins had to implement the first WPA projects, and the necessity of cooperating with state and local governments, made the WPA's immersion in Democratic politics inevitable. [12] More importantly, Congress had mandated provisions regarding the appointment of WPA administrators. The Emergency Relief Appropriation Act of 1935 stipulated that any WPA state or regional administrator whose salary was $5,000 a year or more "must be appointed by the President, by and with the advice and consent of the Senate." [13] This requirement reflected the tradition of senatorial courtesy in making federal appointments.

Hopkins realized that he needed to comply with senatorial courtesy in his appointments because Congress appropriated WPA funds on a monthly basis until 1938. Recognizing the need to cooperate with Democratic members of Congress and their state party organizations, Hopkins began to defer to them more in the selection of state administrators and the approval of WPA project proposals.[14] He began to abandon the defiantly nonpartisan approach he had pursued as FERA-CWA administrator and cooperate with Democratic politicians and organizations in order to cultivate and solidify political support for the WPA and the New Deal in general. According to Paul Kurzman, a Hopkins biographer, "For while he felt that patronage and nepotism had no place in personnel management, he was convinced that one of the crucial skills of the public administrator was an ability to engage in the political arena to sell a program to the Congress and to the public."[15] Hopkins' role as a political advocate of the New Deal became apparent by early 1936 as he realized the need to re-elect Roosevelt and pro-New Deal Democrats in Congress to assure the continuation of the WPA and the rest of the New Deal policy agenda.

Despite Hopkins's increasingly political role, Congress had laid the foundation for the use of the WPA payroll as patronage. Section 3 of the Federal Emergency Relief Act of 1933 made the employees of the so-called emergency agencies (the PWA, FERA, and later the WPA) exempt from the U.S. Civil Service Commission's merit system and grade classification.[16]

Of the sixty-five new federal agencies that Congress created by the end of 1934, sixty were exempt from existing civil service laws.[17] This exemption covered about 100,000 new federal positions. Paul Van Riper found that by 1936 "only about 60 per cent of a total federal public service of more than 800,000 was on the classified list."[18] The exemption of the personnel of the "emergency agencies" from civil service laws was partially caused by the need to staff as quickly as possible this vast bureaucracy created to dispense relief funds and public works jobs. Morris Fiorina, in a detailed statistical analysis of this sharp decline in civil service coverage, concluded that the gradual expansion which began in the late nineteenth century was reversed and that unclassified federal employment became an integral tool of party-building for New Deal Democrats.[19] The Democrats' desire to exploit such a vast number of unclassified federal jobs was evident when Senator Kenneth D. McKellar of Tennessee proposed in January 1933 that a book be compiled and published that would list federal jobs that did not require civil service tests for appointments.[20] This book soon became known as the "Plum Book," and journalist Herbert S. Hollander remarked that the "New Gold Rush" began as the "Plum Book," and became "the spoilsman's bible."[21]

Patronage and Party-Building

With thousands of politicians, party organizations, and campaign workers clamoring for federal patronage, James A. Farley, Roosevelt's campaign manager, became the chief distributor because of his dual roles as Postmaster General and Democratic National Committee chairman.[22] Unlike Harry Hopkins, who evolved from a defiantly nonpartisan administrator to a major force in using New Deal programs to benefit the Party, Farley had always been an organization Democrat who firmly believed in what he called "party government."[23] He believed that the Roosevelt administration had not only the right but the obligation to appoint as many loyal Democrats as possible to unclassified federal jobs. Farley believed that since Roosevelt had been elected by a landslide it was appropriate for patronage jobs to be given to Democrats who had been active in his campaign.[24] Furthermore, he claimed that a rigidly partisan patronage policy was a good administrative practice, ensuring that Roosevelt's policies would be administered by officials who were loyal to him and his party. According to Farley, "My conception of politics is that it is the mechanism through which the program of a political party is translated into legislation. . . . The most important thing in any organization—industrial, governmental, or political—is the loyalty of its workers. We are more likely get that loyalty for the Administration if we appoint Democrats than if we appoint Republicans."[25]

Farley believed that appointees who were loyal, active party members had a strong incentive to perform their duties honestly and competently because they "work for a higher thing than mere self; they want to have the party and the principles it stands for to succeed."[26] Nevertheless, it was still possible for a person who was not a registered Democrat to receive an appointment from Farley. From the Democratic National Committee chairman's perspective, a job seeker's sponsorship could be even more important than his party affiliation. If a Republican or an independent was sponsored by a Democratic congressman, especially one who had been an early and vigorous supporter of Roosevelt, he could receive a patronage job. Farley bluntly told journalist Henry E. Pringle that giving patronage jobs to such applicants was an effective means of converting pro-New Deal Republicans and independents into loyal Democrats.[27] While recognizing the importance of patronage in increasing the number of Democratic voters and effecting a realignment, Farley was still primarily concerned with using patronage to reward politically active, loyal Democrats because it was "an assistance in building party machinery for the next election."[28]

Farley was not the first person to serve simultaneously as a cabinet member and his party's national chairman to facilitate distribution of patronage. He was the first patronage dispenser to formally and publicly systemize the process of selecting applicants. The applicants obtained "clearance" by acquiring letters of recommendation from their Democratic congressmen or local Democratic party organizations. They also submitted forms specifying their qualifications.

With unemployment so widespread, Farley was inundated with over 250,000 letters of application by November 1934.[29] He conducted the selection process from his office at the Democratic National Committee's building and later at the main Post Office building.[30] As much as possible, Farley secured the appointments of applicants who were both well-qualified and strongly endorsed by their Democratic congressmen and local committees. Of those who fulfilled both of these qualifications, preference was given to applicants who were recommended by Democratic politicians and party organizations recognized as being F.R.B.C.—"For Roosevelt Before Chicago."[31]

Thus, the Democratic national chairman was careful to channel federal patronage to Democratic activists, party organizations, and members of Congress who had been early, diligent supporters of Roosevelt's candidacy before the Chicago convention.[32] Both Farley and Roosevelt had the foresight to realize that it was necessary to staff the greatly-expanded bureaucracy with the staunchest Roosevelt supporters because New Deal policies could elicit opposition from anti-Roosevelt factions within the Party who might undermine the administration of the New Deal if they received important patronage jobs. According to Paul Van Riper, "Franklin D. Roosevelt fully understood the intricate relationship of party, program, and patronage . . . Roosevelt rewarded and punished to support his social program and to bind together the discordant party he had inherited."[33]

Despite the proliferation of "emergency agencies" and their vast number of unclassified administrative and clerical jobs, Farley estimated that there were still about twenty applicants for every position.[34] His chief assistant in consulting with Democratic members of Congress, national and state committee members, and the various federal agencies on patronage was Emil Hurja. Hurja, who first worked as a personnel director in the Reconstruction Finance Corporation and later as an administrative assistant to Harold Ickes in the PWA, was the Democratic National Committee's executive director and statistician.[35] An article in *Time* had caustically asserted that he "was put into the R.F.C. as personnel officer to weed out Republicans, replant Democrats."[36]

Farley realized the potential of patronage distribution to fragment and divide the Democratic party into squabbling factions. In September 1933 he asked Louis Howe to help him secure centralized control over patronage so that the heads of all government agencies and departments would have to defer to the Democratic National Committee for the selection of applicants for patronage jobs.[37] Although Farley exercised a more direct, centralized control over patronage than previous national party chairmen had, he still had to share power with agency heads and Democrats at congressional, state, and local levels.[38]

The patronage policy of the Roosevelt administration was not used only to reward Democrats who had been active in the 1932 campaign. It was also used to recruit unprecedented numbers of economists, agricultural scientists, social workers, college professors, and other "service intellectuals" into government service.[39] The appointment of these individuals to administrative and technical positions represented what Paul Van Riper called "ideological patronage."[40] He found that the "great influx of personnel into the federal government in the thirties contained a smaller than usual proportion of ex-precinct workers, party hacks, and unemployables."[41]

Patronage, therefore, was now being used to attract into the federal bureaucracy academics who, while perhaps not Democratic activists or even registered Democrats, supported the New Deal policy agenda and its ideology of greater federal intervention to effect social and economic reforms. Traditional recipients of patronage were often party committee members, lawyer-lobbyists, and campaign contributors who used their public offices for personal gain. But the service intellectuals were usually less self-interested and more idealistic while serving as administrators, technicians, or policy advisors. Their efforts were often motivated by an ideological desire to implement the ideas of "positive government" they had studied and to participate in a major reform movement.[42]

Conflicts occurred as organization Democrats resented the appointment of professionals who had not been active in campaigns and party organizations.[43] The party regulars believed that patronage must be earned by long, faithful, effective service to the Party. They argued that a patronage policy that bypassed "deserving Democrats" in favor of previously apolitical intellectuals would cause resentment and disharmony within the ranks of those who had worked diligently and faithfully for the Democracy during the long, lean years out of power.[44]

Roosevelt realized the potential of patronage distribution for disrupting party expansion efforts and even the efficacy of policy implementation if two conflicting factions were formed within the administration and the party. To mitigate such internal squabbling, he carefully distinguished the task of developing and implementing New Deal policies from that of "selling" these policies to the public, Congress, and party organizations.[45] Roosevelt had established a similar division of labor during his presidential campaign. While he relied on the Brains Trust to provide him with policy ideas and speeches, he relied on Farley, Flynn, and Howe to coordinate campaign efforts.[46]

Because this division of labor worked well during the campaign, Roosevelt hoped that it would work as successfully and harmoniously within the operations of his administration. During the First Hundred Days, this separation of policy and politics proved to be impressively effective. After the service intellectuals formulated and drafted New Deal legislation, Farley and other appointees from the party apparatus would vigorously lobby Congress and generate grass-roots support by mobilizing state and local organizations on behalf of these bills. Once agencies were established to implement New Deal policies, the duties of an appointed position determined whether a service intellectual or a party regular was appointed to it. Jobs requiring technical expertise, especially in agriculture and public works engineering, were given to service intellectuals.[47] Administrative and clerical positions in programs requiring cooperation with state and local officials were often given to party regulars.

Conflicts between these two groups intensified when some of the service intellectuals began to perform tasks that had been reserved for party regulars. Hopkins began to politicize his administrative role in 1936. His speeches not only defended the WPA and the New Deal in general but also Roosevelt and the Democratic party.[48] He was especially persuasive among pro–New Deal Republicans and independents who had grown skeptical of the integrity and efficacy of New Deal programs amidst charges of partisan exploitation.

As a recipient of Felix Frankfurter's ideological patronage, Thomas G. Corcoran's power and prominence within the White House increased as he served as a legislative draftsman and, by 1935, Roosevelt's chief liaison and lobbyist with Congress. Securing passage of bills that he and Benjamin Cohen, a fellow protégé of Frankfurter, had written, combining the roles of policy-maker and policy-seller, Corcoran overshadowed both the Brains Trust and Jim Farley. He built his own network of political allies within the administration by hiring other alumni from the Harvard Law School. Achieving his peak of power and access to the president by 1938, Corcoran attracted the resentment of the remnants of the Brains Trust, Jim Farley, and the increasingly ambitious Harry Hopkins.[49] As Patrick Anderson stated in his study of White House staff members, "During his heyday, Corcoran wielded a far-ranging, free-wheeling power that few presidential aides have ever matched."[50]

Corcoran moved beyond his multi-purpose policy role and became the president's chief operative within the party, especially during the failed "purge" of 1938. Corcoran's intervention on internal party matters was one of the major causes of Farley's growing alienation from Roosevelt and his resignation as DNC chairman in 1940.[51] The brilliant legal mind and gregarious nature that had served Corcoran well as a legislative draftsman and lobbyist failed to compensate for his inexperience in party affairs and the enmity of the party regulars toward him. Meanwhile, Hopkins's allies within the administration spread stories of Corcoran's alleged statements of disloyalty toward Roosevelt in order to reassert Hopkins's position as the president's chief confidant.[52] With his heavy reliance on the machine bosses and party regulars for his renomination and re-election in 1940, Roosevelt recognized the decline in Corcoran's usefulness and agreed to Ed Flynn's request that Corcoran be given an insignificant role in the campaign.[53] In 1941, Corcoran left the administration and entered private practice.

The rapid rise and fall of Tommy Corcoran demonstrated

the limits of ideological patronage in instilling the liberal ideology of the New Deal into the Democratic party. In their assessment of the New Deal intellectuals in 1939, Joseph Alsop and Robert Kintner stated that because of their inexperience and incompetence in internal party affairs they should become "political eunuchs" who limit themselves to public policy matters.[54] Despite their failure to seize control of the party apparatus, the recipients of ideological patronage, through the application of their intellectual talents, integrity, and idealism to public service, strengthened the public credibility of the New Deal as both a reform effort and the essence of the Party's new ideology. If only self-interested party hacks had received political appointments, the legitimacy of both the above policy and partisan aspects of the New Deal might have collapsed, given the complex nature of its policy efforts and the need to enlist the public's trust in this national reform effort amidst the domestic crisis of the Depression. Because of the precedent set by ideological patronage, political appointments would no longer be the exclusive domain of party regulars as academic elites became influential members of the Democratic coalition.[55]

Congress: The Intraparty Politics of the New Deal

Roosevelt's success in achieving a close correlation between the substance of New Deal policies and the new ideology, policy agenda, and coalition of the Party depended on key allies in Congress. The leading initiators and supporters of major New Deal bills in Congress were often urban liberals or, more frequently, agrarian populists who had long sought the economic policy objectives that the New Deal represented. In short, they had been New Dealers even before there was a New Deal.

Like Roosevelt, these congressional leaders, often products of the Populist and Progressive movements, wanted not only to make the Democratic party the enduring majority party in national politics but also to make its ideology and policy agenda a distinctly liberal alternative to the Republican party. They now perceived Roosevelt's presidency and the

economic crisis of the Depression to be their opportunity to
finally implement reforms such as rural electrification, the
stabilization of farm prices, and the strict regulation of
banks, utilities, and the stock exchange.[56]

The identification of the Democratic party with urban and
labor interests during the New Deal era was facilitated by the
legislative leadership of Senator Robert F. Wagner of New
York. His vigorous advocacy of labor reform and social welfare measures in both the New York state senate and the
United States Senate was inspired by his own experiences as
the son of working-class German immigrants. In 1938, John
C. O'Brien observed that "Wagner cannot be grouped with
other sycophantic officeholders who have beaten the New
Deal drum to keep up with the procession. Throughout thirty
years of public life he has been a consistent advocate of most
of the objectives now proclaimed from every New Deal
pulpit."[57]

During Roosevelt's First Hundred Days, Wagner cooperated with the administration in assuring passage of the Federal Emergency Relief Act of 1933 which distributed $500
million to the states as grants, not loans, for relief.[58] With the
establishment of extensive public works and relief, Wagner
focused his efforts on permanently strengthening the position of organized labor in the American economy. The New
York senator participated with the Brains Trust in drafting
the bill that became the National Industrial Recovery Act on
June 16, 1933. When Wagner had introduced the bill for this
act in May, the most vocal opposition came from Senator
William Borah and other western progressives who contended that the bill's relaxation of anti-trust laws would
create oppressive monopolies.[59]

Wagner, though, was confident that big business could not
exploit the NIRA if this act also legitimized organized labor
so that it could check and balance the power of big business.
In helping to formulate the bill for the NIRA, he focused his
efforts on Section 7. This section contained provisions for the
establishment of minimum wages and maximum hours in
each industry through industrial codes. More importantly,
Section 7 granted labor the right to organize and engage in

collective bargaining. Wagner hoped that these provisions would enable labor unions to protect and promote members' interests in relationships with employers. "The NRA had done a great deal to liberate workers and establish a climate in which they could directly challenge the interests of their employers," states Donald Brand, a contemporary authority on New Deal economic reforms.[60]

Wagner's leadership on labor issues influenced both Roosevelt and fellow Democrats in Congress to become more favorable toward organized labor as an economic interest group and a source of political support. Throughout his political career, Roosevelt, like Wagner, had been supportive of social welfare measures and work safety regulations that benefited factory workers.[61] Roosevelt, though, initially feared that a powerful labor movement might form its own political party, depriving the Democratic party of the votes of union members. Arthur M. Schlesinger, Jr., found that "Roosevelt thought instinctively in terms of government's doing things for working people rather than giving the unions the power to win workers their own victories."[62]

Consequently, Wagner's role in attracting northern urban voters and union members into the Party cannot be overestimated. Although Al Smith had received a majority of votes in the twelve largest cities in 1928, Roosevelt expanded and solidified the Party's ability to attract urban voters, especially working-class ethnics and blacks who had previously been staunch Republicans, in such cities as Philadelphia and Chicago.[63] Wagner's successful efforts on behalf of social welfare, public housing, and labor issues enabled urban voters to perceive a clear correlation between their economic interests and the electoral success of the Democratic party.[64] His accomplishments in these policy areas helped to transform the urban, industrial areas of the Northeast and Midwest into Democratic bastions and to identify clearly the national Democratic party's ideology and policy agenda under the New Deal with labor and urban interests.[65] James Sundquist, in his study of the Democratic realignment under Roosevelt, concludes that "the Democratic party of the industrial North found itself with an extraordinarily high degree of philosophical and ideological unity—for an American party."[66]

The emergency atmosphere of the Depression combined with the Democrats' desire to prove their ability to govern well as the new majority party provided an impressive degree of party unity for passing early New Deal legislation.[67] While Roosevelt's initial legislation received the support of most congressional Democrats—liberal and conservative, northern and southern, urban and rural—an inner circle of prominent southern Democratic senators consistently opposed most New Deal bills during the 1933–1935 session. Led by Carter Glass and Harry Byrd of Virginia, these conservatives were immediately suspicious of and hostile toward the New Deal. As early as August 10, 1933, Carter Glass referred to the New Deal as "an utterly dangerous effort of the federal government to transplant Hitlerism to every corner of the nation."[68] Whereas most southern opposition to the New Deal developed gradually and did not become blatant until Roosevelt's second term, Glass and his like-minded Democratic colleagues in the Senate already held an unyielding ideological predisposition against the New Deal's philosophy of greater federal intervention in the economy. They firmly believed that identifying the Party's principles with the New Deal would betray the Jeffersonian tradition of states' rights and minimal federal intervention in the economy.

The conservative Democrats, however, were too few in number to thwart New Deal legislation during Roosevelt's first term.[69] As E. David Cronon and Dewey W. Grantham, Jr., have cogently and persuasively contended, the perception of the South as monolithically conservative in its politics is misleading.[70] Such a misperception neglects the populist strain of southern politics which pervaded chronically depressed, more remote areas of southern states.[71] Resentful of the political influence that business and landowning interests wielded through conservatives like Glass and Byrd, populist politicians sought to improve public services, such as public education, while increasing taxes and regulations on business, especially utilities and railroads. The conservative elites often succeeded in thwarting the reform efforts of the populists by suggesting that their opponents' policy proposals were threats to racial segregation.[72] Populism, therefore, tended to be more prevalent in hill country areas with fewer blacks, where race relations were not the major issue.[73]

Nevertheless, Roosevelt's vigorous cultivation of the black vote in 1936, the presence of the Black Cabinet, and the First Lady's outspoken advocacy of civil rights made increasing numbers of southerners, including pro–New Deal populists, fear that the New Deal would eventually threaten segregation.[74] In addition, the 1938 congressional elections substantially increased Republican representation in Congress. Republicans and southern conservatives now formed a coalition to obstruct further New Deal initiatives.[75]

Intraparty Legislative Battles

Roosevelt's landslide re-election in 1936 emboldened him to announce a court reorganization proposal shortly after his second inauguration. He was confident that he would have enough support from public opinion and in Congress to assure passage of this bill.[76] Although nothing in this bill violated Article III of the Constitution, Roosevelt's apparent desire to "pack" the Supreme Court with a pro–New Deal majority seemed to confirm the conservatives' accusation that Roosevelt was a power-hungry demagogue who threatened the constitutional system of checks and balances. Within Democratic ranks in Congress, the most damaging impact of the court reorganization bill on party cohesion occurred among moderate Democrats who had generally supported New Deal legislation during Roosevelt's first term. They had chafed under their campaign opponents' charges that they were merely Roosevelt's puppets who rubber-stamped the administration's bills. As the emergency of the Depression stabilized and as public opinion reacted unfavorably to this bill, a substantial bloc of moderate Democrats in Congress decided to assert their independence from the White House on this issue.[77]

Unlike the small conservative cabal of Senate Democrats led by Carter Glass, most Democrats in Congress did not have an ideological antipathy toward the court reorganization bill. Like Roosevelt, they were infuriated by Supreme Court decisions overturning laws and programs they had struggled to enact and regarded as crucial for economic recovery and reform. They knew that the New Deal could not endure unless the Supreme Court became more favorable to it.[78]

Most of Roosevelt's bill dealt with reassigning lower court federal judges and increasing their numbers to a maximum of fifty in order to expedite the appeals process and make the overall federal court system more efficient and expeditious in handling its case load.[79] The controversial section of this bill provided the president with the power to appoint up to six new justices on the Supreme Court if justices reaching the age of seventy did not retire.[80] In his February 5, 1937, message to Congress and in his March 9, 1937, radio address, Roosevelt suggested that the Supreme Court, by striking down laws necessary for economic recovery and reform, was unjustifiably interfering in legislative affairs.[81]

What bothered most Democrats about the court reorganization bill was not its substance or even its political objective of obtaining a pro-New Deal majority on the Supreme Court.[82] Instead, they were angry with the arrogant, clumsy, and deceitful manner in which Roosevelt pursued this issue and sought their support.[83] In particular, House Speaker William B. Bankhead and House Majority Leader Sam Rayburn resented the fact that Roosevelt did not consult them well beforehand about the feasibility of such a bill being passed and about how this bill should be written and presented.[84] On the day before he announced the court reorganization bill to the press and presented it to Congress, he summoned Vice President Garner and the Democratic leadership of Congress into his office. After briefly explaining the content of this bill, the president asked for their opinions. Senate Majority Leader Joe Robinson and Henry F. Ashurst, chairman of the Senate Judiciary Committee, expressed their agreement with the bill while their colleagues remained silent.[85] Roosevelt was confident that they could muster enough votes in Congress to pass this bill.

As a Texas populist and chairman of the House Interstate

Commerce Committee, Sam Rayburn had been instrumental
in securing passage of strict regulations on securities and
utilities. Now, as the Democratic floor leader in the House, it
was his responsibility to mobilize a Democratic majority favorable to the bill. Since Representative Hatton Sumners,
chairman of the House Judiciary Committee, opposed the
court reorganization bill, Rayburn advised the president to
have the Senate consider the bill first.[86] Roosevelt agreed and
promised Joe Robinson the first vacancy on the Supreme
Court in exchange for motivating the Senate majority leader
to persuade the Senate to pass the bill.[87]

Senate opposition to this bill, however, emerged from un-
expected sources.[88] John Garner began quietly lobbying senators to oppose the court reorganization bill as well as
upcoming administration bills on public works and relief
spending.[89] The most damaging public expression of opposition by Garner occurred when he abruptly deserted Roosevelt
for an extended vacation at his ranch in Texas. In a July 7th
letter to Garner, the president pleaded with the Texan to
return to Washington "pretty soon, timing it so that it would
not be said that you were rushing back to save the amended
Court Bill."[90] After this issue ended, though, Garner continued openly opposing Roosevelt's bills on labor, taxation,
and relief spending. Throughout Roosevelt's second term,
Garner would serve as the center of anti–New Deal sentiment
within the administration.

What was more surprising than Garner's recalcitrance
was the fact that the opposition movement within the Senate was led by Democratic Senator Burton K. Wheeler of
Montana, a maverick progressive who had been a reliable
New Dealer.[91] Republicans and conservative Democrats
shrewdly realized that they would be more likely to defeat
the bill if the opposition was led by a prominent liberal.
They hoped that the divisiveness of this issue within the
liberal ranks would permanently weaken Roosevelt's ability to secure the enactment of further New Deal legislation.[92] Consequently, Carter Glass and his fellow anti-New
Deal conservatives quietly coalesced with the Republicans
while letting moderates Thomas Connally of Texas and

Bennett Clark of Missouri lead lobbying efforts against the court reform bill.[93]

Besides his growing personal antagonism toward Roosevelt, Wheeler was primarily motivated by an ideological conviction that "court packing" threatened the system of checks and balances and could be used by future presidents to damage the constitutional order. As a rural progressive hostile to centralized power in both economics and government, Wheeler was convinced that the court reorganization bill must be defeated. In testifying before the Senate Judiciary Committee, Wheeler read a letter from Chief Justice Charles Evans Hughes which persuasively contended that Roosevelt's proposed "reform" of the judiciary would hamper rather than expedite the appeals process.[95]

Meanwhile, the most prominent urban New Deal liberal, Robert Wagner, remained silent and neutral as hardball lobbying tactics by Tommy Corcoran and Assistant Attorney General Joseph Keenan on behalf of the bill alienated some undecided, wavering Democrats.[96] Furthermore, the Supreme Court had upheld several New Deal laws in March and April, including the Social Security Act and the National Labor Relations Act. Liberal Democrats, therefore, no longer felt that passage of the court reform bill was crucial to saving the New Deal. Justice Owen Roberts's "conversion" to the New Deal, as expressed by his decisions in these cases, and conservative Justice William Van Devanter's announcement on May 18 of his retirement, further convinced New Deal Democrats that the Supreme Court was no longer a threat to New Deal legislation.[97]

On July 14, one month after the Senate Judiciary Committee's report condemned the court reorganization bill, Senate Majority Leader Joe Robinson died. Roosevelt had now lost his most powerful ally in the Senate struggle. One week later, the Senate decided, by a vote of 70 to 21, to return the court reform bill to the hostile House Judiciary Committee.[98] Shortly thereafter, the Senate passed and Roosevelt signed the Logan-Hatch bill which reformed lower court procedures but did not increase the number of Supreme Court justices.[99]

It had been apparent as early as March that Roosevelt's bill was doomed. Roosevelt persisted so relentlessly because he realized that his position as party leader was at stake among congressional Democrats. It was evident by the end of 1937 that the bitter division over the court issue had inhibited the passage of any significant New Deal legislation.[100] Even though Roosevelt's party enjoyed a substantial majority in both houses, this tediously prolonged, bitter legislative battle had permanently fragmented party cohesion.[101] Roosevelt and his most stalwart supporters in Congress were now confronted by a strengthened conservative coalition and by moderate Democrats who increasingly asserted their independence from the White House regarding the administration's bills.[102] Furthermore, the 75th Congress's overwhelming Democratic majorities in both houses served to accentuate the ideological and regional differences among the Democrats by weakening their incentive to unite behind the White House against the Republican opposition in Congress.[103]

The death of Joe Robinson resulted in another test of Roosevelt's party leadership in Congress—the election of a new Senate majority leader. As a matter of personal loyalty to Roosevelt, Senator Alben Barkley of Kentucky was one of the few senators who had remained supportive of the court reform bill throughout the struggle, despite misgivings about Roosevelt's clumsy tactics.[104] First elected to the Senate in 1926, Barkley was an early supporter of Roosevelt's candidacy and served as temporary chairman of the 1932 Democratic national convention.[105] He had also delivered the keynote speeches at both the 1932 and 1936 conventions.[106] During his 1936 keynote address, Barkley fired the opening salvo for the court reform attempt by denouncing the Supreme Court's decisions overturning New Deal laws. The Kentuckian asserted that the Supreme Court should regard the Constitution "as a life-giving charter, rather than an object of curiosity on the shelf of a museum. . . . Is the Court beyond criticism? . . . May it be regarded as too sacred to be disagreed with?"[107]

Although Barkley's tenure as Robinson's assistant and his experience as a party insider were assets in his candidacy for majority leader, his position as both a "100 percent New

Dealer" and an operative for Roosevelt in the Senate was
perceived by many of his colleagues as a liability.[108] His
formidable opponent in the contest to succeed Robinson was
Senator Pat Harrison of Mississippi. As chairman of the Senate Finance Committee, Harrison had been a valuable ally of
the New Deal on budgetary matters during Roosevelt's first
term.[109] The first indication of his growing disenchantment
with New Deal fiscal policies occurred when he expressed his
reservations about Roosevelt's Wealth Tax Act of 1935.[110]
Nevertheless, he remained loyal to the president and helped
secure its enactment.[111]

Although Harrison had not been part of the Glass-Wheeler
coalition opposing the court reform bill, he had remained
silent and sullen on the issue. Roosevelt perceived Harrison's
silence and his growing fiscal conservatism to be signs of a
budding disloyalty toward himself and the New Deal policy
agenda. Despite the president's public statement of neutrality in this contest, he had sent a letter to Barkley (which was
made public) in which he recognized the Kentuckian as
"acting majority leader" and urged him to continue the struggle for passage of the court reform bill.[112] Harrison's supporters, therefore, recognized Roosevelt's bias for Barkley and
resented his interference in the contest for majority leader.

Perceiving the turbulent events of the court reform battle
to be a harbinger of future congressional opposition to his
legislation, Roosevelt was determined to make sure that
Barkley, a New Deal loyalist, would be elected Senate majority leader. It was apparent that a slim majority of senators
was committed to Harrison.[113] Unlike Roosevelt, many Senate Democrats did not perceive the Barkley-Harrison contest
as a matter of ideology and a test of their loyalty to the New
Deal and Roosevelt's party leadership. Instead, they regarded
the election of a new majority leader as an internal matter of
their institution which should be immune from presidential
intervention. According to the norms of the Senate, Harrison's greater seniority, personal popularity, and network
of quid pro quo obligations based on his power as Finance
Committee chairman made him more deserving of being
elected.[114]

With Farley refusing to lobby senators on Barkley's behalf, Roosevelt relied on Tommy Corcoran to pressure a targeted number of pro-Harrison senators.[115] In particular, Roosevelt used his connections with the Democratic machines of Chicago and Kansas City to pressure Senators William Dieterich of Illinois and Harry Truman of Missouri. Both men, especially Dieterich, felt a sense of personal loyalty toward Harrison and had committed themselves to his election. The combined pressure of Corcoran and Kansas City boss Tom Pendergast failed to deter Truman from voting for Harrison.[116]

Chicago boss Ed Kelly, though, proved to be a more effective ally of the White House. Kelly and Howard Hunter, the WPA regional director for the Midwest, informed Dieterich that WPA funds for Illinois might be reduced if Barkley were not elected and that the Chicago machine would deny the senator renomination if he voted for Harrison.[117] Dieterich succumbed to this heavy pressure and switched his vote to Barkley.

Dieterich's "conversion" proved to be indispensable as Barkley was elected Senate majority leader by a vote of 38 to 37.[118] Barkley's victory signified an important reassertion of Roosevelt's party leadership and influence in Congress, especially since it occurred toward the end of his humiliating defeat over the court reform bill. Despite his proven legislative skills and populist commitment to the New Deal, Barkley's effectiveness as Senate Majority leader was undermined since many of his pro-Harrison colleagues contemptuously perceived Barkley as a White House errand boy.[119] Embittered by Roosevelt's lobbying for Barkley, Harrison now used his Finance Committee chairmanship to oppose upcoming tax and spending bills.

Although the Barkley-Harrison contest further exacerbated the party factionalism wrought by the court reform bill, it more clearly distinguished the most pro-Roosevelt New Deal liberals in the Senate from their more conservative and independent Democratic colleagues. The issue served as another litmus test of congressional Democrats' fidelity to Roosevelt's party leadership and policy goals. However,

Farley and other party regulars feared that any more intraparty battles Congress would further fragment the unity
necessary for victory in the next elections.[120] Unfortunately
for Farley and other regulars desiring intraparty harmony,
Roosevelt and his liberal allies in Congress continued to
pursue policy objectives that forced the Democratic party in
Congress to reflect more closely the New Deal's liberal ideology of increased federal intervention on welfare, economic,
and labor issues.[121]

The prolonged, bitter struggle over the Fair Labor Standards Act of 1938 was the type of economic and labor reform
legislation which more clearly defined the liberalism of the
Democratic majorities in Congress while further alienating
the southern conservative wing of the Party. Since the
NIRA's provisions for minimum wages and maximum hours
had been eliminated by the Supreme Court in the *Schechter*
decision, Roosevelt, labor leaders, and New Deal Democrats
in Congress wanted to replace these provisions through new
legislation. Although his influence in Congress had weakened, Roosevelt was confident that a new minimum wages-
maximum hours bill could be passed during the 1937–1938
session of Congress.

Despite the *Schechter* decision of 1935, Congress succeeded
in passing the Walsh-Healey Public Contracts Act of 1936.
This act required that all workers employed by businesses
with federal contracts receive at least the prevailing minimum wage established by the Department of Labor. All federal contractors for supplies and equipment exceeding
$10,000 in value had to pay overtime wages if their employees
worked more than eight hours a day or forty hours a week. It
also forbade federal contractors from using the labor of chil-
dren and convicts. Roosevelt and his allies in Congress hoped
that this act provided both the legal and political precedent
for a labor bill which would cover all workers in the private
sector.[122]

The administration drafted such a bill and had it intro-
duced in June 1937, by Hugo Black in the Senate and by
William Connery in the House.[123] Because the more liberal
House of Representatives contained a larger proportion of

urban liberals and southern populists than the Senate, Roosevelt and the other supporters of the labor bill hoped that if the House first passed it then the Senate would be pressured to pass it also. However, the anti-union chairman of the House Rules Committee, John O'Connor, formed a majority of Republicans and southern Democrats on his committee to bottle up the bill and prevent it from reaching the House floor for a vote. All but the most pro–New Deal southerners in both houses, such as Representatives Lyndon Johnson and Maury Maverick of Texas and Senator Claude Pepper of Florida, opposed the Black-Connery bill.[124] They feared that this bill would destroy the competitive advantage of the South's lower labor costs and would force southern employers to pay blacks the same wages as whites.[125] With their pro-union northern colleagues supporting this bill, they became even more convinced that northern labor leaders were dominating Roosevelt's policy agenda and the national Democratic party.

House Majority Leader Sam Rayburn finally succeeded in getting the House members to pass a discharge petition forcing the Black-Connery bill out of the Rules Committee.[126] But when the House voted on the bill, it voted to recommit it to the Labor Committee.[127] The compromise bill was finally passed by the House and Senate in June 1938 and signed into law by Roosevelt as the Fair Labor Standards Act.

The compromises and amendments needed to get both houses to pass this bill reflected concessions to both southern and western agricultural interests. In order to reflect the lower cost of living in rural areas, regional wage differentials were added. In addition, farm laborers and domestic servants were exempted from the provisions of this act.[128] The minimum wage was set at twenty-five cents per hour for 1938 and would rise to forty cents per hour by 1945. The maximum work week would gradually decline from forty-four hours for 1938 to forty hours by 1940. Time-and-a-half wages would be required for any work performed beyond these limits.[129]

In both houses, Democrats divided along regional-ideological lines once again.[130] Curiously, though, supporters of the Black-Connery bill were aided by several northern Republicans.[131] Although they shared the anti-union attitudes of many of their southern colleagues, these Republicans hoped that the Black-Connery bill without the regional wage differentials would weaken the labor cost advantages that growing southern industries had over northern industries. With northern liberal Democrats like Robert Wagner and Joseph Guffey supporting this bill as well as the more controversial public housing and anti-lynching bills, many southerners in Congress felt alienated from the national Democratic party and Roosevelt's party leadership as the legislative agenda became dominated by bills responding to the interests and demands of labor, blacks, and urban areas.[132]

These intraparty legislative battles resulted in a permanent bifurcation in Congress. This division emerged as more conservative Democratic members defied the White House and sought to block further New Deal legislation through their power in the committee system. Meanwhile, liberal Democrats in Congress remained loyal to Roosevelt's party leadership on domestic policy issues. They represented mostly urban industrial districts and states and, therefore, sponsored and supported legislation that redefined the New Deal as a policy platform and ideology in which such issues as civil rights, public housing, labor reform, and federal aid to central cities became more prevalent.[133] Nevertheless, these mostly northern liberals were joined by a small number of southern liberals, such as Lyndon Johnson and Claude Pepper, who did not feel compelled to balance their economic liberalism with strident race-baiting as earlier populists had done.[134] Likewise, western populists especially supported stricter regulations on banking, investment, and electric utility interests.

After the 75th Congress ended, the clear intraparty division in Congress would be obscured by Roosevelt's focus on foreign policy and defense matters. Southern conservatives who had been powerful enemies of his bills during the 75th Congress became some of his staunchest supporters on such prewar defense issues as the Lend-Lease Act, the Selective Service Act, and higher military spending.[135] While the war effort induced both bipartisan and intraparty unity behind

Roosevelt, the resumption of domestic policy concerns during the Truman administration made the division between liberal and conservative Democrats even more evident as southern Democrats frequently cooperated with Republicans to defeat or weaken the Fair Deal.[136] Although the divisive domestic policy issues that Roosevelt and his allies pursued during the 75th Congress permanently weakened intra-party harmony and cohesion among congressional Democrats, it did serve to define more clearly the national party as distinctly liberal in its ideology, policies, and coalition membership. Consequently, the term "party loyalty" for Democrats in Congress would now be even more closely correlated to a Democratic member's support of the increasingly divisive ideology and policy objectives of New Deal liberalism represented by Roosevelt's party leadership and often opposed by conservative committee chairmen.[137]

The New Deal and Black Voters

Blacks who could vote (i.e, those living outside of the South) were willing to end their long-held allegiance to the Republican party and become the most loyal of all Democratic voting blocs once they realized that their political and economic interests would be better served by an increasingly liberal party. Suffering the highest incidence of unemployment, poverty, and malnutrition, black Americans were most receptive to the New Deal's policy agenda of social welfare measures and labor reforms.[138] The U.S. Census Bureau did not compile separate economic statistics for black Americans in 1930. Private surveys, however, clearly indicated that unemployment rates among blacks in major northern cities substantially exceeded the national unemployment rate of 25 percent. The unemployment rate among black males in 1931 ranged from approximately 43 percent in New York City, Chicago, and Philadelphia to over 60 percent in Detroit.[139]

Despite their dissatisfaction with Hoover and their perennial complaint that the Republican party neglected them on patronage matters, most blacks remained loyal to the Republican party in 1932 as 65 percent of them voted for Hoover.[140]

Although Robert L. Vann, Julian Rainey, and a few other black leaders bolted to Roosevelt in 1932, most black newspapers and community leaders endorsed Hoover, although reluctantly and ambivalently.[141] Other than New York City, Hoover had won from two-thirds to three-fourths of the black vote in the major cities of the Northeast and Midwest.[142] Roosevelt, though, had won a higher percentage of black votes than any Democratic presidential nominee since the Civil War.[143] It was too early to conclude whether this minor defection from the Republican party would develop into a permanent realignment of blacks with the Democratic party.[144]

Concerned about quickly alleviating the economic suffering of all Americans, the Roosevelt administration did not make the prevention of racial discrimination a high priority in the administration of the FERA and PWA while these two programs were being formulated. Since the FERA heavily depended on state and local governments to distribute its relief funds, racial discrimination in this program was common, especially in the South. Black applicants were often denied relief payments and public works jobs or were given lower payments and wages than white recipients.[145]

By September 1933, however, Harold Ickes had issued an order forbidding racial and religious discrimination in the PWA and established racial quotas which required contractors to hire a percentage of black workers that correlated to the 1930 census statistics for the area in which a PWA project was being constructed.[146] Outside the PWA, Aubrey Williams, administrator of the National Youth Administration (NYA), was most receptive to the appointment of a racial adviser and chose Mary McLeod Bethune, a black educator, as the NYA's racial adviser.[147] In August 1936, Bethune organized other black officials into an informal lobbying group that became known as the Black Cabinet. It sought to prevent, or at least mitigate, racial discrimination in the implementation of New Deal programs.[148] The Cabinet increased its power by applying external pressure to the administration through news leaks to Congress and the media about discriminatory practices in federal agencies.[149]

With both parties and the media initially anticipating a close presidential election in 1936, the black vote, for the first time in history, was perceived as the key to victory.[150] In order to compensate for its silence on civil rights and segregation, the Democratic strategy in 1936 effectively used political symbolism to convey the impression that the national party was giving blacks political recognition and status in national politics that they had not received during their long affiliation with the Republican party.[151] Southern white antagonism against these ingratiating gestures toward blacks was exemplified by Senator "Cotton Ed" Smith's statement that he could not support a party that provided "acceptance of the Negro on terms of political equality."[152]

Approximately 76 percent of all black voters cast ballots for Roosevelt on election day.[153] Compared to the fact that nearly 65 percent of all black voters had voted for Hoover in 1932, this figure revealed the most rapid, massive party realignment of any voting bloc in American political history. It became clear that the vigorous cultivation of the black vote by the national Democratic party was not merely a temporary tactic employed for this election.[154] This would become a permanent element of Democratic campaign strategy in presidential elections.[155]

During his second term, Roosevelt became even more aware of the importance of black political support as increasing numbers of southern Democrats in Congress openly resisted his attempts to transform the Party into a more consistently liberal one through the enactment of such measures as the Fair Labor Standards bill, higher WPA spending, and the Wagner-Steagall public housing bill.[156]

As black leaders became aware of their race's growing political power and importance to Roosevelt and northern liberal Democrats in Congress, they became more assertive and persistent in lobbying for the passage of civil rights legislation, the desegregation of the armed forces, and stronger efforts by the Roosevelt administration to prevent discrimination in New Deal programs and in civil service hiring.[157] Most initial lobbying efforts by black leaders and interest groups had focused on ensuring that blacks received their fair share of relief and public works jobs. During the 1936 campaign, though, the black masses' adoration of Roosevelt contrasted with black intellectuals' ambivalent, equivocal endorsement of him. The intellectuals focused more on Roosevelt's neglect of civil rights issues than on the economic relief that the New Deal provided.[158]

Despite some defections to Wendell Willkie from the black middle class and intelligentsia, Roosevelt received approximately 67 percent of the black vote in 1940.[159] For most black Americans struggling to earn a living, Roosevelt's record on economic and social welfare issues was still the deciding factor for their voting behavior.[160] Except for Jewish voters, blacks had demonstrated themselves to be the most loyal ethnic voting bloc for Roosevelt, because some Catholic ethnics defected to Willkie over foreign policy issues.[161] As many non-southern white Protestants returned to the Republican fold in 1940, Walter White of the NAACP hoped that this loss of white middle-class support for Roosevelt and the national Democratic party would further strengthen black influence within the Party, thereby pressuring northern liberal Democrats into finally adopting effective civil rights measures.[162] Roosevelt's re-election in 1944 revealed a substantial decline in electoral support for the president in the midwestern farm belt, but the level of black electoral support remained unchanged from 1940 as 68 percent of all black voters cast ballots for Roosevelt.[163]

As Roosevelt attempted to transform the national Democratic party into a clearly and consistently liberal party, blacks emerged as the most cohesive, loyal voting bloc in supporting such an ideological transformation. More than any other ethnic group, blacks unequivocally supported the New Deal's ideology and policy agenda of greater federal intervention to solve social and economic problems. Through their power as a dependable, united voting bloc for Democratic presidential nominees, blacks eventually achieved a degree of influence within the national Democratic party and over its policy agenda that exceeded their proportion of the general population.[164] Although Roosevelt's presidency did not achieve the civil rights objectives of black leaders, it gave black Americans the political recognition they needed in order to eventually transform the national Democratic party from their worst enemy on civil rights issues into their most powerful ally.[165]

A New Democratic Party under the New Deal

During the 1920s, Roosevelt had hoped to transform the Party into the enduring majority party in national politics by uniting its northern urban and southern rural factions and attracting progressive Republicans and independents through the formulation of a policy agenda that appealed to them.[166] He had assumed that by focusing on economic and social welfare policies, which party members generally agreed upon, intraparty unity and cooperation would be maintained; religious and cultural issues that divided this diverse coalition would be avoided.[167] During his first term as president, it appeared that his objective—forming a cohesive Democratic majority united behind a liberal policy agenda—was achievable.[168] Except for a handful of outspoken conservative critics like Carter Glass and Harry Byrd, most southern Democrats in Congress enthusiastically supported New Deal legislation. Traditional party loyalty, the populist strain of southern politics, and the economic backwardness and poverty of their region all combined to make them the most important bastion of support in Congress for the early New Deal.[169]

However, the development of the Party as the new majority party in national politics also initiated the steady decline of southern power and influence within it. As Democratic strength in Congress and the electoral college grew outside the South especially in urban-industrial areas of the Northeast and Midwest, southerners lost the disproportionate amount of power within the national party that they had wielded during the Party's chronic minority status. In 1920, southerners comprised 82 percent of the Democratic representation in the House of Representatives and 70 percent in the Senate. By 1936, only 35 percent of the Democrats in both houses of Congress were southerners.[170] Likewise, in the election of 1920, the South provided the Democratic presidential nominee with 90 percent of his electoral college votes. In the 1936 presidential election, only 23 percent of Roosevelt's electoral college votes came from the South.[171]

The effects of the New Deal and Roosevelt's leadership in changing the ideology, policy initiatives, and coalition members of the Party became apparent during his second term. The decline of southern influence within the national party coincided with the rise of northern urban liberals in Congress who were responsive to the policy interests and demands of labor unions and blacks. Intraparty conflicts over the Wagner-Costigan anti-lynching bill, the Fair Labor Standards Act, increased WPA spending, and other divisive bills, exacerbated the sectional, economic, and ideological differences between the northern and southern wings.[172]

The northern Democratic dominance of the New Deal policy agenda during Roosevelt's second term strengthened the liberal identity of the national party, emphasizing greater federal intervention to regulate and reform the economy by improving working conditions and wages, empowering labor unions, increasing public housing, and assuring federal aid to central cities.[173] The growing importance of the black vote to northern Democrats in Congress induced the overwhelming majority of them to oppose their southern colleagues by supporting anti-lynching legislation.[174] During his "purge" in the 1938 Democratic primaries, Roosevelt also proved to be less deferential to the southern Democrats on racial issues as he publicly compared the "feudalism" of southern society to fascism in Europe.[175]

By the end of Roosevelt's second term, it was evident that the New Deal policy agenda and ideology did not have the unifying effect within the national party that he had assumed it would. Intraparty discord intensified as conservative members, mostly southerners, realized that the New Deal's emphasis on expanding the role of the federal government in the economy and its power in federal-state relations through regulatory controls, matching-fund formulas, higher taxes, social welfare programs, and grants to state and local governments sharply contradicted and threatened the party's long-held Jeffersonian tradition of states' rights and minimal federal intervention in domestic affairs.[176]

Most disturbing to anti-New Deal Democrats was the growing emphasis on the development of a social democracy and a liberal Party. Southern conservatives and business interests realized that their power within the Party was declining. Meanwhile, the Democratic party under Roosevelt was becoming a pluralistic, populist party which served as a source of power, status, and access for blacks, women, urban ethnics, and labor unions.

As Samuel Beer has convincingly argued, the New Deal policy agenda and the ideology that it reflected combined democratizing and nationalizing elements. New Deal liberalism sought to further democratize the political system by increasing the political power of previously disadvantaged groups.[177] It sought to achieve this democratization through governmental nationalism, formulating and implementing domestic policies which centralized more authority in the federal government and often benefited the political and economic interests of the coalition members.[178]

The New Deal policy agenda served to expand the size of the national party and more clearly define it. The growing opposition of southern conservatives toward Roosevelt's party leadership and the New Deal made the Party's liberal identity even more evident. The accomplishments of and conflicts over New Deal policies would serve to identify the national Democratic party for the American electorate long after Roosevelt's presidency.[179]

3 Roosevelt and the Machine Bosses

The Bosses' Role in the Democratic Party

One of the ironies of Roosevelt's expansion and liberal reformation of the Democratic party is that many political machines not only survived but even thrived during the New Deal era. How could his leadership inspire and induce the development of a more humane economy and society if corrupt, even anti-democratic, machines were bolstered by federal funds, patronage, and programs? He had, after all, based his first political campaign on the issue of bossism, presenting himself to the voters of Dutchess County as an idealistic crusader opposed to machine politics in both parties. Following his opposition to the Tammany Hall sponsored attempt to nominate William Sheehan to the U.S. Senate, Roosevelt adapted himself to the political reality of Tammany's continuing power in the New York Democracy. During the 1920s, he quietly cooperated with Tammany Hall while trying to limit its influence in New York state politics.[1]

This dichotomous approach to machine politics, following his previously unconditional, outspoken opposition to machines, resulted in part from two realizations. First, as a state senator, he began to respect and admire Al Smith and Robert Wagner, the Tammany-connected leaders of the New York state legislature who successfully and sincerely led the passage of progressive legislation. Roosevelt understood that without machine support such capable men of humble origin could not have entered and succeeded in politics. Their devotion to progressive policy objectives, especially in social welfare and labor reforms, made him realize that machine politicians could support the same policy agenda that he advocated.[2]

Second, Roosevelt's political struggles and conflicts with

Tammany Hall had taught him a harsh yet valuable lesson. No matter how corrupt and inefficient machines might be in spending public funds and managing public services, they were impressively effective and powerful in their ability to deliver united blocs of delegates at nominating conventions and to mobilize masses of urban voters on election day.[3] During his governorship and presidency, he maintained a relationship with Democratic machines in which he gave them patronage and influence within their jurisdictions in exchange for their support at nominating conventions and in mobilizing voters. After 1936, he became even more dependent on machine-controlled political support to secure his renomination and re-election in 1940 and 1944, when many non-southern WASP voters returned to the Republican party.[4]

By relying on the bosses to maintain his electoral support, Roosevelt was able to focus on national policy objectives. He believed that, as president, he must avoid entangling himself in state and local matters of corruption and bossism. A delegation of civic reformers from New Jersey once conferred with him about weakening the power of Frank Hague, dictatorial mayor of Jersey City, by manipulating federal patronage in their state. Roosevelt refused to comply with their request, suggesting that they focus on convincing Jersey City voters to defeat Hague in the next mayoral election.[5] Roosevelt understood that he needed the political support of notorious bosses like Hague in order to remain in office and to help elect Democrats to Congress supportive of his national policy objectives.[6]

Unlike many uncompromising reformers who shared his political ideals and policy objectives, Roosevelt was willing to cooperate with and even benefit politicians and organizations within the Party whose political practices sharply contradicted values that the New Deal ideology encompassed. Recognizing his need for their political support, the Democratic bosses were also dependent on Roosevelt and the New Deal. Unconcerned about the ideological aspects of the New Deal's policies and Roosevelt's leadership, they highly valued his position as an appealing vote-getter at the top of the ticket who would attract votes to obscure machine-backed candidates on the same ballot. More importantly, though, the cities governed by Democratic bosses had been economically devastated by the Depression.[7] The bosses needed a friendly relationship with the White House in order to receive enough federal funds and patronage to maintain their machines. The sharp drop in property tax revenues and the overwhelming demands of their constituents for economic relief made them desperate for federal aid, especially if their state governments were unable or unwilling to provide it.[8] Tammany Hall's humiliating loss to Fiorello La Guardia and his Fusion ticket in New York City's municipal election of 1933 was caused mostly by the unpopular layoffs of city employees and reduction in public services that the Tammany-controlled city hall implemented in order to adapt to fiscal retrenchment.[9]

It is not surprising that the Democratic bosses became the leading supporters of the cooperative federalism that became part of the Party's liberal ideology and policy agenda during the New Deal.[10] With federal funds and programs, the machines were not only able to alleviate the economic suffering of their constituents and provide patronage jobs for their party workers, but also able to improve and expand their cities' public infrastructure substantially. Through the WPA, PWA, and, later, the U.S. Housing Authority, Chicago, Jersey City, Kansas City, and other machine-controlled cities built new public schools, public hospitals, water and sewer systems, bridges, expressways, subway extensions, parks, and housing projects.[11] In his analysis of the New Deal's policy impact on cities, historian Zane Miller estimated that, by 1936, all of the federal programs combined created about 500 points of contact between the federal government and the cities.[12]

During and after World War II, the federal government's partnership with municipal governments in major cities expanded to include urban planning and urban renewal.[13] Federal influence in urban affairs grew as the amount of federal funds in municipal budgets increased.[14] Democratic bosses became even more dependent on federal funds and programs as low-income southern blacks migrated to their cities to work in defense plants and as tax-paying middle-class home owners left for the suburbs.[15] With their local tax bases shrinking and the service demands of their constituents increasing, big city mayors, mostly Democrats, recognized the necessity of having a president responsive to their cities' interests in order for them to stay in power.[16]

Initially, though, the Democratic machine bosses were not certain if a Roosevelt presidency would be sensitive to the economic needs and policy interests of their cities. As a state senator and governor of New York, his policy efforts had revealed a greater concern for rural areas. His focus on the problems of these areas was linked to his political objective of expanding the state Democracy in upstate New York in order to reduce Tammany Hall's disproportionate power in the state's Democratic party. His policy agenda as governor had focused on forest conservation, rural electrification, tax relief for farmers, road-building in rural areas, and other programs intended to attract traditionally Republican upstate voters into the Democratic party.[17] As a presidential candidate in 1932, his rhetoric was directed more at ending the farm depression than at the economic and structural problems peculiar to the cities.[18] His concentration on agricultural issues during the campaign also reflected his belief that rural living was a more wholesome, healthy, and socially stable way of life for Americans.[19]

But the machine bosses were bothered more by his alliance of supporters than by his personal rural orientation. His base of support at the national convention in Chicago consisted of the same southern Bourbons and western progressives who had opposed Al Smith in 1924 and 1928.[20] Despite his quiet cooperation with Tammany Hall on patronage matters, Governor Roosevelt was still suspected by many bosses of being an anti-machine progressive. They feared that he might use federal patronage to strengthen their progressive opponents within the party. Although Roosevelt procrastinated about getting the state government involved in investigating the corruption of New York City mayor Jimmy Walker's administration, he finally capitulated to public pressure and ap-

pointed Judge Samuel Seabury to investigate the Walker
administration.[21] This incident and his vacillation on the
Prohibition issue until 1930 solidified the bosses' suspicion
that he would not be a reliable ally in the White House.[22]

After Tammany Hall endorsed Al Smith for the Democratic presidential nomination, most machine bosses prominent in national party affairs also announced their support of
Smith. Smith's position in the nomination campaign was
strengthened by the fact that John Raskob, his campaign
manager in 1928, was still chairman of the Democratic National Committee. Through his position as DNC chairman,
Raskob could influence the DNC to choose as a convention
site a city whose machine supported Smith. Regardless of
what city was selected, and no matter how many big city
machines supported him with their delegates, it was highly
unlikely that Smith could win the two-thirds majority
needed to secure the nomination. Smith's attraction of machine-controlled delegations, however, could deny Roosevelt
the two-thirds majority he needed to be nominated.[23]

The only nationally prominent machine boss who committed his delegates to support Roosevelt was Tom Pendergast of Kansas City.[24] Roosevelt, therefore, hoped that the
Democratic National Committee would choose Kansas City
as the site of the 1932 Democratic national convention.[25]
Instead, the Smith supporters on the DNC succeeded in securing Chicago as the site of convention. This meant that the
convention would be held in a city governed by a staunch
Smith ally, Mayor Anton Cermak.[26] Elected in 1931, Cermak
did not want to offend his pro-Smith Irish colleagues and
refused to commit his delegates to Roosevelt until his nomination became inevitable.[27]

Roosevelt's most formidable opponent among the machine
bosses at the 1932 convention was Mayor Frank Hague of
Jersey City, Smith's floor manager. In a speech delivered on
June 24, he bluntly declared that Roosevelt was the weakest
presidential candidate at the convention and could not carry
any state east of the Mississippi River.[28] Despite the efforts
of Hague and other pro-Smith leaders, Roosevelt received
enough delegate support for the nomination after Speaker

John Garner created a bandwagon effect by releasing Texas's delegates to him. Like the other pro–Smith bosses, Hague quickly reconciled himself with the Roosevelt camp after the convention.[29] He organized a rally in Sea Girt, New Jersey for Roosevelt in August and mobilized over 100,000 people to attend it.[30] The Hague machine's support enabled Roosevelt to carry New Jersey in 1932 and in his three re-election campaigns.[31]

The political relationship between Roosevelt and the Democratic bosses gradually became stronger during Roosevelt's presidency as the New Deal policy agenda and the president's party leadership became more controversial and divisive.[32] With many southern conservatives, progressive Republicans, and independents abandoning and even opposing Roosevelt after 1936, the Democratic machine bosses and their urban constituents emerged as the most stalwart supporters of his party leadership and New Deal liberalism.[33] Four Democratic bosses in particular became influential partners with Roosevelt in national party affairs and during his 1940 and 1944 re-election campaigns. They were Frank Hague of Jersey City, Ed Kelly of Chicago, Tom Pendergast of Kansas City, and Ed Flynn of the Bronx. Ironically, Roosevelt's liberal reformation of the national Democratic party would receive its strongest base of political support from the types of urban machines which he had regarded as the chief nemesis of liberalism during his early political career.[34]

Frank Hague: "Hitler on the Hudson"

The infamous Mayor Frank Hague of Jersey City exemplified the notoriously corrupt, repressive machine boss whose political support Roosevelt needed. Hague's machine not only controlled the Democratic party politics and municipal government of Jersey City but also dominated the politics and public policies of the surrounding Hudson County and the state government of New Jersey through the administration of A. Harry Moore, a Hague puppet.[35] Besides being able to "deliver" New Jersey to Roosevelt at national party conventions and in presidential elections, Hague's power in national

party politics was solidified by his positions as Democratic
national committeeman from New Jersey, state chairman of
New Jersey's Democratic party, and vice-chairman of the
Democratic National Committee. Furthermore, the Hague-
controlled Democratic delegation in Congress, especially
Representative Mary T. Norton, comprised one of the most
loyal bastions of support for Roosevelt.[36] In a 1942 letter,
Hague assured the president that liberal Democratic Senator
William H. Smathers of New Jersey "will be re-elected in
accordance with your wish."[37]

For the mayor of a medium-sized city, Hague achieved a
disproportionate degree of power and influence over Roosevelt's party leadership and in national party affairs because of
his machine's efficiency in producing overwhelming Democratic majorities in local, county, and statewide elections.
Because southern New Jersey was mostly Republican, a
Democratic presidential nominee needed a large proportion
of votes in Hudson County in order to carry New Jersey in the
electoral college.[38] Likewise, Democratic candidates for governor and senator often perceived the Hague-controlled Hudson County vote as the key to victory in New Jersey, a state
with a competitive two-party system. Realizing the importance of having a governor loyal to him with the state legislature often controlled by Republicans, Hague used his
organization to help elect most of New Jersey's governors
during his thirty-year career, including one Republican,
Harold G. Hoffman.[39]

Hague's vast supply of patronage jobs extended into the
private sector. He had a network of political allies in most of
the banks, insurance companies, industries, hospitals, and
other private concerns. To obtain employment, an applicant
often had to acquire a job card from city hall through his ward
leader.[40]

Hague's patronage power was further strengthened by the
Depression and the New Deal. The Depression had made
thousands of unemployed Jersey City residents desperate for
the economic security of government jobs, no matter how low-
paying. Through his control of the governorship, Hague had
thousands of New Deal public works jobs and an abundance of

federal patronage at his disposal.[41] The WPA in New Jersey employed approximately 76,000 to 97,000 people a year during the New Deal era. From 1935 to 1939, the WPA spent over $47 million in Hudson County.[42] The PWA, CCC, NYA, and other New Deal programs provided even more funds and jobs for the Hague machine.[43]

PWA grants and loans helped Hague expand the Jersey City Medical Center. Besides using this two thousand bed facility to provide even more patronage, Hague used it to strengthen the machine's humanitarian image among Jersey City's needy residents by providing them with free medical care. On October 2, 1936, Roosevelt visited Jersey City to dedicate the new hospital. Hague made the day a public holiday. In his dedication speech, Roosevelt stated, "Frank Hague has done a great service not only to you good people who are alive today in Jersey City and Hudson County, but a service that is going to last for many, many generations to come."[44]

A month later, Hague's voter mobilization efforts helped provide Roosevelt with over 60 percent of the popular votes in New Jersey in the 1936 presidential election. Although he remained quietly cooperative with Hague concerning federal patronage and New Deal programs in New Jersey, Roosevelt avoided public meetings with him after 1937. The Jersey City mayor's repressive tactics and controversial statements against CIO organizers and anti-machine dissidents stimulated a barrage of unfavorable, nationwide newspaper publicity against him and prompted the media's characterization of him as an American Hitler.[45] By the late 1930s, Roosevelt found himself under increasing pressure from liberal allies and prominent journalists to weaken Hague's power by denying him patronage or by publicly condemning his police state tactics. Identifying himself as a New Dealer, a New Jersey resident urged Roosevelt "to squelch the embers of Nazism in Jersey City."[46]

But Hague's political control of Hudson County remained intact. His national reputation as a major power broker within the Party was enhanced by his key role in securing Roosevelt's renomination in 1940.[47] Hague joined bosses Ed

Kelly of Chicago, Ed Crump of Memphis, and Ed Flynn of the
Bronx in assuring substantial machine support for Roosevelt's renomination at the 1940 national convention.[48] With
Roosevelt's renomination secured, the Hague machine's powerful voter mobilization system delivered New Jersey's electoral college votes to the president in the general election.

Hague again delivered his state's votes for Roosevelt in
1944, although by a narrower margin. Hague's machine began to weaken internally during World War II as its reputation among Jersey City residents for "efficiency" in the
delivery of services crumbled because of manpower shortages
and Hague's neglect.[49] Organizational discipline and obe-
dience to the mayor among the machine politicians slackened
as Hague spent most of his time in Florida and conducted city
business by telephone. Throughout the 1940s, the Republicans controlled the governorship and the state legislature
and filled the state's courts and commissions with anti-
Hague members who investigated Hague's cronies.[50] Recognizing his decline in power, Hague voluntarily resigned in
1947 and chose his nephew, Frank Hague Eggers, to replace
him. John V. Kenny, a disaffected machine member, established a fusion ticket and defeated Eggers in the 1949 mayoral election.[51]

Roosevelt's party leadership and the New Deal's relief and
public works programs consolidated Hague's power throughout New Jersey during the 1930s. His decline and fall can be
attributed to his own neglect and to political forces and issues
peculiar to his city.[52] Despite his personal dislike of Hague,
Roosevelt realized how indispensable Hague's machine was
in delivering New Jersey's electoral college votes and delegates at the national conventions and in electing pro-New
Deal senators and congressmen from New Jersey.

Ed Kelly and the Rise of the Chicago Machine

At the beginning of Roosevelt's presidency, the Democratic
machine of Chicago was a struggling, fledging organization.
Unlike the Hague machine of Jersey City, it was not a well-
entrenched political organization or a one-man fief. The Chi-

cago machine was developing as a party organization that depended on consensus and harmony among its politicians rather than on a single charismatic or autocratic leader.[53]

This consensual approach resulted partially from the multi-ethnic character of Chicago's population and the leadership style of Democratic mayor Anton J. Cermak.[54] Defeating Republican "Big Bill" Thompson in 1931, Cermak sought to alleviate Chicago's Depression-spawned fiscal crisis and expand the voter appeal of the local Party beyond its predominantly Irish base. During the bitterly contested race of 1931, Cermak presented himself as a reformer while denouncing the bootlegging, gangsterism, corruption, and fiscal chaos that had occurred under Thompson's Republican machine. Thompson worsened his own position by sarcastically referring to his Czechoslovakian-born opponent as "Pushcart Tony" and "Tony Baloney." The Republican mayor had hoped that such ethnic-baiting would alienate Irish Democrats from Cermak and attract them to his own candidacy.[55] Instead, large numbers of Slavic ethnics and traditionally Republican Jews flocked to support Cermak's candidacy.[56] During the 1920s, Cermak had carefully cultivated the support of Irish ward leaders, especially Pat Nash, and thus received the support of most Irish voters.[57] With Thompson attracting majorities only from blacks, Italians, and staunch WASP Republicans, Cermak was elected by a plurality of nearly 200,000 votes.[58]

Cermak, who founded and served as chairman of the Cook County Democratic Central Committee since 1928, chose Pat Nash to succeed him. Nash was an Irish-born ward committeeman and a wealthy sewer contractor who was highly respected by Irish Democrats in Chicago. Although Cermak opened up leadership positions in the party and in the city and county governments to non–Irish ethnics, especially Slavs and Jews, he strove to maintain a cooperative relationship with Irish leaders. Nash, because of his long absences from Chicago and his unassuming personality, usually deferred to Cermak's leadership, but Irish Democrats on the city council and in the county and ward committees began to chafe under the mayor's aggressive leadership.[59]

Cermak revealed an obsession with efficiency in the operations and structure of both the city government and the Cook County Democratic organization. He alienated some party regulars through a fiscal austerity program that included budget cuts and layoffs of municipal employees. Cermak had the machine publish its own newspaper, *The Public Service Leader*, and conduct statistical analyses of voter turn-out in Chicago's fifty wards. He used these analyses to reward or punish precinct captains and ward committeemen according to their ability to "deliver" for the Democratic ticket.[60] Cermak sought to convey the impression to Chicagoans that a well-organized political machine was synonymous with an efficient, cost-effective city government.[61]

The mayor realized, though, that efficiency alone would not maintain harmony and unity behind his leadership within the Democratic machine. Mostly to appease the Irish, Cermak distinguished himself at the 1932 Democratic national convention in Chicago as a steadfast, diehard supporter of Al Smith. After Roosevelt's nomination was secured, Cermak sought to impress Roosevelt and Farley by delivering a huge plurality of votes.[62] Although Cermak had conferred with Roosevelt at Hyde Park, he was concerned about rumors that Democratic Senator J. Hamilton Lewis of Illinois would receive all of his state's federal patronage.[63] He traveled to Florida in February 1933 to confer with Roosevelt and Farley. A deranged gunman intending to assassinate the president-elect mortally wounded Cermak instead.[64]

With Cermak's death, Nash became titular head of the city's Democratic party and secured the appointment of Francis Corr, an obscure alderman, as acting mayor until a special election could be held. Nash, though, began to fear that fierce competition in a special election would badly fragment the machine. He succeeded in convincing the state legislature to pass a bill granting the Chicago city council the authority to elect a mayor who would finish Cermak's term.[65]

Nash did not want any one of the ambitious aldermen competing to succeed Corr to be elected mayor by the city council. He feared that such a situation would irreparably divide and weaken both the machine and the city council and decided that the ideal compromise candidate for mayor would be someone who was not an elected official yet was well-known to the machine members and had few enemies. His choice, who was quickly elected by the city council, was Edward J. Kelly, chief engineer of the Metropolitan Sanitary District.[66]

The new mayor managed to end a bitter, almost riotous teachers' strike by securing a $25 million loan from the Reconstruction Finance Corporation.[67] Kelly soon realized that the fiscal health of the city government—as well as the political health of the Democratic machine—depended on a substantial, steady flow of federal funds for Chicago. Consequently, he immediately began to cultivate close, cooperative relationships with Roosevelt, Jim Farley, and Harry Hopkins. In September 1933, Hopkins insisted that the Illinois state legislature raise adequate matching funds in order to receive FERA funds. Kelly was instrumental in lobbying and pressuring the reluctant state legislature into appropriating the necessary funds.[68]

By successfully using federal funds and public works programs to provide jobs, relief, and structural improvements for Chicago, Kelly received over 82 percent of the votes cast in Chicago's 1935 mayoral election. Impressed by Kelly's overwhelming margin of victory and increasingly concerned about carrying Illinois in the upcoming presidential election, Roosevelt and Hopkins decided to grant Kelly more federal patronage and discretion over the the selection of WPA projects.[69] This decision was solidified by Kelly's success in again pressuring the Illinois state legislature into adopting a tax increase in order to raise the matching funds necessary for receiving WPA funds.[70] Hopkins had cut off WPA funds to Illinois on May 1 after Governor Henry Horner and the state legislature had failed to appropriate enough matching funds. Kelly's proven ability to "deliver" for the White House had now made him the top Democrat in Illinois for Roosevelt.

Through his relationship with Hopkins, Kelly was able to control the approximately two hundred thousand WPA jobs in Illinois, a rich source of patronage which extended his machine's influence beyond Cook County.[71] Hopkins appointed

Robert Dunham, a Kelly ally, as Illinois's WPA director, thereby strengthening Kelly's influence over the selection of WPA projects and the appointment of administrative personnel.[72] Jim Farley bypassed other Democratic politicians in Illinois and dealt exclusively with Kelly concerning patronage and DNC matters.[73]

Having secured a beneficial political rapport with the White House, Kelly now focused on consolidating and expanding the Democratic machine's power in Chicago so that it would endure beyond his mayoralty. Just as Cermak had made membership in the local Democratic party attractive to more non-Irish ethnics, Kelly sought to coopt the black community of Chicago. This was a formidable task. Compared to the black voters of other major northern cities, Chicago's blacks were the most staunchly Republican.[74] Only 21 percent of them voted for Roosevelt in 1932. In the Roosevelt landslide of 1936, approximately 76 percent of all black voters throughout the United States voted for Roosevelt; however, only 49 percent of Chicago's blacks did.[75]

Unlike the bosses of other Democratic machines that cultivated black support during the New Deal, Kelly did not limit his realignment strategy to the distribution of relief and patronage. He also aroused white antagonism toward himself by advocating racially integrated public schools. When black parents complained about segregation at the Morgan Park High School in 1934, Kelly rescinded the school board's policy allowing such segregation. He refused to withdraw this decision despite an unruly protest by white students. Similar anti-integration protests by whites occurred in 1945, but Kelly refused to yield to them.[76]

Although his close identification with Roosevelt and the New Deal certainly made him more attractive to black voters, most of Kelly's success in coopting Chicago's black community can be attributed to his own initiative. Affectionately known as "Big Red" by Chicago blacks, Kelly convinced many that their support of and participation in the Democratic machine would enhance their personal ambitions and their community's interests.[77] As the black proportion of Chicago's population began to increase steadily during the 1930s, Kelly realized that the electoral support of Chicago blacks would become even more important for the future political strength of the machine. Kelly consistently received a significantly higher percentage of black votes in Chicago than Roosevelt did. Whereas Roosevelt received only 49 percent of the black vote in Chicago in 1936 and 52 percent in 1940, Kelly received 80 percent in 1935, 59 percent in 1939, and 61 percent in 1943.[78]

Regardless of his personality and skills, Kelly's appeal among Chicagoans, was greatly enhanced by his success in assuring a substantial flow of federal funds into the city.[79] Kelly was able to build a subway, a modernized municipal airport, expressways, new parks, public housing projects, and thirty new public schools from 1933 to 1940.[80] During his first two years as mayor, the city government contributed only 1.4 percent of the relief funds spent in Chicago while the federal government contributed 87.6 percent and the state 11 percent.[81] With the federal government paying for most relief and public works projects, Kelly was able to appease businessmen and home owners by avoiding increases in property taxes.[82] When campaigning for re-election, Kelly and other machine politicians were able to claim that they had created many construction jobs and structural improvements while also keeping local taxes low.

Harry Hopkins's indulgent attitude concerning the requirement of local matching funds for the receipt of WPA funds resulted partially from his own presidential ambitions for 1940. By 1938, Jim Farley also hoped to succeed Roosevelt.[83] With both the WPA administrator and the DNC chairman competing for Kelly's political support, the mayor was assured of receiving further preferential treatment.[84]

Chicago hosted the 1940 Democratic National Convention. In 1939, Kelly built a national network of support for a third term while Roosevelt was still denying that he was interested in one.[85] Kelly "managed" the convention, creating enthusiasm for Roosevelt that united Democrats behind the president and defeated the two prominent hopefuls, Farley and Garner.[86]

As the 1944 election approached, Chicago was again chosen as the site of the national convention. Absorbed in his foreign policy and military responsibilities, Roosevelt relied on Kelly to manage another "controlled" convention united behind his renomination. Kelly realized, though, that not even his political prowess could assure Roosevelt's re-election if Henry Wallace was his running mate. DNC chairman Robert Hannegan, Kelly, and other machine bosses convinced Roosevelt to choose Senator Harry S. Truman of Missouri as the best possible compromise candidate for vice president.

While Kelly's political skills had been instrumental to Roosevelt's success in the 1940 and 1944 campaigns, his control of the Chicago machine began to falter during World War II. Ironically, his political power in Chicago eventually became a victim of his own success in building a stable, enduring Democratic machine. As was Kelly's goal, his leadership was no longer crucial to the life of the machine. The machine forced him into retirement in 1947, partially because of his liberal policies toward racial integration in housing and public schools. Even so, Kelly willingly campaigned for his successor, Martin H. Kennelly, a previously apolitical businessman chosen by the anti-Kelly coalition as the machine's candidate.[87] Kelly's support of Kennelly illustrated a characteristic that distinguished the Cook County Democratic organization—an emphasis on intraparty cohesion, continuity, and a stable mayoral succession.[88] This characteristic would become even more apparent during the twenty-one year reign of Richard J. Daley, a Kelly protégé.[89] Despite occasional internal conflicts, the machine's politicians realized that maintaining their own power depended on maintaining a cohesive, stable structure for the machine.

Roosevelt's favoritism toward Chicago was a crucial factor in transforming the fledgling machine of 1933 into a stable, enduring party organization by the end of his presidency. Besides the tangible benefits that the New Deal provided in the form of relief, jobs, and an improved public infrastructure, the steady flow of federal funds into Chicago enabled Kelly and the Democratic machine to claim to the Chicago electorate that machine rule was conducive to the effective management of the municipal government's finances and its delivery of services. This federal subsidy of municipal spending helped Kelly and the Democratic-controlled city council gain the support of previously anti-machine Republican businessmen by avoiding sharp property tax increases and undertaking structural improvements that stimulated economic growth.[90]

Federal aid, therefore, solidified the durability of the Democratic machine's control of Chicago's municipal government by convincing most voters that the machine's control of city hall was synonymous with capable public administration.[91] After Kelly's administration, the Chicago machine not only maintained control of city government but remained a key player in presidential politics. While the Roosevelt-Kelly partnership proved to be highly beneficial to Roosevelt's party leadership, its most enduring impact was the strong foundation that it helped to develop for the resilient Democratic machine of Chicago.[92]

Tom Pendergast and the Demise of a Machine

Tom Pendergast never enjoyed the rapport with Roosevelt that Ed Kelly did. Nor was he indispensable, as Frank Hague was, for delivering his state's electoral college votes to Roosevelt. Pendergast, however, was the first major Democratic machine boss to support Roosevelt in the 1932 campaign.[93] During Roosevelt's first term, Pendergast was rewarded for his delegate support at the convention by being given control over most federal patronage in Missouri. Matthew S. Murray, a member of the Pendergast machine, was appointed WPA director for Missouri, thereby giving Pendergast power over the WPA payroll and the selection of public works projects.[94] Shortly after the 1936 election, though, Roosevelt funneled federal patronage to anti-Pendergast Democratic politicians in Missouri and allowed federal authorities to investigate and prosecute Pendergast for income tax evasion. Imprisoned in Leavenworth by 1939, his machine crumbled as it candidates lost control of Kansas City's municipal government to a reform ticket.[95]

The brevity of Pendergast's beneficial relationship with

the Roosevelt administration and the humiliating demise of
his machine can be explained partially by the position that
Pendergast held in the Missouri Democratic party. Unlike
Frank Hague and Ed Kelly, Pendergast, even at the peak of
his political prowess, did not control his state's Democracy. He
was forced to compete with powerful politicians and factions
from St. Louis and the rural areas. His machine, therefore,
represented only a balance of power in statewide elections.[96]
Consequently, Pendergast could not consistently maintain
control of his state's governorship during the 1930's, as Hague
had done in New Jersey. This lack of hegemony by Pendergast
in the Missouri Democracy enabled Democratic Governor
Lloyd Stark to launch a vigorous legal attack on the Kansas
City machine after 1936 and motivate Roosevelt to ally himself with Stark.[97]

In July 1931, Jim Farley visited Kansas City to solicit
Pendergast's support for Roosevelt at the upcoming Democratic national convention, perceiving Pendergast as the dominant power in the Missouri Democracy.[98] Al Smith also
believed Pendergast to hold the power and, during one of
Pendergast's 1931 visits to New York, tried to obtain the
support of his fellow Irish Catholic by appealing to a sense of
ethnic solidarity.[99] By the fall of 1931, Pendergast had declared his support of Roosevelt's nomination.[100] According to
Ike Dunlap, a Harvard classmate of Roosevelt and the governor's first contact in Missouri, Pendergast felt compelled to
support Missouri's favorite son, Senator James A. Reed, on
the first ballot at the national convention.[101]

Despite his public facade of supporting Reed's candidacy,
Pendergast worked behind the scenes to assure that the
Missouri delegation would vote for Roosevelt.[102] Throughout
May 1932, Pendergast visited Roosevelt and Farley in Albany
and frequently conferred with them by telephone to arrange
a plan to prevent Reed's candidacy from threatening Missouri's support of Roosevelt.[103] Roosevelt had suggested that
he offer Reed the vice-presidential nomination, but Pendergast rejected the idea. According to the plan they formulated,
the Missouri delegation would support Reed until a critical

point in the nominating process and then switch its votes to Roosevelt.[104]

On the second ballot at the Chicago convention, Missouri gave Roosevelt his biggest increase in delegate support from the first ballot.[105] By the fourth ballot, Roosevelt's nomination was assured. In the presidential election of 1932, Roosevelt carried Missouri by over 460,000 votes. Over 140,000 of these came from Kansas City alone.[106]

Grateful for Pendergast's early support and impressed by his ability to mobilize voters, Roosevelt and Farley were generous in granting patronage, legal favors, and discretion over New Deal programs in Missouri to the Kansas City boss. Through his influence with the White House, Pendergast managed to secure a presidential pardon for Conrad Mann, a political associate who was convicted of involvement in an illegal lottery and was about to be sent to a federal prison.[107] Secretary of Labor Frances Perkins had intended to appoint a Republican, Martin Lewis, as Missouri's director of Federal Re-employment. Pendergast intervened and secured the appointment of Harry S. Truman, a county judge and Pendergast ally. Truman formed a close relationship with Harry Hopkins while working in this position and became a committed New Dealer.[108]

As it was for Hague and Kelly, the WPA served as a rich source of patronage jobs and funds for civic improvements. The number of Missourians on the WPA payroll fluctuated between 87,727 in 1936 and 88,884 in 1940.[109] Under strong pressure from Farley and Pendergast, Harry Hopkins agreed to appoint Matthew Murray as the WPA director.[110] Murray had previously worked as the city manager's director of public works and for a construction company affiliated with the Pendergast machine.[111] Entering the Senate in 1935, Truman had used his influence with Hopkins to secure Murray's appointment. Kansas City, therefore, was assured of a disproportionate share of Missouri's allotment of WPA jobs, funds, and construction projects.[112] Governor Guy Park, a Pendergast ally, would simply refer Missourians seeking federal jobs to Pendergast.[113]

With his control of one Senate seat and the governorship,
and his beneficial relationships with Hopkins and Farley,
Pendergast had reached his peak of power by 1936. Intimidation and beatings of anti-machine voters by Pendergast's
henchmen, however, stimulated a growing public demand for
an investigation of the blatant ballot fraud which customarily
occurred in Kansas City elections. The leadership of this
reform movement came from an unlikely source, Governor
Lloyd Stark. Pendergast had endorsed Stark in 1936, assuming that he could be as easily manipulated as Guy Park had
been.[114] Stark's political objective, though, was to be elected
senator in 1940. Assuming that Truman would run for re-
election in 1940, Stark hoped that he could defeat him in the
primary by generating anti-Pendergast sentiment. Consequently, the governor would devote his administration to the
destruction of the Pendergast machine.

The political showdown between Pendergast and Stark
occurred over the nomination of a candidate to the state
supreme court in 1938. The White House paid close attention
to this intraparty conflict because it would perceive the win-
ner as the dominant power in the Missouri Democracy. Stark
supported the renomination of James M. Douglas, while the
Pendergast machine supported James V. Billings, his opponent.[115] Both the governor and the Kansas City boss used
hardball tactics in mobilizing voters for their respective candidates. State employees were intimidated into making campaign contributions for Douglas. Stark purged the state
payroll of suspected supporters of Billings and ordered state
officials to display Douglas bumper stickers.[116]

Likewise, Pendergast exploited his major asset—the WPA
payroll. WPA foremen warned workers that they would lose
their jobs if they did not vote for Billings. Stark wrote to
Roosevelt frequently during the campaign, informing him of
the Pendergast machine's political use of the WPA and com-
plaining that Hopkins was doing little to stop it.[117] Despite
Pendergast's dominance of the WPA, the governor generated
enough anti-Pendergast sentiment to win the primary for
Douglas. The governor confidently told Roosevelt that Doug-

las's victory "crushed the Pendergast machine by a landslide."[118]

Even before the primary, Roosevelt had been embarrassed and annoyed by the unfavorable publicity about ballot fraud, police collusion with gangsters, and other scandals associated with the Pendergast machine. With the election of Douglas, Roosevelt was convinced that Stark, not Pendergast, would now be the dominant power in the Missouri Democracy. In sharp contrast to his earlier suppression of federal court action against Pendergast associates, Roosevelt now supported a vigorous federal investigation of Pendergast's finances.[119] The Treasury Department investigated the boss's tax returns while the Justice Department continued its investigation of his acceptance of an insurance bribe.[120]

The political uses of the WPA and federal patronage had demonstrated Roosevelt's ability to strengthen and expand Democratic machines favored by the White House. Conversely, the full force of the Justice Department and the federal court system applied against the Pendergast machine demonstrated the president's ability to destroy a boss who was regarded as a liability. By contrast, Roosevelt had prevented federal prosecution of Frank Hague's mail tampering. Despite the public outcry stimulated by the Jersey City mayor's arrogant suppression of CIO activities, Roosevelt had recognized that Hague maintained effective control of his state's party and was essential for a Democratic victory in the 1940 presidential election. Pendergast may have been less despicable as a machine boss than the autocratic Hague, but he was no longer indispensable to Roosevelt as Stark began to supersede him in the Missouri Democracy.

Roosevelt's ultimate treatment of Pendergast reveals the ambivalent and conditional nature of Roosevelt's relationship with the Democratic machine bosses while pursuing his strategy of expanding and liberalizing the Party. He was willing to cooperate with the bosses and benefit their machines in order to maintain the party's cohesion and electoral base in urban areas and to assure his own re-election. Roosevelt's support, however, was contingent on a boss's ability to contribute to the Party's unity and strength without tainting the White House.[121] Therefore, as Pendergast's power declined and his machine's sordid scandals became intolerable to the White House, Roosevelt did not hesitate to use federal investigatory powers to accelerate the destruction of the Pendergast machine.

Ed Flynn and New York Politics

Edward J. Flynn, the Democratic county leader of the Bronx, was similar to Hague, Kelly, and Pendergast only in his party affiliation, ethnicity, and church affiliation. His father was an Irish immigrant who graduated from Trinity College in Dublin and became a successful businessman in the Bronx.[122] Flynn, who was born into a comfortable, middle-class home, graduated from Fordham College and Law School. He was an articulate, urbane, and well-read man. Eleanor Roosevelt remarked that Flynn, unlike Farley and the other Irish politicos, could understand the ideological and policy aspects of the New Deal that transformed the Party during her husband's presidency.[123]

By 1918, Flynn was operating a successful law practice and had not considered a political career. Bronx Democrats, though persuaded him to run for assemblyman. In 1922, with the support of Tammany chief Charles F. Murphy, the young assemblyman was elected sheriff and Democratic county leader of the Bronx.[124] Flynn first became acquainted with Roosevelt at the 1924 Democratic state convention. During Roosevelt's governorship, he served as secretary of state and traveled throughout New York with Jim Farley, expanding the state party and strengthening its party apparatus.[125]

Though Flynn and Farley were somewhat successful in making the New York Democracy under Roosevelt's leadership more attractive to upstate voters, Tammany Hall had been plagued by bitter, divisive factionalism since Boss Murphy's death in 1924.[126] Al Smith's governorship and presidential candidacies in 1924 and 1928 provided some degree of harmony and unity,[127] but it would never again possess the degree of citywide unity, cohesion, and discipline that it had enjoyed under Murphy's firm, capable leadership.[128]

In a 1928 article, journalist Joseph McGoldrick expressed his hope that under Smith's de facto leadership through George Olvany a "New Tammany" would emerge in which "idealism rather than private gain is the dominating motive of its effective leaders."[129] The prospect, though, of a "New Tammany" emerging as an honest, progressive party organization soon appeared unlikely.[130] Busy with his governorship and presidential ambitions, Smith ignored much of the self-serving corruption and internecine conflicts that occurred among the Tammany leaders after Murphy's death.[131] He agreed to the nomination and subsequent election of Jimmy Walker for mayor in 1925 and again in 1929.[132] As mayor, Jimmy Walker became known to the public mostly for his flamboyant personality and utter incompetence as administrator of the city's finances.

But even with a more competent mayor, the changing demography of New York City made it more difficult for a Tammany leader to exercise the strict, centralized control over Democratic politicians that Murphy had. As the Manhattan proportion of New York City's population steadily declined, the populations of other boroughs, especially the Bronx and Queens, grew quickly.[133] Feeling secure in their bailiwicks, the Democratic leaders in the growing, outlying boroughs sought to remain independent of centralized control.[134]

Besides having embarrassed Roosevelt's presidential candidacy through the Walker scandals, Tammany delegates at the Democratic National Convention remained loyal to Smith and refused to make Roosevelt's nomination unanimous. John Curry, elected Tammany leader in 1929, spitefully tried to prevent the gubernatorial nomination of Herbert Lehman, Roosevelt's choice as his successor in Albany in 1932.[135] Smith intervened and forced Curry to accept the nomination of Roosevelt's lieutenant governor.[136]

With Tammany Hall's record of seamy corruption and relentless defiance toward Roosevelt, it is not surprising that the newly-inaugurated president did not feel obligated to

funnel federal patronage to Tammany Democrats. Instead, he
and Farley gave the bulk of federal patronage in New York to
the three leading anti-Curry Democrats: Ed Flynn; Frank
Kelly, the Democratic county leader in Brooklyn; and Eddy
Ahearn, a district leader on the Lower East Side. Roosevelt
hoped to spawn an intraparty purge of the Curry Democrats
by strengthening these party organizations.[137] By coordinat-
ing his efforts with Farley, Flynn hoped to build a reformist,
pro-Roosevelt Democratic organization that could win citywide elections, namely the mayor's office.[138]

Flynn made his first attempt to implant such a Democratic
organization in city hall during the mayoral election of 1933.
At the request of Flynn and Farley, John J. McKee, an anti-
Curry Tammany politician, was nominated as the mayoral
candidate of the Recovery party.[139] Through this third party,
Flynn and Farley hoped to attract enough voters that Tammany Hall would at least be pressured into reforming itself,
even if McKee was not elected. Besides attracting the votes of
Democrats alienated from Tammany Hall, Flynn and Farley
hoped that the Recovery party would attract independent
voters who were anti-Tammany yet pro-Roosevelt.[140]

Since Walker's resignation, the mayor's office had been
held by John O'Brien, a Tammany judge. O'Brien's lackluster
leadership and the unpopularity of layoffs among municipal
employees made victory by McKee seem plausible. The Irish
working class, more dependent on municipal employment
than other ethnic groups, and Tammany's bastion of electoral
support, was especially bitter toward O'Brien's fiscal austerity policy.[141] New York City Jews, who represented a
disproportionate number of public school teachers and social
workers, were also angry about the Depression-induced layoffs.[142]

McKee, though, only succeeded in splitting the Tammany
vote among Irish voters. In the race between O'Brien, McKee,
and La Guardia, McKee placed second with approximately 32
percent of the vote while O'Brien received about 27 percent
and La Guardia won with 41 percent.[143] La Guardia had
built a patchwork coalition of middle-class reformers, Republicans, anti-Tammany Democrats, and non-Irish ethnics,

especially Italians and Jews, through the Fusion party.[144] Throughout his administration, La Guardia provided Italians and Jews with a degree of involvement and employment in New York City's politics and government that they had not enjoyed during Tammany's previous hegemony of city hall.[145]

With La Guardia's widespread popularity and accomplishments as a progressive mayor, Roosevelt realized that there was little hope of a revitalized, reformed Tammany Hall emerging soon and defeating La Guardia.[146] He, therefore, gave La Guardia the same degree of discretion over New Deal programs in New York City, especially the WPA, that he had given such Democratic mayors as Ed Kelly and Frank Hague. Throughout his political career, Roosevelt had been able to attract the votes of independents and progressive Republicans who usually did not vote Democratic. During his governorship, much of his party-building strategy consisted of making the state party attractive to such voters in upstate New York. Now, as president, Roosevelt realized the importance of La Guardia in attracting such voters to his own candidacy.

Consequently, La Guardia played a leading role in attracting pro–New Deal Republicans and independents to Roosevelt in the president's three re-election campaigns.[147] Except for his support of Ed Flynn through a generous flow of federal patronage, Roosevelt maintained a position of benign neutrality in New York City politics. He did, however, become favorable toward Tammany Hall by 1942 when he supported the election of Mike Kennedy, a liberal Democratic congressman, as Tammany leader.[148] The maverick, charismatic mayor remained defiantly independent by refusing to endorse Republicans for state and national offices while supporting the re-election of Democratic Governor Herbert Lehman in 1938.[149]

Even if Tammany Hall was doomed to disintegration and political impotence, Roosevelt still hoped to stimulate a strong, liberal Democratic organization in New York City. His chief instrument in trying to pressure that city's Party into becoming more liberal and attractive to pro–New Deal voters was the American Labor Party (ALP).[150] With the help of

Farley and Flynn, the ALP was organized in 1936 by two Socialist labor leaders, Sidney Hillman of the Amalgamated Clothing Workers union and David Dubinsky of the International Ladies' Garment Workers Union.[151] The original purpose of this party was to attract Socialists and workers from unions outside of the AFL to Roosevelt's candidacy. Hillman was also a leading member of Labor's Non-Partisan League and used the ALP to solicit an impressive amount in campaign contributions and votes for Roosevelt's re-election.[152]

Although the ALP helped to re-elect Roosevelt and Lehman in New York, it was soon evident that the ALP would not allow itself to merely be a liberal-labor wing of the local Democratic party. Flynn was ambivalent about helping to establish the ALP, fearing that it might detract from, rather than contribute to, the electoral support of Democratic candidates.[153] The ALP endorsed La Guardia over Democratic mayoral nominees in 1937 and 1941 and later helped to elect the maverick leftist Vito Marcantonio to Congress.[154] By 1944, liberal political strength in New York City became even more fragmented when the Liberal party was established by more moderate members of the ALP.[155]

After Fiorello La Guardia decided not to run for re-election in 1945, the importance of the ALP for Democratic victory in the race for mayor became evident.[156] La Guardia had defeated Tammany Democrat William O'Dwyer by a very narrow margin in 1941, and the ALP's votes had been indispensable for his second re-election.[157] By adopting more liberal positions, O'Dwyer gained ALP support in 1945 and won an overwhelming victory.[158] Roosevelt's objective of having the ALP become an independent source of electoral support that would pressure the city's Democratic party to become more liberal and reformist had been realized.

With his Democratic organization in the Bronx secure and local politics dominated by La Guardia, Flynn devoted most of his time to national party affairs.[159] This was especially true after 1936 as relations between Roosevelt and Farley became strained.[160] Like Farley, Flynn opposed Tommy Corcoran's idea of "purging" selected anti–New Deal Democrats in the congressional primaries of 1938. He agreed with Farley that such unprecedented intervention by Roosevelt would create resentment and rebelliousness among Party regulars and weaken the president's influence within the Party apparatus.[161]

Despite his reluctance, Flynn agreed to "purge" New York Representative John J. O'Connor, the chairman of the powerful House Rules Committee, who had obstructed New Deal legislation, and help elect James H. Fay to replace him. Flynn made it clear to Roosevelt, though, that he did not want any interference from Corcoran or the other "amateurs."[162] The election of Fay was the only success in the otherwise disastrous purge of 1938.

As Joseph Alsop and Robert Kintner once wrote, the White House "amateurs" like Corcoran and Hopkins were "palace politicians" who were inexperienced and inept in conducting such intraparty operations. Although Roosevelt did rely on political advice from Corcoran and Hopkins during his second term, he realized that the actual execution of a political strategy within the Party should be led by an experienced Party professional like Flynn. With Farley defiantly contesting him for the Democratic presidential nomination in 1940, Roosevelt relied on Flynn to organize support for his renomination from the machine bosses and Party regulars at the national convention. Flynn was initially reluctant to become national chairman, but he was persuaded by Frank Walker, the DNC treasurer who succeeded Farley as Postmaster General.[163]

After Flynn managed Roosevelt's re-election campaign, he was determined to maintain the strength and cohesion of the Party apparatus that Farley had built as DNC chairman. Like his predecessor, Flynn disliked the interference of the White House New Dealers in patronage distribution and party affairs. Flynn, however, was more persuasive and successful than Farley in persuading Roosevelt to check with the DNC and Democratic state committees before making federal appointments. Flynn hoped that this would prevent the New Deal "amateurs" from appointing federal officials who were unacceptable, or even hostile, to Party organizations within their jurisdictions.

During his less than three years as DNC chairman, Flynn
tried to improve communications and coordination between
the DNC, Democratic state committees, and Democrats in
Congress. Whereas Farley had focused on increasing the size
of the Party apparatus by expanding special divisions for
specific voting blocs, Flynn was trying to achieve greater
consolidation and coordination among the disparate elements
of the Party.[164] He especially sought greater cooperation between Democratic members of Congress and the DNC on
raising funds for the Party treasury. Roosevelt, though, busy
with foreign policy and defense matters, could not always give
Flynn the attention and support that he needed to accomplish
these objectives for the party apparatus.[165]

Although he did develop a friendly, productive political
relationship with Harry Hopkins, Flynn experienced cold,
strained relations with the other New Dealers, especially
Harold L. Ickes.[166] While Ickes and other New Dealers in the
administration contemptuously regarded Flynn as a Party
hack, the DNC chairman perceived them as pretentious and
politically inept "prima donnas" who threatened intraparty
harmony by their clumsy intrusion into Party affairs. For
example, to reduce DNC expenses, Flynn decreased the number of paid radio broadcasts for Ickes, Hopkins, and other New
Dealers.[167] Being both more assertive and more persuasive in
his relationship with Roosevelt than Farley was, Flynn often
received Roosevelt's support in his conflicts with the New
Dealers over patronage and party matters.[168]

The controversy in the Senate over Flynn's aborted nomination as ambassador to Australia in 1943 impelled the Democratic national chairman to submit his resignation. This
quiet, bookish Bronx politician had never really enjoyed
being in the public eye. Nevertheless, he continued to serve
Roosevelt in Party affairs after he was succeeded by Frank
Walker as DNC chairman. With Bob Hannegan, the new
DNC chairman in 1944, and leading machine bosses, Flynn
helped to organize Roosevelt's re-election campaign in 1944
and to persuade him to choose Harry S. Truman as his running mate.[169] After Roosevelt's death, Flynn withdrew from

national politics yet remained chairman of the Bronx County Democratic Committee until his death in 1953.

Unlike Kelly, Hague, and Pendergast, Flynn was not a machine boss who controlled the margin of victory in his state for determining electoral college and delegates' votes at national conventions. Instead, he was important to Roosevelt's party leadership because of his political skills in serving as the president's liaison with Democratic bosses and party regulars. Because La Guardia dominated New York City politics during Roosevelt's presidency, Flynn immersed himself in national party affairs.[170] With his experience in party organizations and his intellectual grasp of the ideological and policy aspects during the New Deal era, Flynn used his talents as an intermediary and coordinator for the benefit of Roosevelt and the Party.

The Bosses and a Liberal Democratic Party

Roosevelt's dependence on the political support of the machine bosses and their urban constituents grew steadily during his presidency. The bosses, who had been the president's opponents at the 1932 convention, were his most powerful allies in his 1944 campaign. In the 1932 election, only 25 percent of Roosevelt's plurality of votes came from the nation's twelve largest cities. In the 1944 election, however, approximately 65 percent of his margin of victory came from these cities.[171]

As the New Deal became more controversial and divisive after 1936, it seemed to lose the consensual appeal it had previously held among the electorate. This was especially true among rural, non-southern white Protestants, who returned to the Republican party in presidential elections after 1936.[172] Urban voters, especially working-class ethnics and blacks, however, remained loyal to Roosevelt and the more liberal Democratic party that had emerged from the New Deal policy agenda.[173]

While Roosevelt had become more dependent on machine bosses and their constituents for electoral support, the major

cities of the Northeast and Midwest had become permanently
dependent on the federal government for their fiscal health.
In 1933, Harold F. Gosnell wrote that urban party machines
thrived during periods of rapid economic growth and that
"the economic crisis which began in 1929 has greatly reduced
our national income and has made the burden of taxation
appear relatively much greater than it did in the past."[174]
Thus, the survival of urban party machines was threatened
by the greater demand for relief combined with the sharp
drop in property tax revenues during the Depression.

But Gosnell did not anticipate the massive infusion of
federal funds into the cities in the form of federal programs
for relief, public works, education, public health, public housing, and other policy areas which affected both the cities'
public infrastructure and the welfare of their low-income
residents.[175] By subsidizing municipal budgets, New Deal
programs helped the urban machines to maintain their credibility with constituents and thus stay in power. Many machines, therefore, not only survived but even thrived and
expanded during the New Deal era. The Chicago machine, for
example, used New Deal programs and public works jobs not
only to satisfy the demand for relief and jobs among its low-
income constituents but also to coopt traditionally Republican businessmen and middle-class home owners by avoiding
property tax increases.[176]

A Democratic machine emerged in traditionally Republican Pittsburgh in 1933, cultivated an especially close relationship with Roosevelt, and enjoyed a generous flow of federal funds and patronage. During the New Deal era, the
astute use of federal aid by the Pittsburgh Democratic machine enabled it to establish an enduring credibility with the
city's residents. It remained in power until the 1970s.[177]

Cities' dependence on federal aid and their machines' sym-
biotic political relationship with Roosevelt resulted in a new
federal-city relationship. Consequently, the city bosses became the most ardent advocates of the New Deal's form of
cooperative federalism in which the federal government
played a greater role in the cities' public policies, public infrastructure, and fiscal affairs.[178] It would not be until the

Great Society programs of the 1960s that Democratic mayors would begin to object to federal intervention in their cities.[179] During Roosevelt's presidency, though, they recognized the political advantages of claiming credit for the policy accomplishments and economic benefits that New Deal programs provided for their cities.

The political relationship which developed between Roosevelt and the Democratic bosses was not just a matter of mutual self-interest, however. The perception of "bosses" and "reformers" in urban politics as being clearly distinct from each other can be misleading because these opposing political leaders may use similar tactics and seek similar policy objectives.[180] Tom Pendergast, for example, strongly supported the adoption of a city manager government for Kansas City while Frank Hague vigorously suppressed drug dealing and prostitution in Jersey City. Ed Kelly's forced retirement as mayor of Chicago in 1947 was partially caused by the opposition of machine politicians and their white ethnic constituents toward Kelly's liberalism on the racial integration of public schools and housing.

The multi-ethnic and, by the 1940s, increasingly black demography of major northern cities made the Democratic urban bosses more receptive than their southern colleagues to Roosevelt's objective of making the national Democratic party a more liberal, pluralistic, and inclusive party. Unlike demagogic, race-baiting southern Democrats, the machine bosses and machine-supported members of Congress were sensitive and responsive to the ethnically, religiously, and racially diverse political environments in which they operated. The major anti-lynching bill of the 1930s was sponsored by Robert Wagner, the Tammany-affiliated Democratic senator from New York, and was strongly supported in the House of Representatives by such machine-supported members as Mary T. Norton of Jersey City and Adolph Sabath of Chicago. Roosevelt found the northern, machine-connected members of Congress to be his most reliably and consistently liberal supporters, on both domestic and foreign policy issues. They not only supported New Deal programs which benefited their constituents but were among the first members of Congress to denounce Nazi aggression and support the controversial defense build-up and the Selective Service Act of 1940.[181]

In 1942, political scientist E.E. Schattschneider stated that "the fact that the local boss engages in politics at all levels of American government is one of the foundation stones of his authority and longevity."[182] Because of the ability to influence national party politics Democratic bosses and the members of Congress affiliated with their machines became the most crucial supporters of public policy initiatives, which more clearly defined the national party as a liberal party. This was especially true of the civil rights issue during Truman's presidency. The intraparty struggle over the adoption of a strong civil rights plank at the 1948 Democratic National Convention was led by machine-connected liberal Democrats like Senator Paul Douglas of Illinois and Joe Clark, an ADA activist and later a senator from Pennsylvania.[183] In order to maintain friendly relations with Democratic presidents, the Democratic machine bosses recognized the importance of helping the political careers of such well-respected, nationally prominent liberals as Paul Douglas and Adlai Stevenson.

By providing a substantial and reliable base of electoral support for both Roosevelt and liberal Democratic members of Congress, machine bosses contributed to both the expansion and the liberalization of the national Party during Roosevelt's presidency. A diversity of factors led major machine bosses to embrace New Deal liberalism: their cities' fiscal dependence on federal aid, the use of the WPA for patronage and structural improvements, and the economic needs and multi-ethnic composition of their working-class constituents. Roosevelt was grateful for the crucial political support that the machine bosses provided for his campaigns. Consequently, he was willing to ignore the machines' political exploitation of New Deal programs, especially the WPA.[192]

Lyle Dorsett, a scholar of Roosevelt's relationships with machine bosses, exaggerates the quid pro quo nature of Roosevelt's relationship with the machine bosses. He perceives Roosevelt as a self-centered opportunist who cultivated the bosses *only* for the purpose of his own renomination and re-election campaigns.[193] He fails to explain that Roosevelt

also needed the machine bosses and their congressional delegations to receive support for controversial, liberal domestic
policy initiatives and his pre–Pearl Harbor foreign policy and
defense measures. Roosevelt's motives, therefore, for forging
and maintaining an alliance with the machine bosses went
beyond a self-centered concern with his own political career.
The alliance enabled him to develop the urban-industrial
areas of the Northeast and Midwest as enduring bastions of
support for a more liberal Democratic party and for later
liberal, national policy initiatives, such as civil rights for
blacks.[186]

In a 1950 article in *Commentary*, Irwin Ross analyzed the
role of the Democratic machine bosses in presidential party
leadership and liberalism during the Roosevelt and Truman
administrations. On almost every policy issue during the
New Deal and Fair Deal, the bosses and their congressional
delegations were the most powerful and reliable supporters of
Democratic liberalism. Ross persuasively contends that the
more astute, successful Democratic machines adapted to the
political changes of this era by becoming advocates of liberal
reforms and closely allying themselves with these two liberal
Democratic presidents.[187] Ross concludes that the political
support of machine bosses and their urban constituents will
remain indispensable to the liberal identity of the national
Democratic party and that "the changes that have overtaken
the machine have in turn had a significant impact on American liberal politics. That impact can be simply phrased: for
the foreseeable future, the Democratic party will probably
remain the main vehicle for liberal advance—and the new
streamlined Democratic urban machines will be there to keep
the party in power."[188]

4 Roosevelt and the Democratic National Committee

FDR's Concept of the DNC's Role

As a private citizen during the 1920s, Roosevelt worried that the Democratic party would remain a chronically weak, minority party unless it clearly distinguished itself as a liberal organization and improved its appeal among voters dissatisfied with Republican policies. He suggested the Party address economic grievances and interests ignored or damaged by Republican policies and recognized the importance of building Party organizations that could influence the selection of delegates for conventions, the choice of party nominations, and the formulation of policy platforms. Believing that the masses of Democratic activists were more liberal than the wealthy elites who dominated the DNC, he frequently proposed that the national committee democratize its decision-making and fund-raising processes through such reforms as issues conventions and the solicitation of small campaign contributions through local party committees. He believed the liberal activists could influence the formulation of the Party's policy platforms if such proposals were adopted.

While the Democratic party was out of power in Congress and the presidency, Roosevelt wanted the DNC to serve as a vehicle for making economic policy proposals more liberal and thus more attractive to the electorate. The DNC chairmen during this time, however, rejected his proposals. Roosevelt feared that, without such democratic reforms for the economic policy preferences of rank-and-file Democrats and become a vehicle of conservative reaction that would make the Party's policy platforms as subservient to big business interests as those of the Republican party. Because it would fail to provide the American electorate with a clear alternative in ideology and public policy, the Party would remain an electorally unsuccessful minority party.

After he overcame DNC chairman John J. Raskob's opposition to his presidential candidacy and received the Democratic nomination in 1932, Roosevelt adopted a new concept of the role of the DNC. Because he could now appoint the DNC chairman, he no longer had to fear that the committee would become a vehicle for conservatism within the Party. With the Committee now under his control, he agreed with Jim Farley and his successors that the DNC should be used for maintaining intraparty harmony instead of used for democratizing the Party's apparatus and decision-making process. Also, because the Democrats now controlled the presidency and both houses of Congress, Roosevelt no longer found it necessary for the DNC to become a major vehicle for liberalizing Party ideology. The formulation and pursuit of the New Deal policy agenda by the Roosevelt administration and Democrats in Congress and the emergence of interest groups and voting blocs favoring New Deal liberalism would become the chief means for the liberal transformation of the national Democratic party.

The DNC created or expanded special divisions whose purpose was to cultivate the electoral support of specific voting blocs and interest groups, namely, women, blacks, labor, and young voters. The most politically active and effective special division of the DNC during Roosevelt's presidency was the Women's Division under the leadership of Mary Dewson. Dewson won the respect and support of Roosevelt, Farley, and other male Democratic politicians by convincing them that the voting power and political activism of Democratic women could contribute to the overall electoral strength of the Party. In 1936, approximately 80 percent of all Democratic campaign literature was produced and distributed by the Women's Division. The assiduous, effective efforts of the Women's Division in fund raising, publicity, and voter mobilization resulted in Democratic women gaining greater influence in formulating platforms at the national conventions and greater success in receiving patronage jobs.

While the Labor Division sought to cultivate the electoral support of the rapidly increasing number of unionized workers during the 1930s, its role in attracting voters and campaign contributions from organized labor was overshadowed by Labor's Non-Partisan League in 1936 and the CIO under Sidney Hillman's leadership in 1940 and 1944. While the CIO was technically independent of the DNC, it would become a major source of campaign funds for Roosevelt as the proportion of contributions from business interests sharply declined after 1932. Thus, the national Party's growing dependence on organized labor for financial contributions and campaign services, such as canvassing and mobilizing voters, would accelerate its liberal transformation by solidifying its commitment to labor reforms and social welfare measures.

Besides its growing dependence on organized labor for raising funds during presidential campaigns, the DNC also became more dependent on contributions of less than $100 each. Thus, the DNC was beginning to achieve Roosevelt's objective, conceived and proposed during the 1920s, of increasing the number of small contributions from individual voters and decreasing its financial dependence on large contributions from a small number of wealthy patrons. During the 1944 campaign, the CIO conducted a vigorous effort, urging its approximately six million members to make individual contributions to the DNC's campaign treasury for Roosevelt. With financial independence from big business interests, the Party could formulate and pursue New Deal policy objectives opposed by big business but supported by labor unions.

The four DNC chairmen who served during Roosevelt's presidency neither initiated nor opposed the liberal transformation of the Party under Roosevelt's leadership and the stimulus of the New Deal policy agenda. Instead, they focused on maintaining the intraparty cohesion necessary for raising funds—rewarding Party activists with patronage jobs, managing national conventions, and mobilizing voters. During Roosevelt's first term, Jim Farley strengthened and expanded the Party apparatus by distributing a vast supply of federal patronage to Party regulars and improving its fund-raising ability through the establishment of annual Jackson Day dinners held in Washington and by state and local Democratic committees as well as by the sale of campaign books, which was finally prohibited by the Hatch Act of 1940. Farley's alienation from Roosevelt after 1936 and his resignation as DNC chairman in 1940 was impelled by his personal resentment about being neglected by Roosevelt and not by an ideological antipathy toward New Deal liberalism.

Because of the decline of intraparty harmony and the growth of southern conservative opposition to Roosevelt's party leadership by 1940, Farley's three successors would focus on improving the intraparty harmony and cooperation among the various factions and interest groups necessary for assuring Roosevelt's renomination and re-election in 1940 and 1944. DNC Chairman Ed Flynn sought to improve cooperation and coordination between the committee and congressional Democrats, while his successor, Frank Walker, helped to resolve a bitter conflict between the Democratic and Farmer-Labor factions of the Minnesota Democratic Farmer-Labor party. During the 1944 campaign, Chairman Bob Hannegan would oversee the micromanagement of voter mobilization efforts by the thousands of Democratic precinct committees in order to assure a voter turn-out high enough to re-elect Roosevelt.

By 1945, the DNC's apparatus was smaller and had fewer funds than it had during its peak of size and wealth during the 1936 campaign. The growing power of the CIO within the Party and the proliferation of pro-Roosevelt campaign committees technically independent of the DNC—formed in order to evade campaign finance reform laws—reduced the role of the DNC and its special divisions in raising funds and canvassing voters. However, the special DNC divisions that had been created or expanded during Roosevelt's presidency had helped to make the Party's fund-raising efforts and decision-making processes more open, democratic, and participatory.

Thus, interest groups and voting blocs that favored a more liberal Party gained more active and influential roles in national Party affairs. The DNC, especially its special divisions, responded to the growing power and influence of such liberal groups by granting them a greater role in Party activities, especially at national conventions. Consequently, by creating a more democratic Party, Roosevelt achieved his objective of removing the threat of the DNC as a vehicle for conservative reaction and of making the Committee reflective of a more inclusive, liberal Party.

The DNC under Farley

After 1932, Roosevelt no longer focused on transforming the DNC into a vehicle for liberalizing the Party. Instead, he agreed with Farley's policy of using the DNC to maintain intraparty harmony and unity while expanding its apparatus in order to consolidate the Party's gains among women, blacks, labor, and young voters.[1]

In particular, Farley oversaw the expansion of special DNC divisions.[2] The activities and structural changes of the committee during Roosevelt's presidency would reflect both the expansion of the Party's electoral base and the growth of intraparty conflicts over the changes the New Deal and Roosevelt's leadership induced.[3]

The extent to which Farley could make the DNC and the other Party committees responsive to his leadership depended on the extent to which he could control the distribution of federal patronage and maintain a close relationship with Roosevelt and Democrats in Congress. Farley first sought to achieve a more centralized relationship with local Party committees during the 1932 campaign. He had the DNC compose a list of the approximately 140,000 Democratic activists and a description of their campaign duties,[4] then sent campaign literature directly to these Party workers instead of sending it in bulk form to state committees.[5]

Farley, who also served as Postmaster General, gained even more patronage power than previous DNC chairmen who served during Democratic administrations. The high unemployment rate, the sharp increase in the number of federal jobs, and a declining proportion of federal jobs covered by the civil service merit system all combined to enhance Farley's patronage power and thus his influence within the

Party apparatus.[6] Emil Hurja, the DNC's assistant chairman and statistician, became a personnel director in the PWA, thereby extending Farley's power into an agency whose director, Harold Ickes, was hostile to him.[7] In 1933, he tried but failed to formalize his patronage power with a centralized system in which the heads of all federal agencies and cabinet departments would have to defer to the DNC on appointed positions.[8]

Despite the substantial patronage power he possessed, Farley wielded it cautiously and tactfully. He was careful to consult Democratic senators and congressmen about making appointments in their states and districts because he regarded as his chief function the maintenance of intraparty harmony and cooperative relations between the DNC and Democratic politicians at the congressional, state, and local levels. Until his later alienation from Roosevelt and the emergence of his own presidential ambition after 1936, Farley's use of his patronage power was further tempered by his self-subordination to Roosevelt and his role as the president's loyal representative in internal Party affairs.[9]

In addition to the distribution of federal patronage, the DNC chairman's major responsibilities between presidential campaigns entailed managing the activities of the national Party headquarters. A full-time, permanent Democratic national headquarters had been established by John Raskob, Farley's predecessor. Prior to Raskob's chairmanship, a national party headquarters existed only during presidential campaigns.

The purpose of the Executive Committee was to manage the funding and operations of the DNC's staff. Jouett Shouse focused on managing a publicity campaign against Hoover.[10] He and Raskob created a full-time Publicity Division with Charles Michelson as its director.[11] Shouse and Michelson then created a Research Bureau to provide information for anti-Hoover publicity. Having expanded the DNC's activities and functions between presidential campaigns, Raskob left Farley an active and well-funded organization.[12] Farley would seek to maintain the strength and efficacy of this party apparatus through the astute distribution of federal patronage; the maintenance of cordial, cooperative relations with Democrats in Congress, urban machines, and state and local party committees; and diversification of the sources of funds for the DNC.

DNC Finances (1932-1944)

Despite Raskob's organizational and financial accomplishments for the DNC, Farley needed a steady flow of contributions to the DNC to maintain its various political activities, especially publicity. The DNC's growing financial dependence on organized labor and many small contributions enabled it to adapt to and reflect the liberal transformation of the Party. The DNC treasurer was elected by the membership of the Committee and, according to its 1936 convention rule, was "empowered to perform all the necessary duties of his office . . . in such a manner and under such terms as he may deem proper and advisable."[13]

With this high degree of discretion in fulfilling his duties, the DNC treasurer was often a close associate of the Committee chairman and perhaps the presidential nominee as well. He was usually a corporate lawyer, banker, or businessman with contacts in big business. Frank Walker, the treasurer in 1932, was a lawyer and an executive in the motion picture industry.[14] Lawrence W. "Chip" Robert, Jr., the owner of a large engineering firm, served as assistant treasurer under Walter Cummings from 1936 to 1940. Oliver A. Quayle, Jr., was a printing company executive who served as treasurer from 1937 to 1941. He was succeeded by Richard J. Reynolds, a tobacco tycoon who loaned approximately $300,000 to various Democratic state committees during the 1940 campaign.[15]

Despite the domination of this office by wealthy Democratic businessmen, the proportion of the DNC's funds contributed by business interests steadily declined after 1928. In 1928, the DNC spent a total of $5,342,350; 25.3 percent of this was derived from bankers and stockbrokers. In 1932, the Committee only spent $2,245,975; yet a similar proportion, 24.2 percent of its funds was derived from these financial interests. However, the DNC spent over $5 million in 1936, even though only 3.3 percent came from bankers and stock brokers. The figures for the total DNC expenditures for the 1940 and 1944 campaigns were, respectively, $2,783,654 and $2,169,077. Campaign contributions from the foregoing financial interests accounted for 3.1 percent and 5.2 percent of the total expenditures, respectively.[16] V.O. Key, Jr., observed in 1947 that as business hostility to the New Deal and to an increasingly liberal Democratic party intensified, "the general sharpening of political conflict along class lines manifested itself in the pecuniary loyalty of finance and heavy industry to the Republican party."[17]

Besides the sharp drop in business contributions to the DNC during Roosevelt's presidency, there was also a significant decline in financial support from large individual contributors. In 1928, 52.7 percent of the cash contributions to the DNC came from individuals giving $5,000 or more. Surprisingly, only 45.8 percent of the Republican National Committee's cash contributions in 1928 came from this source. During the 1940 campaign, as a result of businessmen's antipathy toward Roosevelt and the campaign finance reforms of the second Hatch Act, only 13 percent of the DNC's cash contributions came from individuals giving $5,000 or more.[18]

Meanwhile, the DNC became more dependent on large numbers of contributors giving less than $100 each. The proportion of cash contributions received from these small donors nearly doubled, from 12.5 percent in 1928 to 23.3 percent in 1940.[19] The Party appeared to be moving gradually toward Roosevelt's objective of making it more dependent on small contributors in order to make it more responsive to its rank and file's policy preferences.[20]

The DNC also devised new fund-raising methods after 1932. In order to financially prepare for and then liquidate the debts of the 1936 presidential campaign, Farley arranged to have a campaign book published for the 1936 convention.[21] Copies of this book and advertising space within it were sold to raise funds for the DNC. Three editions of the book sold at different prices: $2.50, $5.00, and $100. After the election, though, some deluxe editions of this campaign book sold for $250 each.[22] Louise Overacker, an authority on campaign

finance during the Roosevelt presidency, estimated that
the 1936 Democratic campaign book netted the DNC about
$250,000.[23]

To raise funds for the 1940 campaign, Farley began to sell
advertising space for the next campaign book. Sales netted
the DNC $170,000.[24] The Hatch Act of 1939, however, pro-
hibited the DNC from selling copies of and advertising space
in such books.[25] Because the committee began planning and
selling advertising space for the 1940 campaign book prior to
the passage of the first Hatch Act, it considered contesting
this provision, but instead gave away copies, thus realizing
little profit in the venture.[26]

After the prohibition of revenue from campaign books, the
DNC relied more on the Jackson Day dinners as a source of
funds.[27] Farley also wanted to use the dinners in Washington
as a way of promoting intraparty unity and camaraderie and
of attracting favorable publicity. The first annual dinner of
this kind was held in 1936, cost those who attended $50 per
plate, and raised about $100,000 for the DNC. In 1937 and
thereafter, Roosevelt supporters paid $100 each to attend. In
early January of every year, while the Jackson Day Dinner
was being held in Washington, similar dinners were sponsored by state and local Party committees nationwide at as
little as $2 per plate. Approximately 300,000 Democrats at-
tended these dinners in 1936.[29]

Except in 1939, when the DNC received only $322,000,
these dinners attracted about $400,000 annually, peaking at
$422,000 in 1940.[30] Besides being an effective form of fund
raising, the Jackson Day dinners enabled the DNC to build
closer ties with state and local committees. The DNC also
sought to solidify the loyalty of these Democrats to Roosevelt's party leadership by broadcasting his speech at the
Washington dinner to them.

Although Farley wanted Roosevelt to use his Jackson Day
speeches to promote intraparty harmony, the president often
used the occasions to speak on controversial and divisive
topics. In his 1937 address he sought Party support for the
"court packing" bill that he claimed was essential for the
Party to "long remain a natural rallying point for the cooper-

ative effort of all those who truly believed in political and economic democracy."[31] Following the Republican resurgence and the failed "purge" of conservative Democrats in the 1938 congressional elections, the president used his 1939 Jackson Day address to urge fellow Democrats to "give intense and genuine devotion to the cause of liberal government."[32] In these speeches, Roosevelt revealed a common theme—the compatibility of the Party's liberalism under the New Deal with the populism of Jefferson and Jackson.

Despite the success of the Jackson Day fund raisers, these dinners did not compensate for the sharp decline in financial support from large individual contributors and business interests. Consequently, throughout Roosevelt's three re-election campaigns, the DNC became increasingly dependent on organized labor as its largest single source of campaign contributions. Total union expenditures on behalf of Roosevelt's re-election increased from over $770,000 in 1936 to over $1,300,000 in 1944.[33] Much of the labor contributions in the 1936 campaign came from Labor's Non-Partisan League whose major contributors were three CIO unions: the United Mine Workers, Amalgamated Clothing Workers, and International Ladies Garment Workers union.[34] Besides indirectly benefiting from pro-Roosevelt campaigns financed by the American Labor Party, by Labor's Non-Partisan League, and later by the CIO's Political Action Committee (CIO-PAC), the proportion of DNC campaign funds derived from labor unions increased from 10.2 percent in 1936 to approximately 16 percent in 1940. These figures, however, do not include "unclassified" and "unidentified" individual contributions from labor leaders and union members.

Throughout Roosevelt's presidency, organized labor steadily strengthened its position as a major source of Democratic campaign funds and thus strengthened its position in national Party affairs, solidifying the Party's commitment to social welfare and labor reform legislation favored by labor unions.[35] Daniel J. Tobin, president of the Teamsters' union and vice-president of the AFL, served as chairman of the DNC's Labor Division during all four of Roosevelt's presidential campaigns.[36] Despite Tobin's top positions in the AFL

and DNC, his stature in the Democratic party was overshadowed by Sidney Hillman, vice president of the CIO from
1936 to 1940. After John L. Lewis decided to support Wendell
Willkie in 1940, Hillman became Roosevelt's chief contact in
the CIO. A cofounder of the American Labor Party in New
York, Hillman molded the CIO into a tightly disciplined,
politically active labor organization which superseded the
AFL in its impressive ability to raise campaign funds and
mobilize voters for Roosevelt in 1940 and 1944.[37]

Special DNC Divisions

Although "advisory committees" for foreign language groups,
small businesses, and other specific voting blocs dissolved
immediately after a presidential election, other groups,
namely women, blacks, youths, and labor unions, were
granted permanent divisions within the DNC's apparatus.
Foreign language groups did not receive a permanent DNC
division until 1952, whereas a Women's Division was established in 1922, shortly after the membership of the DNC was
doubled to include a national committeewoman from every
state and territory.[38] After the 1932 presidential campaign,
the DNC's Labor Division became a permanent organization
under Daniel J. Tobin, the Teamsters' president.[39] During the
1932 campaign, the Young Democratic Clubs of America were
established in 32 states in order to "form a self-governing
organization of young people interested in taking an active
and purposeful part in politics and public affairs."[40] This
association of clubs was formally recognized as the DNC's
division for youth at the 1936 national convention. In order to
attract traditionally Republican black voters into the Democratic party, the DNC established the Colored Advisory Committee during the 1932 campaign and then expanded it into
the Colored Division.[41]

   Not all of these divisions, however, were equally successful
in advancing their constituents' public policy interests and
influence within the Party. The major factor influencing a
division's effectiveness as an advocate of its constituency's
interests and as a mobilizer of its voters on election day was

the quality and continuity of its leadership. Of these four divisions, the Labor Division had the most stable, enduring leadership pattern during Roosevelt's presidency. Tobin served as its director during all four of Roosevelt's presidential campaigns.

The quality of a director's leadership and of the division's political efficacy was often determined by the amount of time, concentration, and innovation that a director applied to his division's activities during presidential campaigns as well as the period between elections. Tobin, though, like most directors of DNC divisions, did not consider his duties as a division director to be his chief responsibility during the years between presidential elections. His duties as president of the Teamsters' union and vice-president of the AFL as well as a brief term as an administrative assistant to Roosevelt in 1940 kept him busy.[42]

Unlike other directors of DNC divisions, Mary W. Dewson regarded her positions as the Women's Division director (1932-1934) and as chairman of its Advisory Committee (1934-1937) to be important responsibilities that required the full use of her time, effort, and ingenuity. Under her vigorous leadership, the division became the most politically effective of the DNC. She accomplished this by expanding the purpose of the division's activities beyond increasing the power and influence of women within the Party. She shrewdly realized that the Women's Division would gain the respect and support of Roosevelt and Farley if its activities contributed to the overall electoral strength of the Party.[43]

During her early career as an activist in reform movements for women's suffrage and minimum wages—maximum hours legislation for female workers, Dewson recognized the importance of bread-and-butter policy issues for attracting voters into the Party.[44] She believed that if the Women's Division conducted an information and public relations campaign between presidential elections that explained and promoted the benefits of the New Deal to women it could attract independent and liberally inclined Republican women into the Party. Dewson wrote to Roosevelt, "I still believe the Women's Division is on the most fertile ground for winning independent, stay-at-home and possible Republican voters."[45]

Her close friendship with Eleanor Roosevelt was another valuable asset in her development of the division as a major force within the DNC. At Eleanor Roosevelt's press conference on January 15, 1934, Dewson announced the Women's Division's new "Reporter Plan."[46] Two weeks later, she explained the details of the plan in a circular letter to all Democratic committeewomen.[47] Every Democratic county women's organization would assign a "reporter" for each federal agency. Her duties would be to become knowledgeable about that agency's programs and to be prepared to explain and defend its programs to voters when she visited them or spoke at public meetings. The ultimate objective of the plan was to facilitate the election of Democratic candidates by generating a favorable image of the New Deal, especially for undecided voters. Almost one year after the inception of this publicity program, Dewson stated that the Reporter Plan made Democratic women "the mouth to mouth, house to house interpreters and apostles of the New Deal."[48]

The division's publicity efforts were accelerated and expanded during the 1936 campaign. Its chief propaganda campaign consisted of the distribution of Rainbow Fliers. These colorful leaflets explained and defended various New Deal programs.[49] Fliers on the Social Security program were distributed to blue-collar workers to counter Republican charges that contributing workers would never receive Social Security benefits.[50] With approximately 80,000 Democratic women active among the state, county, ward, and precinct Party organizations, over $1 million worth of Rainbow Fliers were distributed during the 1936 campaign,[51] accounting for approximately 80 percent of all Democratic campaign literature in 1936.[52]

In addition to fliers, the Women's Division published the *Democratic Digest* on a monthly basis. This newsletter had first been established by the Women's National Democratic Club during the 1920s. The Women's Division assumed responsibility for publishing it in 1935 and increased its circulation from 1,600 to 16,500 by 1938.[53] The *Democratic*

Digest provided facts to Reporter Plan activists about federal programs, Supreme Court decisions, legislation in Congress, and other public policy matters. It also publicized the political accomplishments of Democratic women.[54]

With the Women's Division more active during the years between presidential elections than any other DNC division, Dewson expected female Democratic activists to be rewarded for their contributions to the Party. To finance the division's expanded, ongoing activities, Dewson requested a $50,000 budget in 1934. Farley refused, but Roosevelt mediated a compromise so that the division received $36,000.[55] In 1935, the Donkey Bank program was introduced to help local women's organizations to finance their political activities.[56]

Besides demanding adequate funding for the Women's Division from the DNC, Dewson asserted that Democratic women should have equal representation on state, district, county, and precinct Party committees. "No state can claim perfect organization that has not a chairman and vice chairman of opposite sex, or a committeewoman wherever it has a committeeman."[57] She led the effort of Democratic women to pressure state organizations to adopt rules requiring "50-50 representation" on committees at all levels as well as in leadership positions such as chairman and vice-chairman.[58] In a letter to Caroline O'Day, elected to Congress in 1935 and a veteran of New York Democratic politics, Dewson even suggested that the Women's Division and other separate Democratic organizations for women be dissolved once the "50-50" goal was attained and women were fully and equally integrated into the Party apparatus and its decision-making process.[59] By 1939, only nine states did not ensure that women would have equal representation on all Democratic committees.[60]

Dewson also expected the DNC to allow women to wield more influence at national conventions. At her insistence, women were appointed as alternates to members of the Resolutions Committee for the first time at the 1936 convention.[61] The Women's Advisory Committee formulated planks and lobbied the Resolutions Committee for their adoption in the Party platform. The women drafted and submitted planks

concerning consumer rights, the abolition of child labor, and
federal aid to education, and succeeded in convincing the
Resolutions Committee to adopt most of them.[62]

By presenting herself as a social reformer dedicated to the
advancement of the New Deal rather than as a feminist only
seeking women's interests, Dewson emerged as the most
prominent and politically effective division leader. She
gained the support and respect of Roosevelt, Farley, and other
male Democratic leaders by making them aware of how the
Women's Division's activities contributed to the Party's electoral strength. Through her vigorous leadership of the division, the number of female Democratic campaign workers
increased from 73,000 in 1936 to 109,000 in 1940.[63] Dewson
wrote to Roosevelt in 1936, "The party organization has been
revivified by women who now see it as an instrument to
attain their hopes and dreams of a measure of economic
stability and security for every-day persons."[64]

Although Roosevelt hoped to coopt blacks into the Party
permanently, the role of the DNC's Colored Division was not
the dominant factor in this partisan realignment. The New
Deal's public works and relief programs, the president's charismatic leadership, Eleanor Roosevelt's activism among
blacks, and the establishment of the Black Cabinet were
major factors contributing to the Democratic realignment of
blacks.[65] During Roosevelt's presidency, moreover, there was
a substantial gap between blacks' expression of support for
Roosevelt and their identification with the Party.[66]

While Roosevelt and the DNC chairmen during his presidency wanted to attract blacks, they did not want their cultivation of the black vote to outrage and alienate southern
whites, the traditional base of their party. This cautiousness
further limited the role of the Colored Division within the
DNC. Instead of promoting causes dealing with such divisive
issues as anti-lynching laws, desegregation, and voting rights
for southern blacks, the Colored Division limited its publicity
campaigns to detailing and praising the economic benefits
that the New Deal provided for blacks. Likewise, this deference to southern racial views impelled the Colored Division
to avoid conducting voter registration and canvassing ac-

tivities among southern blacks, except in the few southern cities where blacks could vote.[67]

These limitations on the Colored Division prevented it from gaining the type of stable, dynamic leadership the Women's Division enjoyed under Mary Dewson and her successors. In 1933, Director Joseph L. Johnson suggested that the division became a larger, permanent part of the DNC and establish "organizations in pivotal states where the Colored vote is a determining factor."[68] Johnson's suggestion was not accepted by the committee.

The Colored Division was nearly neglected by Roosevelt and Farley until the 1936 campaign. Black electoral support for Roosevelt peaked at 76 percent in 1936 and declined slightly to approximately 65 percent in 1940 and 1944.[69] Hampered by frequent changes in leadership and inadequate funding, the division was usually inactive between presidential campaigns.

The DNC's deference to southern white racial views, inadequate funding, and an unstable leadership pattern were not the only factors that contributed to the division's failure to achieve the degree of power and prominence which the Women's Division enjoyed between presidential elections. The prospect of the Colored Division becoming a powerful vehicle of black political strength during Roosevelt's presidency was further weakened by the decentralization and diffusion of canvassing efforts among blacks by numerous political organizations that were independent of the DNC. Such organizations included the Good Neighbor League, the National Council of Negro Democrats, the Colored National Democratic League, urban Democratic machines, and CIO unions.[70] Even though the Colored Division did not develop into a powerful, influential division, black affiliation with the Party would increase after 1945.

The DNC's Labor Division experienced the most stable leadership pattern of all the divisions with Daniel J. Tobin as director. Shortly after being appointed chairman of the Labor Bureau of the Democratic National Campaign Committee in 1932, Tobin sent a circular letter to the presidents of forty different unions asking them to "become associated with us in this campaign as a member of Organized Labor's National Advisory Committee of the Democratic National Committee."[71] He also established a Women's Division of the Labor Bureau, which was headed by Betty Hawley, vice-president of the New York State Federation of Labor.

The rapid increase in the number of unionized workers because of Section 7a of the National Industrial Recovery Act and the National Labor Relations Act, however, did not correspond to a rapid increase in the Labor Division's power within the DNC. Although most labor unions supported Roosevelt and other Democratic candidates, they wanted to retain their independence and, thus, refused to allow themselves to become a subordinate appendage of the Party. Labor's desire to maintain its independence from the DNC manifested itself in the formation of Labor's Non-Partisan League and the American Labor party in 1936 in order to attract labor support for Roosevelt's re-election while avoiding an official affiliation with the Party. Formed by John L. Lewis and Sidney Hillman, the League asserted that it "is not associated with any political party. It is a separate and distinct organization."[72]

Tobin's ability to exercise strong, centralized control over labor's political activities was also prevented by conflicts within the movement, especially between the AFL and the newly formed CIO. Lewis and Hillman established the league partially because they distrusted Tobin, vice-chairman of the AFL.[73] Lewis's endorsement of Willkie in 1940 made Hillman the leader of the CIO's campaign activities on behalf of Roosevelt in the 1940 and 1944 elections. The requirements of the Hatch Act of 1940 impelled the CIO to make its fund-raising and campaigning activities even more independent of the DNC's Labor Division. As an AFL leader, Tobin had his position as the Labor Division director further undermined by the fact that Hillman's CIO unions contributed more votes and funds to Roosevelt's 1940 and 1944 campaigns than the more conservative, loosely organized AFL unions did.[74]

With the CIO overshadowing the Labor division in its campaign efforts for Roosevelt, Tobin's role in Roosevelt's last two campaigns consisted merely of trying to coordinate the individual activities of the pro-Roosevelt labor unions. Roosevelt tried to increase Tobin's stature by appointing him as a White House administrative assistant in 1940.[75] In 1942, the president appointed Tobin as his representative to investigate labor conditions in Britain. However, the CIO's and the AFL's independent yet pro-Democratic political action committees would continue to overshadow the DNC's Labor Division during presidential campaigns.

Richard Roper, the executive secretary of the DNC, took a personal interest in the strength and vitality of the Young Democratic Clubs.[76] He did not believe that these clubs should simply help attract votes for Democratic candidates. He told the Young Democratic Clubs of Texas that they should become "an outlet for liberal thought and opinion."[77] In a speech given to the Young People's Democratic League of Illinois in 1934, Roper urged young Democrats to "open the membership rolls to every young American who feels his obligation of citizenship, Republican and Democrat alike, Progressive, Communist and Socialist."[78]

Comprised mostly of liberal college students, the Young Democrats became even more enthusiastically supportive of Roosevelt when his liberalism became more pronounced after 1936 as he was besieged by conservative opposition within the Party.[79] Consequently, Roosevelt delivered several major speeches to Young Democrats in 1938 and 1939 concerning the need to keep the Party distinctly liberal. He told a convention of Young Democrats in 1939 that if the Party should nominate a conservative for president in 1940 he would "find it impossible to have any active part in such an unfortunate suicide of the old Democratic Party."[80] In 1944, however, a Pennsylvania Democrat complained to Dorothy Vrendenburg, president of the Young Democratic Clubs of America, that unless these clubs were better coordinated "a young organization with communistic ideals" might replace them.[81]

The different degrees of strength and activity of these four DNC divisions during Roosevelt's presidency reflected the growing diversity of the Party's membership and the increasing intraparty influence of groups supporting the development of a more liberal Party under the New Deal. As Roosevelt's party leadership and the New Deal became more controversial and divisive after 1936, the four voting blocs that these divisions represented became even more important. The crucial electoral support that the constituencies of these divisions contributed to Roosevelt's re-election in 1940 and 1944 enabled them to increase their power, status, and influence within the Party.

DNC Chairmen (1932-1945)

In his 1905 analysis of the national Party chairmen's duties, Jesse Macy wrote that "it is the national chairman, himself, who determines just what role he will play in executing them."[82] Because of this ambiguity and flexibility regarding the DNC chairman's duties between presidential campaigns, the four chairmen who served under Roosevelt fulfilled their duties according to the extent to which Roosevelt involved hiself in intraparty affairs. During his first term, Roosevelt worked closely with Jim Farley in revitalizing and expanding the Party apparatus.[83] Roosevelt agreed with Farley's patronage policy of providing federal jobs to both Party regulars and activists who had supported Roosevelt in 1932 but were not registered Democrats—at least not yet. Mary Dewson commented in 1938 that "Farley's concern was not only to build a powerful organization but an organization powerful enough to establish the New Deal."[84]

Farley, like his three successors, Ed Flynn, Frank Walker, and Bob Hannegan, was more concerned about maintaining intraparty unity than he was about making the Party distinctly liberal by forcing conservative Democrats to support New Deal liberalism or leave the Party. It is misleading, however, to perceive him as a conservative who clashed with Roosevelt after 1936 because of an ideological antipathy toward liberalism.[85] Instead, he was a nonideological power broker who perceived his primary responsibility to be the preservation of intraparty unity and harmony in order to win elections. In a speech delivered to the American Political Science Association in 1933, he stated that political principles "are translated into action only by organized effort."[86]

Farley believed that organizational strength and internal

harmony were more important in party politics than ideological purity. This conviction led him to oppose Roosevelt's attempt to "purge" selected conservatives in the Democratic congressional primaries of 1938. Farley was convinced that the "purge" would irreparably weaken intraparty harmony and Roosevelt's party leadership.[87] In general, his relationship with Roosevelt deteriorated as the president relied more on the "White House crowd", especially Tommy Corcoran and Harry Hopkins, as his operatives on Party matters.[88]

Even though Farley's role as the DNC chairman diminished during Roosevelt's second term because of these factors, Roosevelt realized that the movement Farley and Garner led against a third term for him made essential the appointment of an experienced Party professional as Farley's successor. Thus, he chose Ed Flynn, the county Democratic leader of the Bronx and a veteran of Tammany politics.

Flynn was experienced in internal Party affairs. He had first become acquainted with Roosevelt during Al Smith's campaign for the Democratic presidential nomination at the 1924 national convention. Roosevelt, who admired the organizational skills and political savvy of this aloof, urbane Irishman, appointed Flynn New York's secretary of state in 1929.[89] During his governorship, Roosevelt directed Flynn and Farley to expand the apparatus of the state Party in traditionally Republican areas of upstate New York. He originally asked Flynn to travel throughout the nation and build a network of contacts with Democratic politicians and Party activists in preparation for his 1932 presidential campaign, but Flynn suggested the appointment of the more gregarious Farley for this task.[90]

Although he had supported Smith in 1928, Flynn opposed Tammany Hall in 1932 by actively supporting Roosevelt for the presidential nomination.[91] He remained New York's secretary of state until 1939. Thus, he mostly involved himself in the local Democratic politics of New York City rather than in national politics. With the support of Roosevelt and Farley, through a generous flow of federal patronage, Flynn sought to reform and reorganize Tammany Hall in order to reassert Democratic control of the city's politics and government but failed to do so during Fiorello La Guardia's mayoralty.[92] In order to attract pro–New Deal, non-Democratic voters to Roosevelt in 1936, Flynn helped Farley, Sidney Hillman, and David Dubinsky establish the American Labor Party in 1936.[93]

Eleanor Roosevelt would later contend that Flynn, unlike Farley and other Irish politicos, did not focus only on patronage distribution and understood the importance of principles and ideas in Party politics.[94] Nevertheless, Flynn, like Farley, was a Party regular who disliked the idea of "purging" fellow Democrats. He agreed to manage the 1938 purge campaign against Representative John J. O'Connor of New York, however, because of his personal loyalty to Roosevelt and his antipathy toward O'Connor. He made it clear to Roosevelt, though, that he would not share the management of James Fay's primary campaign against O'Connor with Corcoran.[95] O'Connor's defeat was the only successful purge of an incumbent congressional Democrat targeted by Roosevelt.

Farley resigned as DNC chairman and actively opposed Roosevelt's renomination in 1940. Thus, Roosevelt realized that he needed an experienced Party professional to unite the machine bosses and Party regulars behind his candidacy and crumble the Farley-Garner movement against him. Closely cooperating with Ed Kelly and Harry Hopkins, Flynn managed a smooth renomination process for Roosevelt at the 1940 convention.[96]

Flynn officially replaced Farley as DNC chairman on August 17, 1940. He was initially reluctant to succeed Farley; but he was persuaded by Frank Walker, the former DNC treasurer who succeeded Farley as Postmaster General.[97] Despite his political skills and personal loyalty to Roosevelt, the introverted Flynn was temperamentally ill-suited to perform the extensive traveling and public relations tasks of the DNC chairman.[98] Instead, he focused on the less public functions of distributing patronage and improving cooperation between the DNC and congressional Democrats in raising and distributing campaign funds. Flynn proved to be more successful than Farley in persuading Roosevelt to cooperate with the DNC and Democratic state organizations on federal appointments and to avoid allowing White House New Dealers like Harold Ickes to distribute patronage.[99]

In 1941, David Berenstein, a St. Louis Democrat, wrote to DNC chairman Ed Flynn and stated, "the Democratic Organization's weakest link, at the present time, is its inability to get and hold the active interest of the citizens in the affairs of government."[100] Berenstein suggested that the DNC revitalize the party apparatus at the local level by establishing a highly participatory, decision-making process and set a minimal membership fee of $5 each for up to one million activists in these organizations.

When Senate consideration of his appointment as ambassador to Australia was stalled in 1943 because of questions about his personal finances, Flynn quietly resigned as DNC chairman.[101] Even after he was replaced in this position by Frank Walker, Flynn continued to serve Roosevelt politically. With Walker and Bob Hannegan, another future DNC chairman, Flynn persuaded Roosevelt to choose Harry S. Truman as his running mate in the 1944 presidential campaign.[102]

Frank Walker served as the DNC chairman for less than a year. A wealthy lawyer and businessman who served as the DNC treasurer during the 1932 campaign, he had succeeded Farley as Postmaster General in 1940.

As the Postmaster General during World War II, Walker was too busy to devote himself to his chairmanship.[103] Nevertheless, in January 1944, he sent a form letter to the 3,048 Democratic county chairmen, asking for their "frank views on the outstanding problems in your County which affect the national political situation."[104] In conjunction with Elmer F. Kelm, the Democratic state chairman of Minnesota, Walker helped to resolve conflicts between Democrats and the Farmer-Labor factions of the Minnesota Democratic-Farmer-Labor party.[105]

Walker served less than a year as DNC chairman when he was succeeded by Robert E. Hannegan, commissioner of internal revenue, on January 22, 1944. A veteran of St. Louis Democratic politics, Hannegan was instrumental in persuading Harry Truman to accept the vice-presidential nomination at the 1944 convention. Like Walker, Hannegan also asked state and local party chairmen about local political conditions and for their advice about how to strengthen the Party apparatus.[106] He resigned in 1947.

In conclusion, Farley's three successors used their positions as DNC chairmen to resolve intraparty conflicts and assure Roosevelt's renomination and re-election in 1940 and 1944. Farley had already expanded the Party apparatus to accommodate new voting blocs and interest groups attracted to the Party by the New Deal and Roosevelt's leadership.[107] His three successors did not have the degree of patronage power and intraparty unity that Farley enjoyed during Roosevelt's first term. But they did enjoy a greater degree of discretion in fulfilling their duties as chairmen and thus wielded greater influence over Roosevelt's Party leadership as he concentrated on foreign policy matters after 1940 and deferred to the chairmen on Party affairs.

By 1945, however, the concentration on the war effort caused a decrease in the size, activities, and funding of the DNC and its various appendages. DNC chairman Bob Hannegan reduced, rather than expanded, the size of the staff and budget of the DNC because of fiscal constraints. Nevertheless, when Hannegan asked local Party chairmen about the health of their organizations, many of them claimed to have strong, active Democratic committees.[108] Although the DNC itself remained the domain of Party insiders, the activities of its special divisions and its encouragement of greater participation by state and local Party committees combined with the pursuit of the New Deal policy agenda stimulated the development of a more open, inclusive, and participatory Party in which leaders needed to become more responsive to the policy interests of active, rank-and-file Democrats.

5 The Formation of an Electoral Coalition: 1932-1936

The 1932 Election

Although the Depression began earlier than he had assumed it would, Roosevelt had originally planned to run for president in 1936 because he believed that a depression would begin by the early 1930s.[1] He and Louis M. Howe, his chief political operative, realized, however, that the widespread economic suffering and anti-Hoover sentiment that emerged after 1929 would assure the victory of almost any Democratic presidential nominee in 1932.[2] The Party, though, needed a nominee who could appeal to and unite its diverse, conflicting interest groups and voting blocs. Throughout the 1920s, Roosevelt had been carefully positioning himself so that he would eventually be regarded as the strongest candidate, and one who could appeal to all elements of the Party.[3]

Shortly after Roosevelt's landslide re-election as governor in 1930, Howe and Farley began to visit Democratic politicians throughout the nation to assess the strength of Roosevelt's prospective presidential candidacy. By distributing booklets providing impressive voting results from Roosevelt's re-election as governor, Farley initiated letter-writing relationships with state chairmen, DNC members, and other activists in the Party apparatus to cultivate their support for Roosevelt and to learn about local political conditions relevant to his campaign.[5] To impress Democratic contacts in rural areas with Roosevelt's success as a vote-getter, Farley provided statistics from the 1930 gubernatorial election,[6] pointing out that, in the landslide victory, he had not only received an unprecedented 725,001 plurality but had distinguished himself as the first Democratic gubernatorial nominee to receive a majority of votes in upstate counties.[7] The preconvention strategy of the campaign was to convince party leaders, through Howe's voluminous correspondence and Farley's extensive travels, that Roosevelt was the only Democratic candidate whose appeal was broad enough to unite the diverse factions of the Party and attract enough votes from anti-Hoover Republicans and independents to assure victory.[8] Because only a few states would select their delegates to the national convention through primaries, Howe and Farley realized how essential this personal lobbying strategy was for obtaining the endorsements of committee officials and politicians who could influence the selection of delegates at caucuses and state conventions.[9]

Farley and Howe cultivated the support of Party leaders representing regions of political strength for the Party. They gained the endorsement of Senator Cordell Hull of Tennessee, who mobilized Democrats in Congress behind Roosevelt's candidacy.[10] In particular, the Tennessee senator lobbied southern Democrats who, like himself and Roosevelt, opposed the high-tariff, protectionist policy proposals of the Raskob-dominated DNC.[11] Meanwhile, Senators Burton K. Wheeler and Thomas Walsh of Montana and Joseph O'Mahoney of Wyoming organized the support of western progressives.[12]

Southern and western Democrats admired Roosevelt's knowledge about and sensitivity to the agricultural problems that plagued their states. In addition to frequent public statements and articles throughout the 1920s warning that the farm depression threatened to lead to a severe, general depression, Governor Roosevelt introduced innovative programs for New York farmers intended to stabilize farm prices, reduce farm surpluses, and provide tax relief.[13] Although he did not specify exactly what programs he would implement to solve agricultural problems nationally, he stressed that the farm depression should be the federal government's top priority because the industrial and commercial sectors of the economy were so dependent on the purchasing power of rural consumers.[14]

A certain degree of evasive ambiguity by Roosevelt on agricultural policy statements was necessary because of the baffling ideological diversity of the southern and western Democrats who supported his nomination. His coalition included segregationist southern conservatives such as Senators Joseph Robinson of Arkansas and Byron "Pat" Harrison of Mississippi, as well as maverick, trust-busting western populists such as Senators Walsh and Wheeler.[15] Widely perceived as a radical by southern conservatives, Wheeler briefly left the Democratic party in 1924 to become the vice-presidential nominee of Robert La Follette's National Progressive party.[16] Ideologically, though, the southern conservatives and western populists had in common a contradictory desire to solve the agricultural problems of their states through federal action while avoiding a greater centralization of power in Washington.[17]

To stimulate a nationwide bandwagon effect behind Roosevelt's candidacy, Farley and Howe created the impression that Roosevelt's nomination was inevitable by distributing polls indicating the widespread support for Roosevelt among leading businessmen as well as delegates and alternates who attended the 1928 national convention.[18] Throughout the preconvention campaign, Roosevelt attracted a broad coalition by advocating greater federal intervention in the economy to relieve poverty and unemployment and end the Depression while promising to cut federal spending, balance the budget, and reduce the size of the federal bureaucracy.[19] Columnists portrayed the New York governor as an unprincipled opportunist, but his dichotomous rhetoric enabled him to maintain the support of states' rights conservatives in the South while attracting the support of Democrats and disaffected Republicans, who demanded greater federal efforts to combat the Depression than the Hoover administration was employing.[20] Because only about 34 percent of the voters were registered as Democrats in 1932, the Party would need a candidate who had proven his ability to attract the votes of Republicans and independents.[21]

Although Al Smith would not publicly announce his presidential candidacy until February 1932 when he entered the New Hampshire primary, Roosevelt and his campaign aides had always suspected that Smith would challenge Roosevelt for the nomination. As early as 1931, anti-Hoover sentiment and a desperate desire for a change in presidential leadership had become so widespread that virtually any Democratic nominee could win the 1932 election. For the first time in fourteen years, the Democrats won a majority of seats in the House of Representatives, while reducing the Republican majority in the Senate to one seat in 1930.[22] With such favorable electoral developments for the Party, it would be difficult for Smith to resist entering the race.[23]

Despite his resounding defeat to Hoover, in 1928, Smith still enjoyed a strong base of support within the Party, which he could rely on for electoral support in northeastern primaries and delegate support at the national convention. Although Roosevelt had actively sought to endear himself to Catholic Democrats through his courageous advocacy of Smith's presidential candidacies in 1924 and 1928, his inspiring denunciation of religious bigotry during his 1928 gubernatorial campaign, and his appointments of Catholics to prominent positions in New York's state government and Democratic party apparatus, it was clear that most Catholic Democrats would support Smith, their coreligionist.[24] The rules of the Democratic National Committee required that a presidential candidate must receive the votes of at least two-thirds of the delegates in order to be nominated; Smith could gather enough support to deny Roosevelt the nomination, even if he could not win it.[25]

There was a growing possibility that Smith would enter the race to deny Roosevelt's presidential nomination because of his vindictive, personal bitterness and his emerging conservative ideology.[26] Smith resented Roosevelt's rising political status while his own career was eclipsing and was angry that Roosevelt had not consulted him on public policy and party issues in New York. Smith had underestimated Roosevelt by perceiving him as an aristocratic dilettante who could not have succeeded in politics without the Tammany Democrat's support.[27]

Besides this personal rancor, Smith had undergone an ideological transformation that would motivate him to challenge Roosevelt in the 1932 nomination race and later to join the American Liberty League as a prominent critic of the New Deal and an opponent of Roosevelt's re-election. Smith's association with DNC chairman John Raskob, a former Republican and a General Motors executive, led to the abandonment of the urban liberalism he had exhibited as a state representative and governor. During Smith's 1928 presidential campaign, Roosevelt and other Democrats were dismayed that Smith and Raskob solicited the bulk of their campaign contributions from big business interests and devised an economic platform as conservative as the Republican one.[28] Consequently, Smith's political strength was an aggregation of his anticipated support from machine bosses, Catholics, including a majority of New York's delegates, big business conservatives who distrusted Roosevelt, and Raskob's intraparty influence.

Although Al Smith had been defeated by Hoover by a wide margin in 1928, he had distinguished himself as the first Democratic presidential nominee to win a plurality of votes in the nation's twelve largest cities.[29] He had announced his presidential candidacy in February 1932 and had defeated Roosevelt in the Massachusetts primary in April, despite the efforts of Boston mayor James M. Curley, a Roosevelt ally.[30] Ethnic solidarity and a strong suspicion that Roosevelt was an anti-machine reformer induced the major machine bosses to support Smith.

As the dangers that the Smith forces could pose to his nomination at the upcoming convention increased, Roosevelt's popularity and delegate strength among southern and western Democrats also increased in reaction to this development.[31] Perceiving Smith as Raskob's puppet, these Democrats, mostly "dry" on the Prohibition issue, resented the DNC chairman's arrogant, high-handed efforts to impose an unequivocally "wet" position for the entire Party. Although "dry" Democrats realized that Roosevelt and most Democrats would support repeal of the 18th Amendment, they disliked Smith's and Raskob's manipulation of the issue in order to embarrass Roosevelt and obscure their own conservative positions.[32] The Smith-Raskob economic platform was especially repugnant to southerners who wanted a reduction in tariff rates and westerners whose specific economic policy goals included an inflated currency backed by silver, strict regulations on private utility companies, and government-sponsored hydroelectric power.[33]

With the upcoming convention in June scheduled to be held in a city governed by a pro-Smith mayor, the Roosevelt campaign now sought to prevent the election of Jouett Shouse, executive secretary of the DNC and a close associate of Raskob and Smith, as permanent chairman of the convention. Shouse, in conjunction with Raskob, had been trying to block Roosevelt's nomination by urging pro-Roosevelt party leaders to send their delegates to the convention uncommitted to any candidate.[34] Many party leaders and delegates resented the blatantly biased manner in which Raskob and Shouse had been using their positions to damage Roosevelt's candidacy and favor Smith's. The Roosevelt forces, though, succeeded in having the Arrangements Committee recommend and the delegates elect Senator Thomas Walsh of Montana as permanent chairman and Senator Alben Barkley of Kentucky as keynote speaker.[35]

Despite these victories and the growing popularity of Roosevelt's candidacy among the delegates, he still lacked the two-thirds majority needed to secure the nomination on the first ballot. On the eve of the national convention, he had approximately 690 delegates committed to him; but he needed at least 768 votes in order to be nominated.[36] Approximately 209 delegates were committed to or favorable toward Smith's candidacy.

Some delegates were initially committed to vote for their states' favorite sons, such as Senators J. Hamilton Lewis of Illinois and James A. Reed of Missouri. Other candidates included Melvin Traylor, a Chicago banker; Owen D. Young, chairman of General Electric; and Newton Baker, a corporate lawyer who had served as Woodrow Wilson's Secretary of War.[37] Baker remained aloof in the conflicts between the Roosevelt and Smith forces, evidently hoping that he would be chosen as a compromise candidate in the event of a deadlock over the nomination.[38]

Some party leaders who opposed both Smith and Roosevelt

united behind the candidacy of Representative John N. Garner of Texas, the Speaker of the House.[39] Garner entered the race with the strong backing of William Randolph Hearst, wealthy newspaper publisher and political enemy of Roosevelt. With Texas' forty-six delegates committed to Garner, Hearst's sponsorship enabled him to gain the support of California's forty-four delegates.[40]

Some pro-Roosevelt party leaders suggested that the delegates vote to repeal the two-thirds rule before the balloting began.[41] Because changes in convention rules required only the votes of a simple majority, advocates of this tactic were confident that there were enough pro-Roosevelt delegates to overturn the rule, then nominate Roosevelt by a simple majority.[42] Roosevelt and Farley briefly supported this repeal movement, but ordered their delegates to stop the effort when it became obvious that many pro-Roosevelt southern delegates opposed repeal, which, historically, had enabled southern Democrats to prevent the nomination of candidates objectionable to them.[43]

After the third ballot was taken, it was evident that Roosevelt would not be nominated unless he received some delegate support from either the Smith or the Garner camp.[44] With Smith delegates determined to continue their opposition, they enlisted Representative Sam Rayburn of Texas to persuade Garner to support Roosevelt on the fourth ballot in exchange for being selected as his running mate. Concerned about the need for party unity against Hoover, Garner agreed to cooperate.[45] The transfer of Garner's 101 delegate votes to Roosevelt stimulated a bandwagon effect among the delegates of minor candidates so that Roosevelt was easily nominated on the fourth ballot with 945 votes.[46]

The platform formulated at this convention reflected the contradictory proposals Roosevelt had made during the preconvention campaign. He still supported "an immediate and drastic reduction of governmental expenditures" while also proposing a reduction of the federal bureaucracy and an expansion of federal public works programs.[47] His speeches and policy proposals after the convention, though, were bolder and more specific.[48] In major campaign speeches he envisioned a policy agenda in which the federal government prevented monopolistic abuses by big business, ensured stable, adequate farm prices for farmers, guaranteed economic security for wage earners, and provided affordable electricity for rural Americans.[49]

Roosevelt's rhetoric during the general election campaign reflected a suprapartisan approach in which he sought to persuade the voters that he was concerned with solving the nation's economic problems and restoring Americans' faith in presidential leadership and not merely seeking an electoral victory for himself and his party. This rhetorical strategy was evident when he stated in his acceptance speech that he would not use the words "Republican Party" in his campaign addresses.[50] Asserting that the Democratic party was the "bearer of liberalism and of progress" that would save the American political and economic systems from "unreasoning radicalism," he invited the support of "those nominal Republicans who find that their conscience cannot be squared with the groping and the failure of their party leaders."[51] Furthermore, he warned staunchly conservative Democrats that "they are out of step with their Party."[52]

Although Roosevelt's frequent identification of himself, the Democratic party, and his policy proposals with liberalism—however vaguely defined—may have alienated some of the most conservative Democrats, it helped to attract endorsements and voter mobilization efforts from prominent progressive Republicans, such as Senators Hiram Johnson of California, George Norris of Nebraska, and Robert La Follette, Jr., of Wisconsin.[53] Roosevelt's rhetoric pleased western progressives with his promise of implementing federally sponsored hydroelectric power projects.[54] Roosevelt's gubernatorial record and his fight against private utility companies opposed to low-cost electricity for rural areas gave credibility to this rhetoric.[55] Norris organized the National Progressive Republican League as a vehicle for cultivating the support of anti-Hoover, progressive Republicans for Roosevelt.[56]

Despite the opposition of some of his advisers who wanted him to conduct a "front porch campaign" in Hyde Park, Roosevelt embarked on a cross-country, whistle-stop campaign on September 12, 1932. He hoped that a vigorous speech-making effort from coast to coast would assure the voters of his physical stamina and acquaint them with his ebullient personality, rhetorical talent, and leadership qualities.[57] Voters would then note the sharp contrast between Roosevelt and the dour, lackluster Hoover.

Two of Roosevelt's campaign speeches revealed how he perceived and would address the economic crisis. While speaking at Ogelthorpe University, he outlined three economic concepts which would later be reflected in the National Recovery Administration.[58] First, he suggested that the causes of the Depression were domestic, not international, and required the federal government to pursue a recovery policy of economic nationalism, not one stressing international economic agreements, which Hoover had pursued.[59] Second, he contended that the federal government must increase its power over business in order to regulate stock market practices and effect such reforms as the national abolition of child labor. Finally, by advocating a program of economic planning between government, business, and labor, he rejected the trust-busting approach to economic reform of earlier progressives.[60]

On September 23, 1932, Roosevelt provided a more lucid, articulate synthesis of his policy response to the Depression in his address to the Commonwealth Club of San Francisco.[61] He expressed a more conciliatory tone toward businessmen, and urged them to regard their economic power as a public trust and to exercise it with social responsibility. If business did not comply, government would be forced to intervene to protect the public interest. The reassuring tone of this address, however, implied that a cooperative partnership between government and business would achieve economic recovery. In short, Roosevelt welcomed business support, provided that businessmen were willing to contribute to the reform of American capitalism.[62]

Near the end of the campaign, a columnist stated that Roosevelt intended to make the Democratic party "the liberal party, the party which will restore the balance of power between the rich and the poor and bring prosperity to the 'forgotten man' as well as to the Wall Street banker."[63] Widespread economic suffering and opposition to Hoover enabled Roosevelt to win the electoral college votes of forty-two states and 59 percent of the popular votes.[64] With only about one-third of the voters registered as Democrats, the unusually high voter turn-out and the electoral support from anti-Hoover Republicans and independents contributed to Roosevelt's wide margin of victory.[65]

While blacks gave 65 percent of their votes to Hoover, the electoral support for Roosevelt among non-southern whites[66] was distributed broadly in urban and rural areas, among WASPs and ethnics, and among the middle and lower classes.[67] It was unclear, though, if the traditionally Republican voters had realigned themselves with the Democratic party and preferred a liberal policy agenda or had simply wanted to defeat Hoover.[68]

Roosevelt's objective during the 1932 campaign was to harmonize and unite the elements of the Party that had been bitterly divided by the Prohibition issue and Smith's nomination in 1928, especially northern ethnics and southern WASPs. Before he could transform the ideology and policy agenda of the Party into distinctly liberal alternatives to those of the Republican party, he first had to unite these diverse Democratic factions behind his Party leadership. Through campaign rhetoric, he mixed the conservatism of states' rights, a balanced federal budget, and less bureaucracy with social welfare liberalism in order to build a broad coalition. Overall, though, his policy proposals expressed a desire to increase the power of the federal government to stimulate and regulate the economy and to address the economic grievances of farmers and wage earners.[69]

Ernest K. Lindley stated in 1933 that Roosevelt's "consistent ambition for many years . . . was to form a new liberal party by attaching the Republican Progressives and miscellaneous liberals to the Democratic party, thus effecting a new political alignment which had meaning."[70] Roosevelt realized that to transform the Party and gain broad public support for the early New Deal he needed to attract liberally inclined Republicans and independents.[71] During the 1936 campaign, Roosevelt found the New Deal to be a powerful vehicle for expanding and liberalizing the Party and ensuring his own re-election.

The 1936 Election

The outcome of the 1936 presidential election would reveal whether Roosevelt's victory in 1932 was merely the public's reaction against Hoover's presidency or whether it foreshadowed an enduring realignment of the two-party system. To maximize bipartisan support behind the early New Deal, especially the NRA, Roosevelt did not want to appear to be a narrowly partisan president who was exploiting the economic crisis to benefit his party. Realizing that he needed the cooperation of big businessmen, who were predominantly Republican, in order for the NRA to succeed, he wanted to appear to be a statesman who was mainly interested in achieving economic recovery.[72]

As Benjamin Cohen later explained, Roosevelt shrewdly realized that his projection of a suprapartisan image was necessary for attracting the electoral support of liberally inclined Republicans, independents, and third party members.[73] He believed that the transformation he desired for the Party was not possible without the support of these non-Democratic voters.[74] In a 1934 letter to a Nebraska Republican, Roosevelt wrote, "I have tried, more than most people believe, to eliminate partisanship in the relief of human needs and the improvement of the economic structure."[75]

In addition to his cultivation of a less partisan image and leadership style as president, Roosevelt's nationally broadcast "fireside chats" and frequent, media-covered inspection visits of New Deal projects made him familiar to the American public. Many believed he was personally aware of and responsive to the economic problems they were suffering.[76] Despite the failure of the NRA's price and wage codes to induce economic recovery and reports of faulty bureaucratic coordination within his administration, Roosevelt was perceived as an inspiring, ubiquitous problem-solver, unlike any previous president.[77] His leadership style and public image provided a sharp contrast to his grim, withdrawn predecessor.

New Deal programs gave credibility to Roosevelt's rhetoric promising broad, immediate federal action against the economic crisis. During his first term, the New Deal had strengthened support for him in the South and West, his regional political base at the 1932 convention. Reflecting his belief that solving the farm depression was a prerequisite for general economic recovery, the most innovative New Deal programs focused on permanently reforming the agricultural economy.[78]

Furthermore, the New Deal provided low-cost electricity, soil and forest conservation, irrigation, flood control, paved roads, and new public buildings for remote, rural areas of the South and West.[79] Southern Democrats, both Bourbon conservatives and hill country populists, and western progressives, Republican and Democrat, cooperated in Congress to enact such programs. Not until after the 1936 election did a growing number of southern and western Democrats begin to perceive the New Deal and the increasingly liberal national Party as excessively and unfairly biased in favor of northern cities and labor unions.[80]

The benefits of the New Deal solidified Roosevelt's previously monolithic electoral support in the one-party South for the 1936 election, and its assistance to rural interests proved especially advantageous in western states for gaining broad electoral support for Roosevelt in 1936 and for pro–New Deal Democratic candidates in the 1934 and 1936 congressional and state elections. With a regional tradition stressing maverick independence in politics, many western states possessed an unpredictable and unstable partisan configuration regarding the voting behavior and party affiliation of their voters.[81] Progressive politicians in both major parties denounced mining, banking, and electric utility interests for abusing their economic power.[82] Despite their support of New Deal programs favorable to the interests of their states, Republican and Democratic western progressives shared a distrust of centralized power, both on Wall Street and in Washington.[83]

The West was a region in which voters had proven to be most likely to leave the two-party system and support populist third parties. Theodore Roosevelt's Progressive party in 1912 and Robert La Follette's National Progressive party in 1924 received their strongest electoral support from western states where these third-party presidential candidates heavily outpolled their Democratic opponents.[84] Consequently, Roosevelt had to be concerned about the prospect of losing votes in the West in 1936 if a strong, populist third party emerged that was more appealing to the regional interests and political principles of westerners.[85]

Roosevelt's suprapartisan image and solicitation of support from progressive Republicans and independents during the early New Deal led to conflicts over patronage distribution between Jim Farley and less partisan cabinet members, especially Harold Ickes, as well as between Farley and non-Democratic politicians favored by Roosevelt, such as Fiorello La Guardia.[86] Likewise, some state and local Democratic organizations complained that Republicans controlled federal relief programs in their states and, in some cases, discriminated against Democratic voters in the distribution of relief and public works jobs.[87]

Despite complaints from party regulars, Roosevelt understood that many Democratic candidates outside of the South would need the votes of non-Democratic voters to win the congressional and state elections of 1934. This was especially true in rural areas of the Midwest and West. Although this region was traditionally Republican, many distressed farmers supported such leftist third parties as the Farmer-Labor Party of Minnesota, North Dakota's Nonpartisan League, and the Progressive party in Wisconsin established by Philip and Robert La Follette in 1934.[88] Roosevelt implicitly supported the re-election of Floyd Olson, Minnesota's Farmer-Labor governor, against John Regan, the conservative Democratic nominee who opposed Roosevelt in 1932.[89]

In 1936, Roosevelt directed Ed Flynn and Jim Farley to

establish the American Labor Party in New York City to
pressure Tammany Hall into becoming more liberal and reformed, and to attract non-Democratic voters, especially Socialists in the labor movement, to his candidacy.[90] By taking
these actions during his early presidency, Roosevelt was not
neglecting or weakening regular Democratic organizations
and their candidates. Instead, he was trying to pressure these
Democratic organizations and candidates into becoming
more liberal and supportive of the New Deal and his party
leadership while making membership in the Party more
attractive to liberally inclined, non-Democratic voters.[91]

   The ability of Roosevelt's presidential leadership and New
Deal liberalism to attract Republicans and independent
voters into the Party was especially pronounced in Pennsylvania. As the largest overwhelmingly Republican state,
Pennsylvania was one of only six in which Herbert Hoover
received a majority of popular votes in 1932, and had not
given a Democratic presidential nominee its electoral college
votes since 1856.[92] Two ambitious Democratic party-builders,
Joseph Guffey and David Lawrence, closely identified the
Pennsylvania state Democratic party with Roosevelt and the
New Deal in the hope of sweeping their state's congressional
and state elections in 1934.[93] After coopting traditionally
Republican blacks, union leaders, and non-Irish urban ethnics while attracting a significant minority of rural WASPs,
the Pennsylvania Democrats won a majority of their state's
congressional seats and a majority of seats in Pennsylvania's
House of Representatives.[94] Guffey was elected to the U.S.
Senate and soon distinguished himself nationally as a "100%
New Dealer."[95] George Earle was elected as the first Democratic governor since 1890 and launched a "Little New Deal"
in state government.[96]

   As in other heavily Republican states, Pennsylvania Democrats conducted an extensive voter registration drive to prepare for the 1934 and 1936 elections. The percentage of
Pennsylvania voters registered as Democrats doubled from 21
percent in 1932 to 42 percent in 1936.[97] In California, where
Democrats had controlled only 10 of the 138 elective state and
federal offices in 1930, Upton Sinclair, a former Socialist and

the Democratic gubernatorial nominee in 1934, conducted a highly successful voter registration campaign. By 1934, for the first time in California history, Democratic voters outnumbered Republican voters.[98]

Even though Republican voter registration still exceeded Democratic registration in 1934, the Democrats actually increased their majorities in Congress and their control of state governments.[99] Though Democratic candidates had attracted Republican and independent voters by advocating the New Deal, Roosevelt was confronted with opposition in the 1936 election from both the left and the right.[100] Prominent Democrats like Al Smith and John Davis formed the American Liberty League to oppose his re-election by denying him the Democratic business support he had received in 1932.[101] A number of leftist, populist movements led by Dr. Charles Townsend, Governor Huey Long of Louisiana, and Father Charles Coughlin threatened to attract ordinarily pro-Roosevelt voters by nominating a presidential candidate for 1936.[102]

By 1935, the prospect of a leftist third party and growing newspaper and business criticism of the New Deal led both parties and the media to anticipate a close outcome for the 1936 presidential election.[103] Because the economic crisis had abated and stabilized by 1936, it was possible that many middle-class Republicans who had voted for Roosevelt in 1932 would return to the Republican fold in 1936.[104] To attract traditionally Republican middle-class voters and blacks, the Roosevelt campaign established the Good Neighbor League and various "Republicans for Roosevelt" state organizations.[105] With many recently unionized workers still not registered as Democrats, John L. Lewis, a Republican, and Sidney Hillman, a Socialist, established Labor's Non-Partisan League to support Roosevelt.[106] To symbolize the realignment they sought to effect, the Democrats selected the staunchly Republican city of Philadelphia as the site of their 1936 convention.[107]

Roosevelt realized that the types of enemies he had made in big business, banking, Republican-owned newspapers, and the Supreme Court would make him more attractive to voters if he portrayed himself as their champion against powerful interests. In his campaign speeches, he denounced the shortsighted selfishness of "economic royalists." He asserted that reforming American capitalism through the New Deal was essential for preserving American democracy.[108]

Throughout his first term, and especially during the 1936 campaign, the president concentrated his rhetoric on assuring Americans that the New Deal would preserve and strengthen democracy, capitalism, and basic values. The concept and tangible development of a big, interventionist federal government disturbed many middle-class Americans, who had absorbed the traditional American ideology of "negative government," and believed that big government would threaten individual liberty, states' rights, economic freedom, and democratic rule. To respond effectively to the Republican and American Liberty League denunciations of the New Deal as a radical philosophy detrimental to the values and institutions of a democratic, capitalistic society, Roosevelt devoted much of his campaign rhetoric to the theme that the New Deal was compatible with such traditional American values as the work ethic and individualism.[109]

Roosevelt adopted this theme in his first official speech of the general election campaign, delivered in Syracuse, New York, on September 29, 1936. He asserted that liberalism as manifested through the New Deal was the philosophy of a farsighted conservative and that "never has a Nation made greater strides in the safeguarding of democracy than we have made during the past three years. Wise and prudent men—intelligent conservatives—have long known that in a changing world worthy institutions can be conserved only by adjusting them to the changing time."[110]

In his speeches defending New Deal liberalism as a modern adaptation of traditional American political and economic values to new conditions, he assured his listeners that the social welfare, labor reform, and regulatory policies of his administration would save the free enterprise system, not destroy it. Although he realized that he would convert few corporate executives into New Deal liberals, he sought to convince businessmen that it was not necessary for them to perceive the New Deal and the labor union movement as threats to capitalism. In a campaign address given in Cleveland, he stated that the "interest of every business man is bound to the interest of every wage earner."[111] He asserted that higher wages and greater economic security for workers would improve productivity and consumer demand, thus increasing profits for businessmen.

Roosevelt used another rhetorical theme to legitimize New Deal liberalism in the minds of the voters as a current reflection of the American political tradition. He frequently described a correlation between economic democracy and political democracy. No longer could Americans believe that economic injustices and grievances would not affect the vitality and integrity of their democracy. In Dallas, Texas, the president asserted that "Any elemental policy, economic or political, which tends to eliminate these dependable defenders of democratic institutions, and to concentrate control in the hands of a few, small powerful groups, is directly opposed to the stability of government and to democratic government itself."[112]

Roosevelt also compared his administration's struggle to end the Depression and permanently reform the economy to such earlier crises as the Revolutionary War and the Civil War. As the campaign progressed, he began to adopt a more antagonistic portrayal of anti-New Deal businessmen, accusing them of hindering the advance of political and economic democracy by their opposition to the New Deal.[113] Drawing parallels between the philosophy and policies of the New Deal and the ideas of such highly respected presidents as Jefferson and Lincoln, Roosevelt hoped to inspire the voters to associate the New Deal with familiar, attractive patriotic figures and perceive its opponents as threats to the American political tradition.[114]

This class-conflict theme in Roosevelt's rhetoric was evident in his acceptance speech at the 1936 Democratic National Convention. He asserted that "economic royalists" had undermined and distorted the American economy by transforming it into "privileged enterprise, not free enterprise."[115] According to Roosevelt, it was the responsibility of the federal

government to intervene effectively on behalf of average
Americans against the "economic tyranny" of wealthy business elites. Consequently, the purpose of the New Deal was
not only to preserve American capitalism by reforming it but
also to win "a war for the survival of democracy."[116]

Such inflammatory rhetoric against economic interests
opposing the New Deal certainly appealed to the delegates of
the convention. Sidney Milkis estimates that about 50 percent of them were federal job holders.[117] The composition of
the delegations also indicated the emergence of blacks and
women as prominent party activists. Two hundred nineteen
women delegates attended the 1936 Democratic National
Convention while only sixty attended the Republican National Convention that year.[118] For the first time, Democratic
women served as alternates to the members of the Resolutions Committee.

The historical "firsts" that blacks enjoyed at this convention, however, were more noticeable. For the first time, thirty
black Democrats served as delegates and black reporters
were admitted to the press box.[119] Roosevelt's recognition of
the importance of the black vote in this election was more
powerfully symbolized by his choice of a black minister to
deliver the opening prayer and of Arthur Mitchell, the first
black Democrat elected to Congress, to deliver the welcoming
speech.[120]

The 1936 convention was the first since 1832 to conduct its
nomination process without the two-thirds rule, which required a nominee to receive votes from at least two-thirds of
the delegates at a national convention. Roosevelt supporters
had attempted to overturn the rule at the 1932 convention but
had failed because of their fear of alienating southern conservatives.

The repeal clearly demonstrated the growing ability of
voting blocs and interest groups to overcome the resistance of
Party conservatives. It also demonstrated Roosevelt's ability
to secure reforms that would increase the intraparty power of
groups favoring the nomination of liberals committed to the
New Deal.

The two-thirds rule gave united southern delegations veto

power during the nomination process if they opposed a candidate who was supported by only a simple majority. They maintained that their region, the most loyally and consistently Democratic, should have the right to ensure the nomination of presidential candidates acceptable to the South.

Opponents argued that the rule weakened intraparty unity by enabling a determined, united minority of delegates to prevent the nomination of a popular candidate with voter appeal beyond the South. Even House Speaker Champ Clark in 1912 and Senator William Gibbs McAdoo in 1924, both popular among Southern delegates, had received wide delegate support at their respective conventions. But Clark and McAdoo failed to be nominated because they did not have enough delegate support outside of the South and thus lacked the necessary two-thirds majority.[121] The presidential nomination was denied to them by northern and progressive Democrats. At the 1932 convention, an obstructionist minority comprised of the backers of Al Smith and John Garner had threatened to deny Roosevelt the two-thirds majority.

In 1936, however, approximately 900 of the 1,154 delegates attending the convention were committed to the abolition of the two-thirds rule.[122] Roosevelt, Farley, and Senator Bennett Clark of Missouri, chairman of the Rules Committee, were confident that the rule could be quietly repealed with a minimum of intraparty conflict. As Harold F. Bass, Jr., has persuasively contended, Roosevelt's choice of Clark to lead the repeal effort was "truly inspired" and assured its success.[123] Clark received favorable media attention and widespread sympathy within the party for his determination to end the two-thirds rule because it had denied his father the Democratic presidential nomination in 1912. Also, Clark's ideological status as a conservative weakened the claim of southern opponents that the repeal movement was a nefarious plot by northern liberals like Joe Guffey who wanted to liberalize the Party by increasing the intraparty power of blacks, labor, and urban ethnics while weakening southern influence.[124]

Although opposition to the repeal was led by southerners, especially Representative Eugene E. Cox of Georgia and Sen-

ator Harry Byrd, a significant minority of southern delegates
favored repeal.[125] One Arkansas delegate even told the Rules
Committee that he "favored the reform as an incentive to
party building above the Mason-Dixon line."[126] Clark's skill-
ful leadership of the Rules Committee, Farley's lobbying
efforts, and Roosevelt's status as a popular incumbent intimidated and inhibited diehard supporters of the rule and facilitated its repeal.[127]

In 1938, Senator Josiah Bailey of North Carolina, an anti–
New Deal conservative and a defender of the rule, bitterly
lamented that the repeal would result in the Party and its
national conventions being controlled by "very objectionable
men whose politics are entirely distasteful to the Southern
Democracy. They get elected by the negro vote in New York,
Pennsylvania, Boston, Chicago, and the cities of the Middle
West."[128] At the 1944 Democratic national convention, Eugene E. Cox made a futile attempt to restore the rule, even
though only 21 percent of the delegates attending the convention were from the South. He ruefully concluded that the end
of the rule meant that "the South completely lost its power
independently to influence party affairs."[129] Assessing the
impact of the repeal on the ideological and regional character
of the Party in presidential elections, Arthur M. Schlesinger,
Jr., concluded that the end of the two-thirds rule would "accelerate the transformation of the Democracy into a more thoroughly northern party."[130]

Repeal of the rule proved to be crucial to the liberalization
of the Party's ideology and domestic policy objectives. At the
1940 and 1944 conventions, Roosevelt did not feel compelled
to choose a southern conservative as his running mate in
order to appease southern delegates and assure his renomination and instead, was free to choose a committed New
Dealer. The selection of presidential and vice-presidential
nominees and the adoption of major policy planks in the
platform now had to be acceptable, or at least not objectionable, to the dominant liberal elements of the Party.[131] In
short, Roosevelt's successful effort to repeal the two-thirds
rule was a major factor in preventing conservative Democrats

from regaining control of national Party affairs after his 1936 campaign.

Roosevelt's willingness to risk alienating southern conservatives, such as Senator "Cotton Ed" Smith who angrily left the 1936 convention during the black minister's opening prayer, revealed that southern support was not indispensable to his re-election because Democratic electoral strength outside of the South had rapidly increased increased during his first term. The repeal of the two-thirds rule and the fact that only 23 percent of his electoral college votes in 1936 came from the South indicated the beginning of the South's decline in influence at Democratic national conventions.[132]

The prominence of blacks, women, urban ethnics, and labor leaders at the 1936 convention also indicated the increasingly pluralistic character of the Party's membership that both coincided with and accelerated the onset of the South's decline in power over national Party affairs. This intraparty power shift from the mostly conservative southern Democrats to more liberally inclined voting blocs and interest groups emerging at the 1936 convention illustrated the "redistribution of power" thesis formulated by Samuel Beer.[133] This redistribution of power resulted from the New Deal's bias toward farmers, laborers, and small businessmen and against big business interests, and was demonstrated by such policies as the Wagner Act, the Social Security Act, the WPA, the AAA, as well as higher taxes and stricter regulations on big business. The bias stimulated the growth of countervailing powers—especially labor unions and farm organizations—against big business.[134]

Just as the New Deal's policies broadened the distribution of economic power in American capitalism, the growing power of blacks, women, urban ethnics, and organized labor within the national party signified the convergence of what Beer called the democratic and national ideas in American party politics. Prior to the New Deal, the southern-controlled Democratic party had been "democratic" in the sense that it stressed local-level democracy, states' rights, and minimal federal intervention. The Republican party expressed the "national" idea of using a strong federal government to develop and consolidate the nation, or at least its economy.[135]

By 1936, the Party under Roosevelt had combined the democratic and national ideas through its espousal of New Deal liberalism as the essence of its ideology and policy agenda. It emerged from the 1936 convention as a more inclusive, pluralistic party which democratized national politics by embracing previously disadvantaged, neglected groups. According to Beer, the Party encouraged these voting blocs to become party activists and achieved this democratization through governmental nationalism, formulating and implementing federal policies which redistributed economic power and wealth more broadly and thus benefited these new coalition members.[136]

Although he employed more combative rhetoric in 1936 than he had in 1932, Roosevelt understood the ability of the New Deal, as the dominant campaign issue, to build a consensus behind his candidacy. His class-conflict theme appealed to Democratic and liberally inclined, non-Democratic voters. The New Deal had served a broad spectrum of socioeconomic groups.[137] For example, FHA mortgage subsidies helped middle-class home owners while AAA price supports, soil conservation, and rural electrification benefited farmers. Federal relief and public works jobs aided working-class ethnics and blacks.

Recognizing the widespread popularity of New Deal programs, even among such traditionally Republican voters as rural, non-southern WASPs, the Republican party pursued a rhetorical strategy attacking such problems in New Deal programs as partisan favoritism in the administration of public works projects and Roosevelt's failure to fulfill his 1932 campaign promises of reducing federal spending and the size of the federal bureaucracy.[138] While asserting that they subscribed to the humanitarian goals the Democrats claimed were offered by the New Deal, Republicans denounced the New Deal as a politically corrupt, incompetent, and fiscally extravagant means for reforming capitalism. In short, Republican speakers directly challenged Roosevelt's frequent contention that the New Deal was a necessary adaptation of the American political and economic systems to modern conditions.

Republican party leaders realized that they must not nominate a presidential candidate who fit Roosevelt's depiction of a callous "economic royalist" with Wall Street backing. They knew that a clearly pro–big business conservative would be doomed to a landslide defeat. The best Republican candidate was perceived to be someone who had the image and background of a moderate progressive but was also a reliable party regular and New Deal critic who espoused such traditional Republican policies as a balanced federal budget and high protective tariffs.[139]

With little hope of receiving electoral majorities in the South and major urban areas of the Northeast and Midwest, the Republican party focused its strategy on farm states of the Midwest and West. Because Roosevelt had attracted the endorsements of prominent progressive Republicans in 1932, Republican party leaders realized that they must prevent the realignment of moderate to liberal Republican voters, many of them living in the Midwest and West, with the Democratic party. To appeal to farmers in these states, the Republican platform was most specific and elaborate in its discussion of agricultural issues, promising farmers high protective tariffs against agricultural imports, low-interest loans, and subsidy payments.[140] It also promised black Americans, Hoover's most loyal voting bloc in 1932, "equal opportunity . . . and protection of their economic status and personal safety."[141]

Republican party insiders and their allies among newspaper publishers decided that Governor Alfred "Alf" Landon of Kansas was the ideal presidential nominee for 1936. Landon, who appeared to be an effective vote-getter, was the only Republican governor elected in 1932 who was re-elected in 1934, even though Roosevelt carried his state in 1932.[142] Republican supporters hoped that Landon would attract pro-Roosevelt Republicans because he had been a leading Kansas operative for Teddy Roosevelt's Bull Moose campaign of 1912 and Robert La Follette's third party presidential candidacy of 1924.[143] Almost unanimously nominated by Republican delegates on the first ballot, Landon chose another former Bull

Mooser, Frank Knox, as his running mate. The progressive political backgrounds of Landon and Knox, combined with the mildly reformist Republican platform advocating farm subsidies, old age pensions, and federal regulation of securities and utilities, held the possibility of a competitive race between Landon and Roosevelt.

Landon, however, soon destroyed whatever potential he had to prevent significant Republican defections to Roosevelt. His choice of an unpopular conservative, John D.M. Hamilton, as RNC chairman and campaign manager as well as his solicitation of big business contributions led many liberal Republican politicians to dismiss Landon as an insincere opportunist.[144] As in 1932, such nationally known liberal Republicans as George Norris, Fiorello La Guardia, and the La Follette brothers organized voter mobilization campaigns for Roosevelt.[145]

The Republicans hoped that their nominee would appeal to the midwestern farm belt. But many traditionally Republican farmers there preferred Roosevelt, mostly because of the New Deal's agricultural policies.[146] Landon weakened his own appeal and credibility by inconsistently alternating his rhetoric between orthodox conservatism and progressive proposals. Each time he attacked a New Deal policy, especially the Social Security Act, he further weakened his own voter appeal and strengthened Roosevelt's image as the common man's champion.[147] As the campaign progressed, Landon's anti–New Deal rhetoric isolated him more and more from the electorate and accelerated the momentum behind Roosevelt's re-election.[148] By the end of the campaign, Roosevelt was not just the presidential nominee of the Democratic party but also "the leader of a liberal crusade which knew no party lines."[149]

Roosevelt's assertive, eloquent defense of the New Deal's policy agenda and ideology, the broad consensus behind his re-election, and a high voter turn-out combined to provide him with over 60 percent of the popular vote and the electoral college votes of all but two states.[150] The Democratic party formally became the majority Party in national politics as registered Democrats outnumbered registered Republicans.[151] Although Catholics, Jews, blacks, and low-income Americans were more likely to vote for Roosevelt, his electoral support from middle-income WASPs was high enough to assure his victory in midwestern and western states.[152]

The voting statistics for the 1936 presidential election indicated a reduction of ethnocultural and regional differences in the voting behavior and party affiliation of Americans. Nonsouthern white Protestants significantly reduced their previously overwhelmingly Republican voting behavior and gave Roosevelt half of the total WASP vote outside the South. Sixty percent of low-income non-southern WASPs supported Roosevelt, while only 35 percent of the high-income members of the group did.[153] Roosevelt's attractiveness to Catholics was evident as approximately 80 percent of them voted Democratic.[154]

Blacks and Jews, who had previously been the most loyal ethnic voting blocs for the Republicans in major northern cities, voted for Roosevelt by margins of 76 percent and 90 percent, respectively.[155] Roosevelt's combined plurality of votes in the nation's twelve largest cities nearly doubled from 1.8 million in 1932 to 3.5 million in 1936.[156] In all, the results of the 1936 presidential election suggested that the Democratic party could consistently succeed as the majority party in national politics if it could continue to transcend regional and ethnocultural differences among the electorate by identifying itself with an ideology and policy agenda that addressed commonly held economic problems and grievances.

Roosevelt's overwhelming victory, however, revealed that there were political forces and changes which would soon weaken the popular, unifying appeal of the New Deal and his Party leadership as well as divide the Democratic party, whose size had expanded so rapidly during his first term. The repeal of the two-thirds rule at the national convention and the vigorous cultivation of the black vote suggested the decline of southern power within the Party. With Roosevelt receiving only 23 percent of his electoral college votes from the South and with only 35 percent of Democrats in the upcoming Congress from the South, it appeared that Roosevelt had a nationwide mandate for the continuation of New

Deal liberalism and thus could successfully defy and circumvent southern conservatives in Congress.[157] Roosevelt's pursuit of further New Deal policy initiatives, however, would prove to be as divisive for intraparty relations during his second term as it had been conducive toward unity and party-building during his first term.

6 The Purge Campaigns of 1938

Roosevelt's relentless yet unsuccessful effort to persuade the Democrats in Congress to pass the court reform bill early in 1937 permanently weakened his ability to convince the Democratic Congress to pass further domestic policy proposals from the White House.[1] The bitter intraparty struggles over the failed court reform bill and the close election of Alben Barkley, a New Deal populist, as Senate majority leader over Pat Harrison, a southern conservative, accelerated the bifurcation between northern liberals and southern conservatives.[2] These intraparty conflicts also made conservative Democrats more openly hostile to Roosevelt's party leadership and more likely to cooperate with the Republican minority in opposing White House bills.[3]

Despite the invigoration of the conservative opposition that these conflicts stimulated, Roosevelt became more aggressive, combative, and publicly critical toward his conservative Democratic opponents. The legislative defeats that he suffered at their hands during the 75th Congress made him more determined to eliminate, or at least subordinate, the power of anti–New Deal conservatives within the Party. Less cautious about maintaining a consensus within the Party than he had been during his first term, he delivered several major addresses from 1937 to 1939 which emphasized his determination to continue the development of a distinctly liberal Party despite conservative opposition in the party.[4]

Roosevelt had become angry and frustrated with Democrats in Congress who had rhetorically associated themselves with the popular president and the New Deal in order to be renominated and re-elected but then weakened or opposed White House bills during the legislative process. Roosevelt referred to these members of Congress as "yes, but—" Democrats. As Roosevelt stated in 1941, the "quarrel in 1938 was

with those who said they were liberals, but who, nevertheless, proceeded to stand in the way of all social progress by
objecting to any measure to carry out liberal objectives."[5] For
Roosevelt, therefore, a presidential effort to "purge" or at
least discipline anti–New Deal Democratic incumbents was
necessary to strengthen the clarity and integrity of a two-
party system in which the Democratic party represented
liberalism in public policy and the Republican party represented conservatism.

In 1938, Roosevelt claimed that the Party's identification
with New Deal liberalism was essential for its continuation as
the majority party and in order for it to attract the votes of
liberal Republicans and independents.[6] He stated in a 1939
address to the Young Democrats that a liberal identity was
essential for his own support of the Party.[7] He stated unequivocally that he would not endorse a conservative presidential nominee in 1940.

All of these factors motivated Roosevelt to embark on the
most politically courageous yet reckless endeavor of his presidential leadership—his intervention against selected conservative incumbents in the 1938 Democratic congressional
primaries. Previously, Roosevelt's cautious, calculating political acumen had impelled him to remain neutral in primaries,
even when pro–New Deal incumbents were threatened by
conservative opponents.[8] At this time, Roosevelt wanted to
emphasize a consensual, inclusive Party leadership that
could expand the electoral base of the national Party by
attracting liberally inclined voting blocs while maintaining
the loyalty of southern conservatives.[9] He did not want to
damage his party leadership and threaten New Deal bills
during his first term by intervening in primaries and antagonizing powerful conservative Democrats in Congress.

But the conservative Democrats' increasingly successful
opposition to further New Deal policies and to the liberal
transformation of the Party had emboldened Roosevelt to
seek the defeat of several prominent conservatives by openly
supporting their liberal challengers. The decision to take
such unprecedented action in intraparty affairs, however,
was not entirely of his own volition. His decision to purge se-

lected congressional conservatives was influenced by Tommy Corcoran, Harry Hopkins, Harold Ickes, and his son, James Roosevelt.[10] These White House New Dealers, especially Corcoran, had begun to overshadow Jim Farley as Roosevelt's operatives in intraparty affairs and in White House relations with Congress. Farley and other party regulars opposed a presidential purge of Democratic primaries; because of their interest in maintaining intraparty harmony and unity, they preferred the renomination of Democratic incumbents.[11] The White House purgers, more concerned than Farley with the ideological transformation of the Democratic Party, were willing to risk arousing further intraparty discord to attain this objective.

Corcoran had quickly moved beyond his position as legislative draftsman and Capitol Hill lobbyist for White House bills. He sought an influential role in Party affairs as Roosevelt's liaison.[12] He assumed that the defeat of the court reform and the original executive reorganization bills were harbingers of further defeats of White House legislation if pro–New Deal Democrats were not elected to Congress.

After their modest success on January 4, 1938, in Alabama's special Democratic primary for a Senate seat, Corcoran, Hopkins, and the other members of the purge campaign were confident that they could help nominate Democrats loyal to Roosevelt. After Hugo Black vacated his Senate seat in order to become a Supreme Court justice, Congressman Lister Hill and J. Thomas Heflin, a former U.S. senator, competed in a special Democratic primary to replace Black. Hill was a New Deal supporter who stressed his advocacy of the wages-and-hours bill. This bill was repugnant to Alabama industrialists, who perceived the South's lower wages as an advantage against their northern competitors.[13]

Heflin, a shrill race baiter and an opponent of the wages-and-hours bill and most New Deal policies, succeeded in gaining the endorsements and campaign contributions of Alabama business interests. Heflin, ironically, was embarrassed by an attempt of his business supporters to damage Hill's voter appeal by criticizing his support of the wages-and-hours bill. In November 1937, Heflin's business supporters distributed copies of Republican Congressman J. Will Taylor's speech criticizing this bill and Hill's support of it.[14]

Because of his endorsement of Herbert Hoover in 1928, Heflin's fidelity to the Democratic party was already questionable. Use of a Republican congressman's speech to attack Hill led Hill supporters to denounce this tactic as Republican carpetbagging. They also repeatedly reminded the public of Heflin's support of Hoover.[15] With the Civil War and Reconstruction not yet forgotten in the Deep South, this was an effective rhetorical tactic by the Hill campaign.

Even though Heflin was on the defensive for the remainder of the primary campaign, Hill sought White House help to secure his nomination. The congressman met with Hopkins, Ickes, and Attorney General Robert Jackson at Roosevelt's suggestion. They decided to distribute pamphlets in Alabama in which Roosevelt would state the importance of passing the wages-and-hours bill as an implicit endorsement of Hill.[16] Hill's support of this bill also gained the endorsements of the AFL and CIO unions of Alabama. Under pressure from Corcoran, Governor Bibb Graves broke his neutrality and agreed to use his organization to support Hill.[17] Hill also had the opportunity to accompany the popular president on a well-publicized train ride across Alabama.[18]

The January 4 primary resulted in an impressive victory for Hill. He won 61.8 percent of the votes.[19] Heflin, who was ill with pneumonia at the time, received only 34.2 percent.[20]

While the president's assistance had been an asset for Hill, it was not crucial to his nomination. Union endorsements, the support of the Graves machine, rumors of a Republican "conspiracy" to aid Heflin, and Heflin's clumsy campaign behavior were the main ingredients of Hill's landslide victory. Nevertheless, involvement in Hill's nomination campaign encouraged the White House political team to commit itself to a more challenging electoral objective—the renomination of Senator Claude D. Pepper of Florida.

Pepper, an Alabama native and a brilliant graduate of Harvard Law School, had distinguished himself as the most consistently liberal southern senator, especially on labor issues. Unlike such New Deal populists as Senator Theodore

Bilbo of Mississippi, Pepper did not balance his economic liberalism with racist rhetoric. Although he joined his fellow southern senators in defeating a 1937 anti-lynching bill, an action which he later regretted, Pepper emphasized the achievement of New Deal policy objectives as the means for improving the economic security of southern farmers and workers.

Pepper wrote in his diary in November 1937 that New Deal liberalism would be the theme of his renomination campaign. "The issue is the New Deal or not—liberalism vs. reaction. . . . I think this campaign shall determine the political character of Florida for some time to come. I want to make the state liberal, which it has never been, and now is my chance."[21] The Roosevelt administration perceived Pepper as a model New Deal politician for the New South in which a concern for economic justice superseded racial antagonism.[22]

Whereas the issue of the wages-and-hours bill had proven to be an asset for Lister Hill, it appeared to be a liability for Pepper. Like their counterparts in Alabama, Florida business interests vehemently opposed a minimum wage law.[23] The major beneficiary of the Florida business community's financial support was Representative Mark Wilcox, who had opposed the wages-and-hours bill in the House of Representatives.[24] Wilcox had also opposed the court reform bill and the executive reorganization bill in 1937.[25] He accused Pepper of exploiting the state's WPA for political support. Despite his general fiscal conservatism, Wilcox sought to attract Florida retirees by pledging to support the Townsend Plan, which promised generous old age pensions to the elderly.[26]

David Sholtz, who served as governor from 1933 to 1937, had an ideology midway between those of Pepper and Wilcox. Telling Pepper that DNC chairman James Farley supported him, Sholtz remained noncommital on the wages-and-hours bill.[27] Sholtz was a political pragmatist who recognized the popularity of the New Deal and simply allowed the federal government to spend money on relief and public works in his state.[28] His reluctance to provide the necessary state matching funds for the implementation of WPA programs in Florida infuriated Hopkins.[29]

Nevertheless, Sholtz wanted the voters to associate him with Roosevelt as he repeatedly referred to the president as "My good friend in the White House."[30] A leading member of the Florida Chamber of Commerce, he was a tireless, amiable campaigner. Unlike Wilcox, he already enjoyed statewide name recognition. These factors made Sholtz appear to be a formidable primary opponent of Pepper.

Although his campaign organization was solid, Pepper wanted some indication of White House support to counteract Farley's favoritism toward Sholtz and his public prediction that the former governor would defeat Pepper in a second, runoff primary.[31] After some prompting from Pepper, James Roosevelt announced to the press his hope that Pepper would be re-elected.[32] Earlier, in a December 27, 1937, letter, the young Roosevelt urged his father to give public support to liberal candidates such as Pepper in Democratic primaries.[33]

Soon, the purgers mustered the federal forces in Florida to assist Pepper. Corcoran organized federal appointees, especially U.S. attorneys, IRS officials, and postmasters, behind Pepper. Well-publicized meetings between Roosevelt and pro-Pepper Florida Democrats were held in Washington. Pressured by Roosevelt, Farley used the dedication of new post offices in Florida as an opportunity to praise Pepper's Senate record.[34]

The White House support helped to accelerate the momentum that favored Pepper's renomination. Because Pepper's pro-labor appeal was most attractive to low-income voters, the abolition of the poll tax and the implementation of voting machines induced an unusually large voter turn-out.[35] Consequently, Pepper won a decisive victory in the May 3 primary with over 58.4 percent of the vote, compared to 12.7 percent for Sholtz and 26.6 percent for Wilcox.[36] Pepper's majority obviated the need for a runoff primary.

The White House was elated that Pepper's electoral success in a campaign in which the beleaguered senator stressed his support of the wages-and-hours bill had emboldened New Deal Democrats in the House of Representatives to pass a discharge petition forcing the conservative Rules Committee to send the bottled-up labor bill to the floor for a vote.[37]

Commenting on the White House purgers' assessment of
Pepper's victory in 1939, J.B. Shannon stated, "It appeared to
make it safe, according to New Deal reasoning, for national
leadership to intervene in local elections. Had not James
Roosevelt's actions in Florida proved it?"[38]

The activities of the purgers helped to facilitate Pepper's
decisive margin of victory. Nevertheless, they certainly were
not indispensable to his renomination. His victory, however,
served to strengthen the purgers' confidence that they could
nominate liberals and defeat conservatives in selected primaries.

Though the purgers were primarily interested in electing
liberal Democrats to Congress to support further New Deal
legislation, they decided to intervene in Oregon's Democratic
primary for governor. Harold Ickes, secretary of the interior,
was especially interested in preventing the renomination of
Democratic Governor Charles H. Martin. Martin had opposed
Ickes's efforts to build a government-owned power plant at
the Bonneville Dam.[39]

Martin, who was elected as governor in 1934 on a pro–New
Deal platform, soon antagonized the coalition that had supported him. The former Republican and retired army general
sought to minimize state spending on relief and acerbically
denounced the organizing efforts and strikes of labor unions
in Oregon.[40] He publicly warned CIO president John L. Lewis
to stay out of Oregon.[41] He had gained national attention and
the disdain of liberal Democrats for his outspoken criticism of
Secretary of Labor Frances Perkins and the National Labor
Relations Board.[42]

Despite his tactless rhetoric and growing unpopularity,
Martin's renomination campaign was bolstered by a law-and-
order platform which appealed to voters' concern about labor
unrest.[43] He also enjoyed the implicit endorsement of Farley.
He emphasized his loyalty to Roosevelt in order to compensate for his conservative policy behavior and rhetoric.[44]

Ickes, though, was determined to defeat Martin and end
this source of opposition to the Bonneville Dam project. Another leading advocate of public power with an interest in this
project, Senator George Norris of Nebraska, a former Repub-

lican re-elected as an independent in 1936, joined Ickes in
endorsing Henry L. Hess, a former state senator, to challenge
Martin in the gubernatorial primary.[45] Federal appointees
were organized behind Hess. In the May primary, Hess narrowly defeated Martin, by 57,727 votes to 50,905 votes.[46]

When Hess was later defeated by the Republican gubernatorial nominee, Farley told Ickes that, if Martin had been
renominated, the Democratic ticket in Oregon would have
succeeded in the general election. Ickes exemplified the perspective of his fellow purgers, saying, "For my part, I want to
see the Democratic party made the liberal party of the country and so it doesn't matter whether a man calls himself a
Democrat or not. It is what he is and not what he accounts
himself that matters."[47]

Roosevelt recognized the difficulty of preventing the renomination of well-entrenched incumbents, especially in the
South where voters highly valued an incumbent's seniority
in Congress. He did not initially identify himself at White
House press conferences with the purge campaign being conducted by his staff.[48] Instead, he gave the purgers a free hand
under Corcoran's leadership during the initial period of the
campaign and allowed them to provide pro–New Deal candidates with assurances of federal patronage for attracting
supporters. Roosevelt, though, waited until the purge campaign indicated the potential for success before he publicly
identified himself as the leader.[49]

In Iowa's June primary, the purgers sought to achieve a
much more difficult objective—the primary defeat of a popular, incumbent senator. Just as the defeat of Martin in the
Oregon primary had been Ickes's pet project, the Iowa-born
Hopkins wanted to deny renomination to Democratic Senator
Guy Gillette. In late May, Hopkins publicly endorsed Gillette's primary opponent, Representative Otha D. Wearin, a
fellow alumnus of Grinnell College and a reliable New Deal
liberal.[50] Likewise, James Roosevelt, as he had done for Pepper, announced his support of Wearin.[51]

Encouraged by their success in assisting Pepper and Hess,
the purgers failed to realize the advantages that a popular,
broadly supported incumbent senator enjoyed. Cautious lead-

ing Democrats, including Senator Clyde Herring, readily endorsed Gillette.[52] Most farm organizations also supported the incumbent. Even Henry Wallace, the secretary of agriculture and an Iowa native, refused to endorse Wearin against Gillette.

It was unusual that Hopkins and the other purgers targeted Gillette. He certainly ws not a conservative ideologue. He had supported most New Deal policies, especially on agricultural and public utility issues.[53] However, he had been a vocal opponent of the court reform bill. For Roosevelt, this was a key indication of disloyalty to his party leadership in Congress.[54]

Gillette, however, like other incumbent senators targeted by the purge, was careful not to single out Roosevelt for criticism. Instead, he castigated the purgers for abusing their administrative positions and trying to dominate intraparty affairs.[55] As most political observers anticipated, Gillette easily defeated Wearin and his two other primary opponents.[56]

Gillette's victory, the purgers' first defeat, impelled Roosevelt to assume full command of the purge campaign publicly by mid-June.[57] Although he had continued publicly to assert his neutrality in Democratic primaries as late as early June, he realized that he was widely perceived in Congress and the press as the prime mover behind the purge strategy.[58] If the campaign proved to be unsuccessful, its failure would be widely interpreted as a major defeat for Roosevelt and lead to a further erosion of his policy influence in Congress, regardless of whether or not he formally and publicly directed it.[59]

Consequently, Roosevelt delivered a nationally broadcast radio address on June 24 explaining his reasons for intervening in upcoming Democratic primaries on behalf of pro–New Deal candidates. He justified his rhetorical intervention in the primaries as attempts to educate primary voters on contradictions that appeared in the legislative voting records of conservative incumbents who had previously been elected on "a platform uncompromisingly liberal."[60] He asserted that the sincerity and consistency of the two-party system in the American republic were jeopardized if winning candidates

did not behave in government according to their party platforms, and that "I feel that I have every right to speak in those
few instances where there may be a clear issue between
candidates for a Democratic nomination involving these principles, or involving a clear misuse of my own name."[61]

His son James withdrew from the purge campaign; Roosevelt relied less on Corcoran and Ickes and more on Harry
Hopkins and such experienced Party professionals as Steve
Early, Marvin McIntyre, and Joseph Keenan, the assistant to
the Attorney General. He was partially motivated to assume
leadership of the purge campaign publicly because of the
importance of the next primary in which the White House
would intervene—the Kentucky senatorial primary.[62] Roosevelt regarded the renomination of Senate majority leader
Alben Barkley as the most important objective of the purge
campaign because of the president's determination to retain a
loyal New Dealer in this position.[63]

As early as February, columnist Arthur Krock had referred to Barkley's primary race as the "Gettysburg of the
party's internecine strife over national control in 1940. Every
prospective element in the impending contest between Senator Alben W. Barkley and Governor Albert B. Chandler
unites to provide an unmistakable test of the President's
political leadership."[64] Barkley, conspicuous in the Senate as
one of a handful of diehard supporters of the doomed court
reform bill, needed to win renomination and re-election in
order to direct New Deal forces in the Senate.[65] If he were
defeated, it was probable that Senator Byron "Pat" Harrison,
an increasingly conservative Democrat, would replace him as
Senate majority leader.[66]

Barkley, a veteran of Kentucky politics, was first elected to
the House of Representatives in 1912 and to the Senate in
1926. Throughout his career in Congress, he distinguished
himself as a sincere and consistent liberal.[67] He was one of
the first Democratic senators in 1932 to endorse and actively
support Roosevelt's presidential nomination. Grateful for
such assistance, Democratic delegates chose Barkley as the
keynote speaker of the 1932 and 1936 Democratic national
conventions.[68]

As a two-term incumbent, the Senate majority leader enjoyed the support of most federal officials. In particular, Barkley was supported by George H. Goodman, the state's WPA administrator; Seldon R. Glenn, collector of internal revenue for Kentucky; and Judge Elwood Hamilton of the U.S. Circuit Court of Appeals for the Louisville circuit.[69] Because the coal industry was a major employer in Kentucky, the endorsement of Barkley by UMW president John L. Lewis was a major asset for soliciting votes and campaign contributions among coal miners.[70]

Despite Barkley's incumbency and his powerful positions in the Senate, his renomination was uncertain.[71] He confronted a formidable opponent in the Democratic senatorial primary, Governor Albert B. "Happy" Chandler. Chandler had a powerful machine consisting mostly of state employees. Furthermore, the Democratic primary for senator would not be a clear-cut ideological contest between a New Deal liberal and an anti–New Deal conservative. Like Barkley, Chandler presented himself as a New Deal populist who supported Roosevelt.[72]

Ironically, both Barkley and Roosevelt had provided crucial support to Chandler in his 1935 gubernatorial campaign when he confronted an unusually strong Republican opponent, King Swope. Chandler, as lieutenant governor, had angered and alienated Democratic Governor Ruby Laffoon when he opposed the sales tax sponsored by Laffoon and enacted by the Kentucky state legislature.[73] Laffoon, however, had antagonized Barkley and the Roosevelt administration by obstructing the implementation of New Deal programs in Kentucky.[74]

Chandler defeated Thomas Rhea, Kentucky's highway commissioner and Laffoon's handpicked successor, in the Democratic gubernatorial primary of 1935, and was then faced with a divided Party.[75] Laffoon and Rhea refused to support Chandler against Swope.[76] Chandler, however, received significant support from Barkley and the Roosevelt administration. Hopkins approved a sharp increase in WPA funds for Kentucky so that the number of WPA workers increased from less than 5,000 in September 1935 to over

30,000 by November.[77] Farley spoke in Kentucky on Chandler's behalf, and Barkley abruptly canceled an official visit to
the Philippines in order to campaign for him.[78]

Chandler, a Democratic governor who was more cooperative in administering federal programs in Kentucky than
Laffoon had been, campaigned for the Senate nomination as a
New Deal Democrat. He contended that Barkley was too old
and neglectful of his home state.[79] The forty-year-old governor was a dynamic, colorful campaigner who frequently entertained audiences with jokes and songs. Chandler even
musically identified himself with Roosevelt by preceding his
visits to Kentucky communities with sound trucks playing
"Happy Days Are Here Again."[80]

Although Chandler certainly was not a conservative ideologue, his rhetorical identification as a New Deal liberal was
somewhat exaggerated and misleading. He eagerly supported the flow of federal funds into Kentucky through New
Deal programs, but he prided himself on being a fiscal conservative regarding state taxes and spending.[81] He considered
Senator Harry Byrd of Virginia, one of the most bitterly anti-
Roosevelt Democrats in Congress, to be his friend and mentor.[82] After gaining the repeal of the state sales tax, he based
many of his fiscal and government reorganization reforms
on Byrd's governorship.[83] Distrustful of Chandler's pro-
Roosevelt rhetoric, the president told Ickes at a March cabinet meeting that Chandler was a "dangerous person," similar
to Huey Long.[84]

Consequently, Barkley could expect most conservative
Democrats in Kentucky to support Chandler.[85] In addition to
his fiscal conservatism, Chandler might be able to attract
some votes by appealing to the race issue. Barkley was the
only southern senator who had voted for the failed Wagner–
Van Nuys anti-lynching bill in 1937.[86] One Barkley Democrat warned Marvin McIntyre, a Kentucky-born White House
aide, that Barkley's support of this anti-lynching bill would
damage his appeal among Kentucky voters.[87] Fortunately for
Barkley, this issue did not become a liability during the
primary campaign, and Chandler did not exploit it.

Barkley would later write in his autobiography that White

House intervention was not necessary for his victory in the primary and implied that Roosevelt's efforts may have actually reduced his plurality of votes.[88] Nevertheless, Barkley clearly behaved in early 1938 like an incumbent worried about losing his Senate seat to Chandler and sought assistance from the Roosevelt administration.[89] In February, Barkley received financial contributions from Bernard Baruch, a prominent Wall Street financier and Democratic insider, and a lucrative fund-raising dinner sponsored by the Democratic National Committee.[90] White House press secretary Steve Early regularly provided the press with statements critical of Chandler's gubernatorial record and campaign rhetoric. Roosevelt sent the director of the DNC's Colored Division to Kentucky to attract black voters for Barkley.[91]

Barkley's rhetorical strategy emphasized how much the New Deal had helped Kentucky and how instrumental he had been in sponsoring or supporting key New Deal policies and assuring that Kentucky received a fair share of federal funds and public works projects.[92] Barkley's use of the WPA, however, as a source of votes and campaign contributions soon became a major source of controversy. In late May, Judge Brady M. Stewart, Chandler's campaign manager, charged that "every agency of the Federal Government dispensing relief is resorting to methods and policies that are crudely reprehensible to force the citizens of the great Commonwealth to support Senator Barkley."[93]

State WPA Director George Goodman, a leading supporter of Barkley, denied that the WPA was being used to promote Barkley's renomination.[94] Investigative reporter Thomas Stokes, however, conducted extensive research in Kentucky, Oklahoma, Pennsylvania, and several other states experiencing contentious Democratic primaries.[95] He concluded that Harry Hopkins knew about, allowed, and even directed the use of the WPA to benefit pro–New Deal Democratic candidates, including Barkley. Although Hopkins articulately denied all but two of Stokes's charges, the Senate committee investigating political exploitation of the WPA, chaired by Senator Morris Sheppard of Texas, sent an agent to investigate the situation in Kentucky on July 15.[96] The agent subse-

quently reported to the Sheppard Committee that not only
the WPA but most other federal agencies in Kentucky, especially the Federal Housing Authority and IRS, were canvassed for votes and campaign contributions by Barkley's
campaign.

Barkley denied any personal instigation of such political
manipulation and frequently asserted that all federal employees and recipients of federal relief in Kentucky had a
right to vote for whomever they wished.[97] The equally well-
known and credible charges that Chandler's campaign was
blatantly soliciting votes and contributions from state employees, especially in the highway department, minimized
any damage to Barkley these charges might have created.[98]
As early as February, a Kentucky Democrat informed Marvin
McIntyre, "Probably you have heard something about the
little 'blue books' that the members of the highway department and other state employees have been given with in-
structions that each man who works on the highway must get
22 people to sign his little blue book agreeing to vote for
Chandler."[99] Chandler also had state employees promoting
his candidacy as they personally delivered Social Security
checks.[100]

In a July visit to Kentucky, Roosevelt made it clear to
Kentucky voters that he favored Barkley over Chandler. The
President reiterated Barkley's theme about the substantial
financial benefits that the New Deal had given Kentucky.
With the governor and senator next to him as he spoke in
Latonia, Kentucky, Roosevelt stated that although Chandler
was a capable governor he would need "many, many years to
match the national knowledge, the experience and the ac-
knowledged leadership in the affairs of the nation" that
Barkley had demonstrated in the Senate.[101] Two weeks after
Roosevelt's visit, a bizarre incident caused the Chandler campaign to lose momentum and support. While giving a radio
address from his hotel room in Louisville, Chandler and two
of his aides drank several glasses of ice water delivered by the
hotel's waiter. All three men were stricken with stomach
pains and fever.[102] Chandler's physicians and body guards
claimed that he had been poisoned. The Louisville police,

however, immediately dismissed and ridiculed the charges of poisoning as a campaign gimmick.[103] Subsequently, Barkley entertained audiences by satirically asking them, "Has it been tested?" before drinking a glass of ice water.[104] This incident would lead more voters to question Chandler's judgment and integrity.

The full exertion of Roosevelt's party leadership and the mobilization of federal resources in Kentucky enabled Barkley to gain a decisive victory over Chandler in the August 6 primary with 56 percent of the votes.[105] Although Barkley later discounted the importance of these federal forces and Roosevelt's intervention, it is very possible that Chandler could have defeated Barkley if the incumbent senator had had to rely entirely on his own efforts.[106] Barkley's WPA support was previously estimated to be worth 200,000 of the 525,555 votes cast in the primary.[107] The political use of the WPA in Kentucky spawned additional Senate investigations which resulted in the passage of the Hatch Act of 1939.[108]

In the cases of Pepper and Barkley, Roosevelt and the purgers were supporting the renomination of incumbent senators.[109] In Democratic senatorial primaries in Maryland, Georgia, and South Carolina, however, they attempted a much riskier venture—the defeat of well-entrenched incumbents—by supporting weak, often obscure candidates. Senators Millard Tydings of Maryland, Walter George of Georgia, and Ellison "Cotton Ed" Smith of South Carolina were all vocal critics of the court reform bill, the wages-and-hours bills, and the New Deal in general. In his campaigns against Tydings and Smith, Roosevelt supported experienced politicians—Congressman David J. Lewis of Maryland and Governor Olin T. Johnston of South Carolina.

Tydings's voting record in the Senate distinguished him as the second most consistently anti–New Deal Democrat, with Carter Glass being the most conservative.[110] Even during the First Hundred Days, he opposed the TVA, NRA, and AAA. Tydings, a corporate lawyer, maintained close ties with Wall Street and persistently opposed virtually all major New Deal measures as being detrimental to American capitalism. He was imperious and aloof, and was intensely disliked by his

more liberal colleagues and the Roosevelt administration.[111]
The purge campaign against Tydings was the only one in
which Farley readily and fully participated, because of his
own rancor toward Tydings.[112]

Tydings had never paid rhetorical homage to Roosevelt
and the New Deal as an easy way to sustain popularity with
his constituents. His unequivocal opposition to New Deal
bills in the Senate was reflected by equally blunt public
statements.[113] Although he was well-financed and confident
of renomination, he moderated his rhetoric somewhat as the
September primary approached by vaguely stating that he
was "not running as an Old Dealer nor particularly as a New
Dealer but I hope as a Square Dealer."[114]

A shrewd, cautious campaigner, Tydings did not want to
jeopardize his already commanding lead by launching an
ideological assault on New Deal liberalism or a personal
attack on Roosevelt.[115] Instead, he explained and justified
his opposition to White House bills as a noble example of
independence and intellectual integrity.[116] He succeeded in
arousing feelings of state pride and resentment toward political interference from Washington that engendered positive
support for his renomination.[117]

Roosevelt and the purgers considered two other candidates
before Representative David J. Lewis was recruited and
agreed to challenge Tydings in the September 12 primary.
Roosevelt's preference was Harry C. Byrd, president of the
University of Maryland.[118] Byrd declined the proposition,
and Roosevelt hoped that the more politically ambitious attorney general of Maryland, Herbert O'Conor, would enter
the race, but he also refused.

The purge campaign's offer was finally made to Lewis, who
accepted. At the age of sixty-nine, Lewis was twenty-one
years older than Tydings. He also differed greatly from Tydings in personal background and political perspective. In
sharp contrast to the urbane aristocrat from the eastern
shore, Lewis was a mostly self-educated former coal miner
from western Maryland who was determined to improve the
economic security and working conditions of manual laborers
through federal policies.[119]

A pro-labor populist and leading supporter of the Social Security Act of 1935, Lewis was hardly known outside of his district. Nevertheless, Roosevelt and the purgers fully mobilized the resources and tactics they had employed for Barkley in the Kentucky primary. CIO unions and federal appointees, such as postmasters and IRS officials, were organized behind Lewis's candidacy.

The Roosevelt-sponsored campaign, however, began only three weeks before the primary. Leading Democrats in Maryland, including Senator George L. Radcliffe, Roosevelt's former business partner, supported Tydings.[120] In an attempt to discredit the big business conservative, Secretary of Commerce Daniel C. Roper generated unfavorable publicity about Tydings's business dealings.[121]

Hoping that a personally delivered endorsement of the liberal congressman would stimulate some momentum for Lewis, Roosevelt traveled to Maryland in early September. Speaking in Denton, a Tydings stronghold, on Labor Day, Roosevelt explained the mutual interests of farmers and urban laborers. He contended that the further development of the New Deal would create a more just and prosperous economy for both groups, and that "Economic lesson number one of the past twenty years is that men and women on farms, men and women in cities, are partners. America cannot prosper unless both groups prosper."[122]

The president then praised Lewis, who as a state representative, sponsored and helped to enact Maryland's workmen's compensation law, the first in the nation, and later the Social Security Act. To emphasize the importance of electing New Deal Democrats like Lewis, Roosevelt stated that the American government needed to secure economic justice to avoid the political oppression and growing international tensions in Europe, and that "the best contribution that we at home can make to our own security is to eliminate quickly all feelings of injustice and insecurity throughout our land. For our own safety, we cannot afford to follow those in public life who quote the Golden Rule and take no steps to bring it closer."[123]

Unfortunately, Roosevelt could not easily transfer his popularity and name recognition to Lewis. Furthermore, Tydings effectively distracted any public attention from his anti–New Deal voting record by charging that federal employees were being pressured by their pro-Lewis superiors to vote for the congressman.[124] To add credibility and prolonged media exposure to these accusations, he formally submitted them to the Sheppard Committee. The committee later found no evidence to implicate Lewis.[125]

Tydings's campaign expenditures exceeded Lewis's by a ratio of almost two to one.[126] Tydings was constantly on the offense with charges of Lewis's exploitation of federal employees and programs. He criticized Lewis's receipt of support from "Reds" in the labor movement and made appeals to state pride. He expressed his resentment against Roosevelt's carpetbagging "invasion" through a puppet candidate. Lewis, meanwhile, struggled simply to hold his hastily organized campaign structure together and to achieve greater name recognition throughout Maryland.[127] Despite their efforts, the purgers failed to win the primary for Lewis as Tydings received 59 percent of the votes cast on September 12.[128]

Lewis had been a congressman with an electoral base, however small, but Roosevelt also supported a New Deal candidate with no current electoral base, U.S. attorney Lawrence Camp of Atlanta, who ran against Senator Walter George in Georgia's September 14 Democratic primary.[129] Roosevelt's first choice to oppose George was Governor Ed Rivers, a popular and loyal New Dealer. However, Rivers's previous affiliation with the Ku Klux Klan was regarded as a liability for a purge effort that wanted to make the Democratic party in Congress more liberal.[130] Furthermore, Rivers then decided to run for re-election.

Unlike Tydings, George was not a thoroughly anti–New Deal conservative. As a matter of fact, he had supported most major New Deal measures during Roosevelt's first term, including the AAA and Social Security Act. Near the end of Roosevelt's first term, however, he had become critical of what he perceived as an anti-business bias in the tax and regulatory legislation that the White House sponsored.[131] He selectively supported New Deal programs according to Georgia's

interests and had been a vocal critic of the court reform bill
and the wages-and-hours bill.[132]

Consequently, it would be difficult for Camp and the purgers to convince most Georgia voters that George was an
enemy of the New Deal[133]; he was able to point to a voting
record in the Senate that had mostly supported it.[134] Roosevelt, however, sensed that George was becoming increasingly
hostile to the New Deal and was determined to unseat him. As
in other purge campaigns, Roosevelt hoped that his chosen
candidate's support for the wages-and-hours bill would attract the votes of most blue-collar Georgians.

In Georgia, however, most poor white voters, especially in
rural areas, were mesmerized by the demagogic appeal of
Eugene Talmadge, a former governor who had entered the
Senate race. Talmadge's rhetoric consisted of a dichotomous,
opportunistic mixture of denunciations of George as a pawn of
big business interests, and castigations of New Deal agencies
for excessively intervening in state affairs and not adequately
addressing the economic problems of poor farmers and laborers.[135] Among his more dramatic promises, Talmadge
pledged that relief would be ended and free farm land would
be given to tenant farmers.[136]

Roosevelt, having long regarded Georgia as his adopted
state and having developed a warm rapport with Georgians,
hoped that a personal endorsement of Camp would provide
name recognition and voter appeal to his Senate campaign
and stimulate public interest in it. The president also wanted
to establish the dominant issue and parameters of debate for
the campaign. He sought to do this in his August 11 speech in
Barnesville, Georgia. Beginning in a friendly, sentimental
tone, Roosevelt proceeded to remind his listeners about the
benefits of the New Deal to Georgia, especially rural electrification.[137]

He asserted that more New Deal economic reforms were
necessary. To substantiate this contention, he referred to an
economic study recently completed by the National Emergency Council which identified the South as the nation's chief
economic problem. Thus, he argued, it was the region in
greatest need of further New Deal measures. To make their

region's economy more just and humane, the voters of Georgia and other southern states must elect loyal New Deal liberals to Congress because the "task of meeting the economic and social needs of the South, on the front that is absolutely necessary, calls for public servants whose hearts are sound, whose heads are sane, whose hands are strong, striving everlastingly to better the lot of their fellowmen [sic]."[138]

Arguing that the policies of New Deal liberalism were necessary for the enhanced well-being of Georgians, the president stated that George "cannot possibly in my judgment be classified as belonging to the liberal school of thought."[139] With George sitting nearby on the same platform, Roosevelt continued his criticism of the Senator by suggesting a clear discrepancy between George's recent voting record and his campaign rhetoric regarding the New Deal.[140] After dismissing Talmadge as someone who "would contribute very little to practical progress in government," the president heartily endorsed Camp as "a man who honestly believes that many things must be done and done now to improve the economic and social conditions of the country, a man who is willing to fight for these objectives."[141]

Until Roosevelt's Barnesville speech, George had been careful not to criticize Roosevelt and even to praise the popular president. In June, suspecting that Roosevelt would support Camp against his candidacy, George had sent a courteous, almost deferential letter to Roosevelt apologizing if his rhetoric and voting record during the 75th Congress had offended the president.[142] Shortly before Roosevelt's arrival in Barnesville, however, George was furious that a close political ally of his, Earl Cocke, had been abruptly removed from the National Emergency Council.[143] The political purpose of this action was obvious since Cocke was replaced by Clark Foreman,[144] an Atlanta native who served as a racial adviser to New Deal agencies and was sent to Georgia by Roosevelt to manage Camp's campaign.[145]

Charges by Camp and Talmadge that George was a tool of business interests and insensitive to the working conditions and incomes of blue-collar Georgians were weakened by the

AFL's endorsement of him.[146] Rivers, concerned about his own gubernatorial campaign, did not want to alienate pro-George voters who might be favorable to his own re-election. Consequently, Rivers, Senator Richard Russell, whom Roosevelt regarded as more loyal to the New Deal than George, and most Georgia congressmen either remained neutral or quietly supported George.[147] The *Atlanta Constitution*, nationally respected as a voice of enlightenment and moderation in southern politics, strongly endorsed George and acrimoniously castigated Roosevelt's purge campaign as an unjustified and inexcusable violation of a state's right to nominate and elect its own officials.[148]

More vehemently than Tydings had done in Maryland, George capitalized on this popular outrage against presidential interference in a primary. He compared the purge to Sherman's infamous march through Georgia and the president and his aides to Reconstruction carpetbaggers.[149] While denouncing the purge, George directed most of his fire at White House aides, not Roosevelt. According to George, Roosevelt had been manipulated and duped into leading the purge by the "little group of Communists" around him, namely, Corcoran and Cohen.[150]

Meanwhile, Camp identified himself as a "100% New Dealer." His initial campaign theme simply claimed that voting for him was the equivalent of voting for Roosevelt.[151] Ridiculed by George and Talmadge as nothing more than a White House puppet, he made a feeble attempt to project political independence by stating his opposition to anti-lynching legislation.[152] Regardless of the content of his speeches, Camp was a dull, uninspiring speaker whose rhetoric lacked the rousing effect of George's righteous indignation against the purgers' invasion of the primary or Talmadge's magnetic charisma among poor whites.

White House efforts to manipulate federal positions and funds to help Camp either failed to generate additional votes or added credibility to George's accusations of carpetbag tactics. Federal appointees, such as Edgar Dunlap of the RFC, were suddenly fired for refusing to end their active support of George's nomination.[153] Extra WPA and PWA funds were

funneled into Georgia in early September, and Camp argued
that Georgia would benefit more from these programs if he
were elected senator.[154]

Unfortunately for Camp and Roosevelt, most WPA and
PWA workers were blacks and poor whites who would not
vote in the primary.[155] The sudden flood of federal funds
created further suspicion that Roosevelt was trying to bribe
them into nominating Camp. A Gallup poll conducted one day
before the primary indicated that, of the Georgia voters questioned, Camp was strongest among lower-income voters in
cities and larger towns. But even there, Camp could not
expect more than 29 percent of the votes.[156] Talmadge was
strongest among lower-income farmers. George, however,
was the most popular candidate among most categories of
voters.

On September 14, at the last primary of the purge campaign, the voting results reflected the statistics of recent
public opinion polls and the assumptions of most political
observers. Of the popular votes, George received 43.9 percent,
Talmadge 32.1 percent, and Camp 23.9 percent.[157] Georgia's
county unit system, however, gave George 59 percent of the
410 unit votes and Camp only 4.9 percent.[158]

George occasionally used the 1937 anti-lynching bill as a
rallying issue in his campaign, but there was only one purge
campaign in which race baiting was a major theme—South
Carolina's Democratic primary for senator. Even more significant in this August 30 primary was that both major candidates, Senator Ellison D. "Cotton Ed" Smith and Governor
Olin T. Johnston, would exploit the race issue in order to
attract support. Although he was a New Deal populist endorsed by CIO unions, Johnston, like traditional populist
politicians in the heavily black Deep South, was careful to
combine his pro-labor economic positions with segregationist
rhetoric in order to counter the accusations of conservative
opponents that he was a radical who threatened southern
society.[159]

Johnston had announced his senatorial candidacy from the
White House on May 17.[160] At that time, however, Roosevelt
did not announce an endorsement of Johnston to the press.

He was less active in the South Carolina primary than in other primaries with an incumbent targeted for purging for several reasons. First, an open endorsement of Johnston might antagonize Smith voters and jeopardize the gubernatorial nomination of Burnet Maybank, the progressive mayor of Charleston, who was admired by Roosevelt.[161] Second, Johnston did not solicit White House intervention in the form of federal funds and personnel. If substantial presidential assistance had been requested and provided, Johnston's chances of defeating Smith might be damaged rather than enhanced by risking additional accusations of a carpetbag invasion. Finally, among all of the pro-Roosevelt candidates who challenged an incumbent opposed by the purgers, Johnston was in the strongest position. He was a popular governor with a strong organization and labor support, significant in a state where the votes of textile mill workers were often decisive in electoral results. Thus, Johnston was already capable of waging a competitive campaign against Smith on his own.[162]

Smith was widely criticized for his callous remarks opposing a minimum wage, and Johnston decided to make Smith's opposition to the wages-and-hours bill his chief issue.[163] In a trip through South Carolina, Roosevelt met Johnston in Greenville on August 11 and asserted the need to elect candidates to Congress who would support the wages-and-hours bill and other New Deal policies beneficial to wage earners and farmers. Although he did not specifically endorse Johnston and rebuke Smith in this speech, the president implied his preference for Johnston.[164]

Realizing his vulnerability to Johnston on the minimum wage issue, Smith effectively deflected attention from this issue by arguing that further federal intervention by the New Deal threatened white supremacy and states' rights.[165] He greatly exaggerated and misled audiences about Roosevelt's minor role in the campaign by accusing the president of invading South Carolina and trying to manipulate voting behavior.[166] The conservative incumbent also denounced Johnston for receiving the support of CIO unions which he suggested were controlled by radicals who sought the end of segregation and the political empowerment of blacks.[167] Determined not to be perceived as a race-mixing liberal, Johnston angrily castigated Smith for supporting a bill earlier in his career which would have ended segregation in railroad cars.[168]

Johnston's prospect of victory was threatened by the Senate candidacy of state Senator Edgar A. Brown.[169] Also running on a pro–New Deal platform, Brown had narrowly lost to Smith in the 1926 Democratic primary for the U.S. Senate. He was, however, a relentless political foe of Johnston and directed much of his criticism toward the governor. Johnston, distracted by Brown's candidacy, was outraged when he withdrew from the race two days before the August 30 primary and then used the media attention to criticize the governor's candidacy.[170]

Meanwhile, Smith was able to solidify his forces during the final days of the campaign. Senator James F. Byrnes of South Carolina, a moderate Democrat who had previously contributed to Tydings's campaign, organized federal appointees behind Smith.[171] The primary's results revealed that Smith had been renominated with 55.4 percent of the votes to Johnston's 44.6 percent.[172]

The purge campaign succeeded in defeating only one congressional incumbent, Representative John J. O'Connor of New York.[173] As chairman of the House Rules Committee, O'Connor had proven to be an obstacle to White House bills, especially regarding business regulations and taxes.[174] Roosevelt's success in defeating O'Connor and nominating James Fay as his successor resulted mostly from the purgers' effective exploitation of local political factors that threatened O'Connor's renomination. O'Connor's working-class constituents resented their congressman's long absences from their district.[175]

Fay, who had narrowly lost to O'Connor in the 1934 primary, was popular in the district and received the support of WPA workers who canvassed voters and solicited campaign contributions for him. O'Connor's charges that this purge was part of a Communist conspiracy won him little support. With Ed Flynn managing his campaign, Fay defeated O'Connor with 8,352 votes to the incumbent's 7,779 votes in the September 20 primary.[176] O'Connor, though, received the Republican nomination in this heavily Democratic district, which elected Fay in November.

Roosevelt's failure to defeat all but one of the conservative congressional incumbents he tried to defeat in the Democratic primaries led most journalists at this time and later scholars to conclude that the purge campaign was a reckless, ill-conceived, badly managed strategy that weakened Roosevelt's party leadership and emboldened southern conservative Democrats in Congress to cooperate more with Republicans in weakening or defeating liberal policy proposals.[177] In 1940, Thomas L. Stokes asserted that Roosevelt's purge campaign "did not liberalize the Democratic Party" but instead "only ripped it wider apart."[178] Arthur M. Schlesinger, Jr., would refer to the purge as "an almost complete failure"; and William E. Leuchtenburg called the purge "a humiliating drubbing" for Roosevelt.[179] E. Pendleton Herring stated that the purge failed "as a disciplinary measure" against congressional Democrats who had defied Roosevelt on New Deal bills, while William Riker claimed that the campaign "had no significant effect, except perhaps in New York City."[180]

Critics of the purge, however, disagree over what Roosevelt's long-term objective was. Jim Farley bitterly claimed that Roosevelt merely wanted to establish a "personal party" and succeeded in weakening the structure and exacerbating the division between the liberal and conservative wings of the Party.[181] James T. Patterson argues that Roosevelt intended the purge to stimulate an ideological realignment of the two-party system but failed by showing that "the New Deal, far from nationalizing or regimenting the nation, was all but helpless when confronted by determined state organizations in the South."[182] Likewise, Alan Brinkley suggests that while Roosevelt wanted the purge to strengthen pro–New Deal, liberal Democrats in the South, his unprecedented intervention in these primaries offended the regional pride of both liberal and conservative Democrats in the region.[183] Raymond Clapper concluded shortly before the congressional

elections of 1938 that Roosevelt intended the purge to achieve
the more modest, limited objectives of making southern Democrats in Congress more supportive of his bills and "of drama-
tizing his struggle to imprint the New Deal indelibly on the
party majority."[184]

Although Roosevelt failed to defeat any of the southern
incumbents, J.B. Shannon argued in 1939 that these electoral
defeats for Roosevelt did not represent a repudiation of Roosevelt and the New Deal by southern voters. He calculated that
53.4 percent of all southern voters in 1938 voted for pro–New
Deal candidates in the primaries while 67 percent of the
southern voters polled by the American Institute of Public
Opinion expressed approval of Roosevelt.[185] He attributed
the victories of conservative incumbents to a myriad of local
political factors peculiar to each contest and to the incumbents' appeals to racial fears and states' rights in order to
avoid discussing Roosevelt and the New Deal. Consequently,
Shannon infers that although Roosevelt's "effort to remake a
political party in the form of political philosophy" failed in
the purge, the widespread popularity of Roosevelt and the
New Deal among southern voters compelled these conservative incumbents to avoid specifically attacking Roosevelt and
the New Deal in their speeches.[186]

In short, Roosevelt's failure to defeat the southern conservative incumbents did not represent a rejection of the New
Deal and Roosevelt's party leadership by southern voters.
Most southern voters in these primaries resented and rejected the principle and practice of presidential intervention
in local politics. By contrast, Charles M. Price and Joseph
Boskin found that northern, urban, working-class Democrats
who were polled in 1938 were more likely to express support
for the purge. This regional difference of public attitudes
toward the purge may partially explain why Representative
John J. O'Connor of New York was the only congressional incumbent defeated in the campaign.[187]

It is evident, therefore, that the conservative incumbents'
victories did not necessarily reflect their constituents' rejection of Roosevelt and New Deal liberalism or even of Roosevelt's desire to make the Party a more distinctly liberal party

so that congressional Democrats would be more supportive of further New Deal measures. But the question remains: Did the purge of 1938 detract from his short-term objective of pressuring Democrats in Congress to become more supportive of New Deal bills and from his long-term objective of making the Party more distinctly liberal?

John E. Hopper persuasively contends that Roosevelt's purge campaign accomplished the first objective because it stimulated the passage of the previously stalemated wages-and-hours bill. According to Hopper, the mere prospect of Roosevelt intervening against recalcitrant Democratic congressmen in their future renomination campaigns pressured enough wavering Democrats in Congress to support the wages-and-hours bill and other bills favored by the White House.[188] Moreover, Hopper cites a fact often ignored by critics of the purge: that Roosevelt's intervention helped ten liberal Democratic incumbents whose renominations were threatened by conservative challengers. Hopper asserts that these victories were crucial for achieving the second, long-term objective of liberalizing the Party by solidifying the strength of New Deal liberals within the Party and assuring their dominance over national Party affairs, thereby preventing conservatives from seizing control of the Party in 1940.[189]

Sidney Milkis claims that the purge campaign stimulated the growth of a coalition of conservative Democrats and Republicans which would dominate Congress and obstruct the passage of further liberal policy proposals for the next twenty years.[190] He further contends that the decentralized nature of American party politics ensures that such presidential intervention intended to centralize control of party affairs under the president will inevitably result in intraparty discord and in even weaker presidential control.[191] According to Milkis, the purge's failure convinced Roosevelt that he should focus on reorganizing the executive branch and expanding its administrative powers over public policy so that the Party would be subordinated into "a temporary waystation on the way to administrative government, that is, a centralized democracy."[192]

Milkis suggests that Roosevelt sought to transcend par-

tisan politics and expand the power and efficacy of the executive branch in policy matters so that the Party would not
be essential for achieving New Deal policy objectives. He also
suggests that "Roosevelt's aggressive partisan efforts were
primarily rhetorical after 1938."[193] This assessment, however, underestimates the vigor of some of Roosevelt's partisan
efforts after 1938, especially the assiduous efforts he and the
White House New Dealers made to control the nomination
and platform-making processes at the 1940 Democratic national convention to prevent conservatives from seizing control of the Party.

Milkis's analysis also overemphasizes the policy role of a
party by neglecting a major role of the increasingly liberal
Party that Roosevelt recognized. Since the 1920s, Roosevelt
had recognized that a liberal Party needed to fulfill the role of
an inclusive, pluralistic party that would serve as a vehicle
for integrating, assimilating, and empowering previously disadvantaged voting blocs and interest groups into national
politics. According to Samuel Beer, the more liberal, pluralistic Party that emerged under Roosevelt's leadership provided such previously politically disadvantaged groups as
blacks, urban ethnics, and labor unions with greater power,
status, and opportunity in the national political process and
in society in general.[194] Would these newly empowered members of the New Deal coalition become merely passive bene-
ficiaries of the administrative state's liberal policies? Or
would they become active participants in the national political process and part of an enduring, liberal Democratic party?

Bernard Donahoe argues that the 1938 purge clarified the
ideological and factional divisions between liberal and conservative Democrats. Instead of permanently frustrating the
Party under presidential leadership, the results of the purge
made Roosevelt and the New Deal liberals determined to
engineer the 1940 Democratic national convention so that
they would firmly control the nominating and platform-
making processes, thus assuring the continuation of liberalism within the national Party. Donahoe writes, "The
conservatives were left without a place on the ticket or a place
in the platform, and it seemed . . . that the days of Democrats

like Garner, Farley, Tydings, Van Nuys, and Harrison were as much a part of the past as those of Al Smith, John Raskob, John W. Davis, and James Reed."[195]

Furthermore, E.E. Schattschneider indicates that the increase in congressional power the southern conservatives enjoyed as a result of their victories in the purge and their growing cooperation with Republicans in Congress did not translate into control of the national Party, and, "as viewed from 1940, the 'purge' of 1938 does not seem to have been a failure."[196] The aftermath of the 1938 purge and the events of the 1940 Democratic national convention indicated the southern conservatives' growing isolation from and declining influence in national Party affairs.

The purge of 1938, therefore, did beneficially contribute to the long-term, liberal transformation of the national Party by dramatically publicizing the ideological-policy differences and conflicts between the liberal and conservative elements of the Party. If Roosevelt had not chosen to attempt a purge, the anti–New Deal conservative Democrats would have continued to identify themselves rhetorically with the president and the New Deal for electoral purposes while sabotaging New Deal bills in Congress.[197] As Rexford Tugwell and Samuel Rosenman have indicated, Roosevelt wanted the conservative incumbents targeted by the purge to be held publicly accountable to their constituents for their anti–New Deal voting records in Congress.[198]

The purge was a milestone in Roosevelt's Party leadership because it was a public expression of his willingness to direct both his rhetoric and political action against well-entrenched Democratic incumbents who endangered his efforts to implant New Deal liberalism as the Party's ideological-policy identity. He realized that the national Party could not become distinctly liberal if southern conservatives continued to be "the ball and chain which hobbled the party's forward movement."[199] Morton Frisch contends that for the purpose of "providing a formulation or definition of what the Democratic party was to stand for, the purge was a significant success."[200]

Even though Roosevelt lost individual battles against several conservative incumbents in 1938, he won the war for control of the ideological character and policy agenda of the Party.[201] Southern conservatives in Congress would feel increasingly alienated from the national Party's liberal domestic policies as they recognized the decline of their power in national Party affairs and the rising power of interest groups and voting blocs, especially labor unions and blacks, which favored a distinctly liberal Democratic Party.[202] The seemingly unsuccessful purge of 1938 served as the harbinger of the truly successful "purge of 1940" in which New Deal Democrats succeeded in renominating Roosevelt, choosing his running mate, and dominating the formulation of the Party's domestic policy platform.[203]

7 The Struggle to Maintain a Liberal Party: 1940-1944

The 1940 Election

The Democratic party that emerged in 1940 to renominate and re-elect Roosevelt to an unprecedented third term reflected the political changes that had occurred since 1936. The intraparty discord wrought by the policy conflicts of the 75th Congress, the 1938 purge, and Farley's alienation made conservative Democrats increasingly rebellious toward Roosevelt's Party leadership. The Republican resurgence in the 1938 congressional elections revealed the return of many non-southern WASPs to the Republican party.[1] Consequently, Roosevelt could not expect to receive the large number of votes from disaffected Republicans and independents that he had received in 1932 and 1936.[2] This was especially true after the Republicans nominated Wendell Willkie, a former Democrat, who proved to be attractive to previously pro-Roosevelt Republicans and independents.[3]

The Democrats had been steadily increasing their number of seats in Congress since 1930. It seemed inevitable that the Republicans would gain seats in Congress after voters became dissatisfied with the New Deal policies.[4] A solid majority of Americans polled continued to approve of Roosevelt's performance, but, between 1936 and 1940, there was growing public opposition to further New Deal reforms. A Gallup public opinion poll conducted on August 28, 1938, revealed that 66 percent of the voters polled wanted Roosevelt to pursue more conservative domestic policies.[5]

The recession of 1937–1938 generated further dissatisfaction with the New Deal, especially among non-southern farmers. After briefly cutting domestic spending in an effort

to balance the federal budget, Roosevelt reluctantly returned
to "pump priming" through higher spending on relief and
public works to reduce unemployment and increase consumption.[6] The high deficit spending, however, did little to satisfy
the grievances of farmers in the Midwest and West who were
suffering low farm prices, especially for wheat and corn.[7]

Exploiting such discontent among middle-class voters to
assure their own electoral success, the Republicans realized
that they must not appear to be conservative ideologues who
simply denounce the New Deal while spouting platitudes
about rugged individualism and laissez-faire capitalism. The
electoral results of 1936 and public opinion polls revealed that
most voters, including most Republicans, accepted the idea
that there was a need for permanent federal intervention in
the economy.[8] In a 1938 poll, 56 percent of all Republican
voters questioned stated that they wanted their party to become more liberal.[9]

This public mood influenced the campaign strategy that
most successful Republican nominees pursued in 1938 and
the type of presidential nominee that their party would
choose in 1940. This moderate, pragmatic approach, which
most Old Guard conservatives disdainfully referred to as "Me
Too-ism," basically agreed with the broad New Deal policy
objectives of greater economic security for farmers and wage
earners and regulations against big business abuses.[10] Instead, Republican candidates criticized Roosevelt's policies as
being fiscally extravagant, politically corrupt because of the
Democratic machines involved in public works projects, and
ineffective as evidenced by the recent recession.[11]

Realizing that the Party under Roosevelt and New Deal
liberalism had proven to be especially popular among the
youngest voters, the Republican party recruited young, dynamic candidates in 1938. Friction between the Democratic
and Farmer-Labor parties of Minnesota enabled thirty-three-
year-old Republican Harold Stassen to win the Minnesota
gubernatorial election of 1938.[12] Enjoying national fame for
crusading integrity and competence as a racket-busting district attorney, Thomas E. Dewey, the thirty-six-year-old Republican nominee for the governorship of New York, lost

to the Democratic incumbent, Herbert Lehman, Roosevelt's chosen successor, by only 64,000 votes—1 percent of the state-wide vote.[13] Without votes from the CIO-created American Labor Party and the Communist party, Lehman would have been defeated. Meanwhile, two nationally prominent "Little New Deal" Democratic governors, Frank Murphy of Michigan and George Earle of Pennsylvania, were defeated.[14]

One successful Republican nominee for senator, Robert A. Taft of Ohio, did not dilute his thoroughly anti–New Deal conservative ideology to adapt to public opinion. In a campaign address delivered on September 14, 1938, Taft criticized New Deal regulations on farmers and businessmen and stated that prosperity in the United States "can be more effectively restored by individual freedom and free competition under the American Constitution and the American way of life than by the importation of ideas from Russia or from Germany."[15] Determined to keep the Republican party distinctly conservative, Taft, like Dewey, became a leading candidate for the Republican presidential nomination of 1940.

The results of the 1938 congressional elections encouraged Republicans about their prospects for winning the 1940 presidential election. They gained eighty-one seats in the House of Representatives, almost doubling their current number of eighty-eight.[16] In the Senate, the Republicans increased their number of seats from fifteen to twenty-three.[17]

Although the Democrats still held a comfortable majority of seats in the House and a two-thirds majority in the Senate, the enlarged Republican presence could diminish Roosevelt's influence on the passage of White House bills in two ways. The increased number of Republicans and conservative Democrats alienated from Roosevelt would make it very difficult for New Deal Democrats in Congress to obtain the number of votes necessary to suspend the rules or issue a discharge petition to a recalcitrant committee chairman in order to facilitate the passage of the president's bills.[18] Also, cooperation between Republicans and conservative Democrats in defeating the court reform bill and heavily amending the wages-and-hours bill set a precedent for bipartisan opposition to Roosevelt in Congress. This coalition would give Re-

publican members of Congress a degree of policy influence
beyond their number of seats.[19]

In the hope of accurately understanding the causes of the
Democratic reverses of 1938 in order to prepare for the 1940
election, Farley asked state and local Democratic committeemen for analyses of Democratic defeats in their states.[20]
For the most part, Democratic defeats were attributed by
these Party activists to candidates and issues peculiar to each
state.[21] In particular, unusually acrimonious and divisive
Democratic primaries, especially in Pennsylvania and Illinois, weakened the ability of Democratic nominees to win
elections.[22]

Nevertheless, Farley's analysis did reveal certain nationwide themes and issues that had hurt the voter appeal of
Democratic nominees. Many farmers outside the South were
angry with the AAA for its regulatory and subsidy policies
and with the WPA for reducing the availability of cheap farm
labor.[23] Some reports even contended that higher WPA
spending did not make WPA workers and recipients more
supportive of Democratic candidates because many of them
were dissatisfied with the amount of their benefits.[24] More
significantly, though, the Party's humanitarian image under
the New Deal was tainted by widespread accounts of Democratic manipulation of the WPA and other federal agencies for
electoral purposes.[25]

What lessons could the Party learn from its 1938 defeats to
prepare for the 1940 election? Although it was not clear that
the election results of 1938 expressed a public rejection of New
Deal liberalism and the Democratic Party, Farley and other
Party regulars perceived the need to shift the Party's policy
agenda and image toward the center and soothe conservative
Democrats in Congress, who were enraged by the purge campaign and the divisive bills of the 75th Congress. They believed that, because a majority of the voters were Democrats,
the key to electoral success for the Party was to maintain a
high degree of intraparty harmony through the judicious
distribution of patronage and the avoidance of presidential or
DNC intervention in conflicts at the state and local levels.[26]
Farley had assumed from the beginning that a purge cam-

paign, especially one led by White House New Dealers like Corcoran and Hopkins, would irreparably fragment the Party and lead to Republican victories. He said, "I trace all the woes of the Democratic party, directly or indirectly, to this interference in purely local affairs. In any political entity voters naturally and rightfully resent the unwarranted invasion of outsiders."[27]

Further angered by Roosevelt's favoritism toward such non-Democratic liberals as Fiorello La Guardia and George Norris, Party regulars could not understand why Roosevelt and the White House New Dealers would risk dividing and weakening the Party to strengthen its candidates' commitment to New Deal liberalism. What Roosevelt believed and Farley failed to realize is that principles and policy objectives were more important for stimulating voter interest and for governing responsibly than patronage distribution and party organization were.[28] A more moderate, cautious Democratic party, reminiscent of its status during the 1920s as a party vague and vacillating in its ideology and policy agenda, would alienate the liberally oriented voters and interest groups that it had coopted since 1932. In particular, organized labor, with its substantial amount of votes, campaign contributions, and campaign services given to liberal Democratic candidates, could desert the Party in 1940 if it nominated a moderate or conservative who was antagonistic toward labor's policy interests.[29]

While the conventional wisdom among party regulars assumed that Roosevelt must become more cautious and moderate in his rhetoric, policy efforts, and party leadership to assure victory in 1940, the president continued to assert that the Party needed to maintain and even further enhance its liberalism in public policy and its ideological identity. Two key addresses by Roosevelt in 1939 underscored this theme. In his speech at the Jackson Day dinner on January 7, he stated that the effect of the Republican resurgence "should be to bring us real Democrats together and to line up with those from other parties, those who belong to no party at all, who also preach the liberal gospel, so that, firmly allied, we may continue a common constructive service to the people of the country."[30]

The president's August 8 address to a national convention of Young Democrats criticized Republican and Democratic conservatives equally as obstacles to the nation's progress. More significantly, Roosevelt firmly stated that his own Party loyalty was not absolute and unqualified. He revealed that he definitely would not support a conservative nominee for president in 1940. He told the group, "If we nominate conservative candidates, or lip-service candidates, on a straddle bug platform, I personally, for my own self respect and because of my long service to and belief in, liberal democracy, will find it impossible to have any active part in such an unfortunate suicide of the old Democratic Party."[31]

As early as 1938, Harold Ickes had publicly stated that there was nothing sacred about the two-term tradition for presidents and that Roosevelt was "the only man capable of carrying on the liberal tradition who can be both nominated and elected."[32] Even without an outbreak of war in Europe, Ickes and several other New Deal liberals believed that Roosevelt was the only liberal Democrat who could win.[33] As early as April 1939, Kelly was advocating a third term for Roosevelt. While the president was publicly denying that he wanted to serve a third term, Kelly was quietly building a nationwide network of support for a "Draft Roosevelt" movement.[34] Most of the early support for a third term came from other machine bosses, such as Frank Hague of Jersey City and Ed Crump of Memphis.

Roosevelt, however, continued to avoid answering questions about any plans for running in 1940.[35] There are two possible reasons for Roosevelt's evasion. He may have wanted to wait until as near as possible to the 1940 Democratic National Convention to see if the development of international affairs justified and warranted a third term.[36] Also, his evasion was a source of power with the press, Congress, and his opponents within the Party. If he had unequivocally stated before 1940 that he would not run again, he would have been branding himself as a lame duck, thereby diminishing his policy influence in Congress.[37] Furthermore, Roosevelt's conservative Democratic opponents would be reluctant to fully finance and publicly endorse a presidential candidate if there was a constant possibility that Roosevelt would suddenly announce his candidacy and secure the nomination.

Another effect of Roosevelt's evasion was to stimulate minor, exploratory presidential candidacies among three Democrats in particular. Harry Hopkins had become increasingly ambitious since the 1936 campaign and was widely perceived as Roosevelt's likely successor. His appointment as secretary of commerce in 1939 was regarded by political observers as his first step toward a presidential candidacy.[38] As the WPA administrator, Hopkins certainly enjoyed greater public name recognition than such presidential possibilities as former Governor Paul McNutt of Indiana and Secretary of State Cordell Hull.[39] If nominated and elected, he would be the candidate most likely to continue New Deal liberalism in domestic policy.

Hopkins, however, faced serious obstacles to the nomination. Within the Party apparatus, politicians were angry with Hopkins for a variety of reasons. Some disliked the reduction in patronage that occurred when Republicans were allowed to serve as WPA personnel. Others resented control over WPA appointments and projects in their states by rival Democratic politicians.[40] Hopkins was also detested by southern conservatives and Party regulars for his prominence in the 1938 purge.

Besides these political factors, Hopkins's status as a divorced man and his deteriorating health due to stomach cancer were additional liabilities.[41] In a Gallup poll released on December 2, 1938, Democratic voters were asked whom they would prefer as the Democratic presidential nominee in 1940 if Roosevelt did not run again. Of the ten most frequently mentioned candidates, Hopkins ranked ninth in order of preference.[42]

If Roosevelt were not a presidential candidate in 1940, Farley and Vice-President John Garner were the chief preferences among Party regulars.[43] As the primary distributor of federal patronage, the genial Postmaster General was respected by many party regulars, had accumulated many political debts, and had carefully remained neutral in most intraparty conflicts.[44] But even if Farley were nominated as a

compromise presidential candidate in the event of a deadlock
at the convention, it was doubtful that his voter appeal would
be broad enough to defeat an attractive Republican nominee.
Having no experience in elective office except as a one-term
assemblyman, his qualifications for the presidency would
certainly be questioned, especially during a period of growing
international crises.[45] Finally, Farley's church affiliation
might limit his voter appeal to his fellow Catholic Democrats.

A more feasible presidential "boomlet" was that of the vice-
president. The conservative Texan had become alienated from
Roosevelt over domestic policy issues since the 1936 election.
He had not only refused to support the president on such key
legislation as the court reform bill, the wages-and-hours bill,
and higher WPA spending to alleviate the recession, but
quietly lobbied members of Congress for the opposition.[46]
The first Garner for President Club was opened in Dallas in
May 1939 by Texas oil barons. It was obvious that Garner's
strongest support came from conservative businessmen opposed to New Deal economic policies.[47]

Although Garner had the potential to attract the endorsements of fellow southern conservatives and Liberty League
Democrats, his candidacy was clearly repugnant to liberal
interest groups, especially organized labor and blacks. The
vice-president avoided public speaking and passively allowed
his supporters to establish campaign organizations in several
primary states during the spring of 1940. In these states, most
notably California, slates of Democratic delegates committed
to Roosevelt trounced the Garner forces.[48]

Roosevelt, meanwhile, was concentrating on foreign policy.
Since the outbreak of war in Europe in September 1939, he
had sought to strengthen the American military and indirectly aid Britain while maintaining neutrality.[49] He realized that he needed to conduct his implicitly pro-Allies
foreign policy cautiously to avoid inflaming isolationist opinion to the extent that it would intimidate Congress into
opposing a military build-up.[50] In October 1939, he succeeded
in persuading Congress to repeal the 1935 Neutrality Act's
arms embargo, enabling the Allies to buy arms from the
United States.[51]

To counter the isolationist opposition of western progressives such as Burton Wheeler, Roosevelt sought to build an internationalist majority in Congress favorable to his foreign and defense policies. He cultivated the support of southern conservatives and eastern Republicans.[52] His appointment of Republicans Frank Knox and Henry Stimson as, respectively, the new secretary of the navy and secretary of war symbolized Roosevelt's effort to establish bipartisan support for his foreign policy.[53] The fall of France to Hitler in June 1940 convinced Roosevelt and most Democratic delegates at the national convention that he should run for a third term.[54]

With both northern liberals and southern conservatives in the Party committed to an internationalist platform, the future course of American foreign policy was not expected to be a divisive issue at the Democratic National Convention.[55] The formation of the Republican platform toward Europe, however, was expected to be a contentious issue among the Republican delegates.[56] Despite the increasingly pro-Allies trend of public opinion, including among Republican voters, most Old Guard conservatives and western progressives in the Republican party were determined to draft an isolationist platform.[57]

To the dismay of the most committed isolationists, the Republican delegates drafted an ambiguous foreign policy platform which equivocally combined internationalist and isolationist elements. Even though Republicans in Congress led the opposition to a defense build-up, their party's platform accused the Roosevelt administration of having "left the Nation unprepared to resist foreign attack" and "ignoring the lessons of fact concerning modern, mechanized, armed defense."[58] With equal vigor, the Republicans expressed their firm opposition to "involving this Nation in foreign war."[59] Alf Landon, whom Roosevelt had originally wanted to appoint as the new secretary of war, had tried to strengthen the wording of the platform's defense plank but was defeated by the prevailing isolationist sentiment.[60]

Isolationist Republicans at the convention still had to make their party's platform on foreign policy and defense vague and flexible in order to accommodate their unorthodox

nominee, Wendell L. Willkie.[61] A utility company executive
and former Democrat, Willkie had not become a registered
Republican until 1940.[62] In fact, the only elective office that
Willkie had held was his position on the Tammany County
Committee in New York City's 15th assembly district in
1935.[63] As recently as 1938, Willkie had voted for Governor
Herbert Lehman and the rest of New York's Democratic
ticket.[64]

Willkie's meteoric rise as a Republican presidential candidate from 1938 to 1940 can be mainly attributed to shrewd
publicity efforts promoting his candidacy and the zeal of his
grass roots campaign activists, many of whom were not party
regulars.[65] In 1936, Alf Landon lost by a landslide as his
rhetoric tried to appease both conservatives and progressives
in the Republican party. Since Landon's spurious dichotomy
succeeded in offending liberal Republicans and driving them
into the Roosevelt camp, it seemed sensible to such leading
Republicans as House minority leader Joseph Martin of
Massachusetts and Republican national chairman John D.
Hamilton that a maverick like Willkie would have enough
popular support among liberal Republicans, independents,
and disaffected Democrats to win an upset victory in 1940.[66]
The rapid proliferation of Willkie clubs and the impressive
enthusiasm and diligence that young Republicans in particular exhibited in campaigning for Willkie's nomination
seemed to confirm these assumptions.[67]

This populist, bandwagon effect behind Willkie at the Republican National Convention overwhelmed more conservative GOP delegates who resented the former Democrat's
candidacy. The presidential candidacies of Senator Robert A.
Taft of Ohio, Senator Arthur Vandenburg of Michigan, and
District Attorney Thomas E. Dewey of New York quickly
disintegrated under the ebullient momentum of Willkie's
candidacy.[68] Willkie was nominated on the sixth ballot,[69] and
he chose Senator Charles L. McNary of Oregon, the Senate
minority leader and a western progressive favoring public
power, as his running mate.[70]

Willkie's rhetoric and campaign strategy generally reflected the "Me Too" approach. He basically agreed with the

humanitarian and reformist objectives of the New Deal while criticizing its level of federal spending, regulatory control, and burdens on business operations. Willkie usually avoided discussing foreign policy issues since he agreed with Roosevelt on the defense build-up and peacetime draft and did not want reminders of these agreements to damage his appeal among isolationists.[71] The amiable nominee's speeches, however, became more strident as he charged that the New Deal was stifling economic growth and that a third term for Roosevelt would lead to totalitarianism.[72]

Whereas Willkie had relied on the enthusiasm of grass roots activists and favorable newspaper publicity to overcome the reluctance of Republican bosses toward his candidacy, the support of Democratic machine bosses and their delegates proved to be instrumental to Roosevelt's renomination. To assure his re-election, Roosevelt had to rely on the machine bosses more in 1940 than he had in 1932 and 1936.[73] Determined to renominate the president as a proven vote-getter to head their Democratic tickets and to continue the benefits of New Deal programs for their cities, the machine bosses emerged as Roosevelt's most powerful, reliable allies in the 1940 campaign. Before the convention opened, Roosevelt realized that he especially needed the bosses' support to counteract whatever appeal Garner and Farley's anti–third term movement might have among disaffected Party regulars and southern conservatives. Through Roosevelt's influence, Chicago, Ed Kelly's domain, was chosen as the site of the 1940 Democratic National Convention even though it did not offer the highest bid.[74] By controlling the galleries and the agenda of the convention, Kelly could minimize the prospect of a "Stop Roosevelt" movement suddenly emerging and growing among the delegates.[75] Roosevelt later confided to Ickes that Kelly's ability to pack the galleries with supporters of a third term was an important factor in the choice.[76]

Roosevelt realized, though, that even Kelly's machinations might not prevent Farley and Garner from bitterly dividing the delegates through their anti–third term coalition. Garner had declared his candidacy at the convention to express his conviction against a third term.[77] Farley had briefly thought that he could run in 1940 as Secretary of State Cordell Hull's running mate. But Hull had revealed no desire to run for president, and his appeal was limited to the South.[78]

Farley's presidential candidacy, however, appeared to be mostly a matter of personal opportunism and bitterness toward Roosevelt as the president relied more on Hopkins and Corcoran for political advice after 1936. Farley had not become a conservative ideologue. He had lavishly praised the New Deal's social welfare liberalism in his first autobiography.[79] During his service as DNC chairman and Postmaster General, he had been oblivious to ideology and public policy. Except for his involvement in the campaign against Millard Tydings, he opposed the 1938 purge because he feared that it would irreparably damage intraparty relations, and not because of an ideological preference for the conservatives targeted by the purge. His cooperation with Garner in the anti–third term movement was caused more by mutual bitterness toward Roosevelt than because of a shared ideology.

Once he decided to run for a third term, Roosevelt was determined to choose a committed New Deal liberal as his running mate. As early as May 1937, the president told Henry Morgenthau that he needed to force conservatives such as Garner out of the Party in order to pursue New Deal policy objectives.[80] Except for a few diehard, anti-Roosevelt conservatives like Millard Tydings and Carter Glass, most southern Democrats who had opposed major New Deal bills in Congress and were outraged by the 1938 purge united behind Roosevelt instead of Garner.[81] Their bitterness toward Roosevelt had been reduced by his solicitation of their support on foreign policy and defense measures.[82] Moreover, the 1938 purge had made them reluctant to incur the president's vengeful wrath in the event of his re-election.[83]

When the Democrats met, therefore, in July 1940, at their national convention in Chicago, they were more united than they had been in the previous year. Growing Nazi aggression and the weakness of Farley's and Garner's candidacies had increased support for Roosevelt's renomination. Senator Jimmy Byrnes of South Carolina, who had supported "Cotton Ed" Smith against the purge, became Roosevelt's floor leader.[84]

Moreover, there was a growing realization among Democratic politicians and delegates that Roosevelt was the only candidate behind whom all of the diverse, conflicting elements of their Party would unite.[85]

The diverse coalition that supported Roosevelt's renomination was personified by its leading organizers—Ed Kelly, Harry Hopkins, and Jimmy Byrnes. Hopkins served as the liaison of the president, who remained in Washington, while Byrnes lobbied the southern delegates.[86] But Kelly had the responsibility for planning and implementing an overwhelming demand among the delegates for Roosevelt's renomination. He had arranged beforehand to have his machine create a bandwagon effect that would provide the necessary momentum. Although Harry Hopkins was not a delegate, Kelly made him a sergeant at arms so that he could be admitted to the floor of the convention and organize pro-Roosevelt delegates for the planned demonstration.[87] As soon as Alben Barkley, the convention chairman, finished delivering a message from Roosevelt telling the delegates that they could vote for any candidate they wished, a voice from the loudspeakers bellowed, "We want Roosevelt!"[87] A boisterous, pro-Roosevelt demonstration began and lasted nearly an hour.[88]

The voice that initiated this "spontaneous" demonstration belonged to Thomas Garry, Chicago's superintendent of sewers. Kelly had arranged for Garry's shout to be the signal that would initiate the demonstration. The burst of enthusiasm, meticulously planned by Kelly, had the desired effect.[90] By the next day, 86 percent of the delegates voted for Roosevelt on the first ballot; and the remaining delegates divided their votes among Farley, Garner, Hull, and Tydings.[91]

Unfortunately for the machine bosses and the White House New Dealers who engineered the proceedings of the convention, the nomination of Roosevelt's running mate could not be implemented as smoothly. Hull, a moderate respected by all factions, had firmly rejected White House suggestions that he run for vice-president.[92] A vice-presidential nomination for Jimmy Byrnes might prove to be offensive to blacks, labor unions, and Catholics because of his position as a segregationist, an opponent of pro-union bills, and an ex-

Catholic.[93] Furthermore, Roosevelt's anger at Garner for his secret lobbying in Congress against New Deal bills had made him determined to choose a liberal running mate who was unequivocally committed to the New Deal.

Roosevelt informed Kelly, Hopkins, and Byrnes that he wanted Secretary of Agriculture Henry A. Wallace as his vice-presidential candidate.[94] He informed his operatives in Chicago that he would not accept his own renomination unless they convinced the delegates to support his choice of Wallace. Wallace's status as a former Republican, his lack of a political base, and his rather eccentric interest in mysticism were regarded by this triumvirate as liabilities for "selling" him to the delegates.[95] With most of the opposition to Wallace coming from southerners and pro-Farley New York delegates, Wallace won the nomination by the embarrassingly close vote of 628 to 459.[96]

Roosevelt, by choosing Wallace as his running mate, hoped to improve his voter appeal in the midwestern farm states. The recession of 1937–1938 had lowered farm prices, which farmers blamed on the New Deal, and led to a strong Republican resurgence in the 1938 congressional elections in these states.[97] Furthermore, this region was strongly isolationist and opposed Roosevelt's increasingly internationalist foreign policy and defense build-up. Roosevelt also had to be concerned about his pro-British foreign and defense policies losing him votes from traditionally Democratic German, Italian, and Irish ethnics.[98]

The limitations on campaign finance imposed by the Hatch Act on the national party committees led to the proliferation of publicity activities by state party committees and independent organizations. It was very difficult for the Roosevelt and Willkie campaigns to control the activities of these autonomous campaign committees and prevent their distribution of scurrilous, irresponsible campaign literature.[99] Some Willkie clubs portrayed Roosevelt as a dictator similar to Stalin and Hitler while the DNC's Colored Division claimed that Willkie's German ancestry made him a Nazi sympathizer.[100]

Willkie, though, avoided personal attacks on Roosevelt and portrayed himself, to the dismay and anger of Old Guard Republicans, as being basically supportive of the New Deal philosophy and of an internationalist foreign policy.[101] He tried to win the election by maintaining Landon's Republican base of 1936 while attracting dissident Democrats and previously pro-Roosevelt Republicans and independents.[102] V.O. Key, Jr., later estimated that approximately 4.7 million Americans who voted for Roosevelt in 1936 cast ballots for Willkie in 1940.[103] Willkie also hoped that John L. Lewis's nationally broadcast endorsement would swing labor support to his campaign. Nevertheless, Sidney Hillman, the CIO's vice president, undermined Lewis's endorsement of Willkie so that approximately 72 percent of the organized labor vote went to Roosevelt on election day.[104]

Despite defections to Willkie from voters who had supported Roosevelt in 1936, the president won the election with approximately 55 percent of the popular votes and the electoral college votes of thirty-eight states.[105] Eight of the ten states that Willkie carried were in the Midwest and West.[106] Although their members of Congress chafed under Roosevelt's increasingly combative liberalism, all southern states provided Roosevelt with their electoral college votes by a wide margin of victory.[107]

Thus, Roosevelt had succeeded in being renominated and re-elected to an unprecedented third term in the presidency, even though his more aggressive liberalism since 1936 had alienated many conservatives within the Party. In choosing a running mate and in affirming his commitment to the continuation of liberal domestic policies, Roosevelt had refused to make concessions to conservative Democrats. These intraparty victories by Roosevelt were enabling him to gradually fulfill the resolution, which he had expressed to Rexford Tugwell shortly after the 1932 election, to make the Democratic party a progressive party after eight years in the White House.[108] "In effect, Roosevelt's drive to liberalize and modernize the Democratic party which had apparently foundered for good in the Purges of 1938 had at last borne fruit."[109]

The 1944 Election

The congressional elections of 1942 resulted in the smallest
majorities in Congress that the Democrats would hold during
Roosevelt's presidency. Due to this Republican resurgence,
Democratic majorities had been reduced to twenty-one seats
in the Senate and only nine seats in the House.[110] During the
1940 campaign, Roosevelt hoped to attract bipartisan support
for his foreign policy by appointing Knox and Stimson to his
cabinet, and he offered Willkie a position as an arbitrator on
the War Labor Board in 1942.[111] After the United States
entered World War II, he increased the appointment of Republicans to defense-related agencies and commissions. This
bipartisan gesture, however, failed to increase Republican
support in Congress for his policies as the opposition frequently criticized him for mismanaging the civilian economy
and war production.[112]

As in the congressional elections of 1938, successful Republican candidates castigated the federal bureaucracy under the Roosevelt administration for being incompetent,
ineffective, fiscally wasteful, and devoid of clear lines of authority and responsibility among the wartime agencies.[113] In
particular, they benefited from the dissatisfaction of farmers
with AAA policies and farm price limits imposed by the
Office of Price Administration. Generally, though, many
voters were dissatisfied with the rationing and shortage of
consumer goods, inflation, higher income taxes, and the
seemingly constant regulation of their daily lives by bureaucratic decisions.[114]

An added feeling of frustration and discontent among the
voters was caused by the sense that these sacrifices and
inconveniences imposed by the Roosevelt administration
were not clearly contributing toward victory in the Pacific
and European theaters of the war. The American assault on
Guadalcanal in the Pacific had sustained heavy casualties
and still faced fierce Japanese resistance by late October.[115]
The long-awaited Allied invasion of North Africa was delayed
until after the 1942 congressional elections because of logis-
tical problems.[116] This stagnant situation made it feasible—

and beneficial—for Republican candidates to criticize Roosevelt's conduct of the war without appearing to be unpatriotic toward their commander in chief.[117]

The Party also suffered from a low voter turn-out in the 1942 midterm elections. Although registered Democrats had outnumbered registered Republicans since 1936, voting behavior revealed that traditionally Republican middle-class voters were more likely to vote than traditionally Democratic working-class voters, especially in midterm elections.[118] Thus, Democratic nominees outside of the South suffered from the fact that only 26,000,000 Americans voted in 1942, half as many as in 1940.[119] Military service and relocation to defense plant jobs led to especially low turn-out rates among two of the most Democratic voting blocs, young voters and factory workers.[120] Consequently, a major goal of Roosevelt's campaign managers for the 1944 election was to increase voter turn-out among these groups.[121]

During the sessions of the 78th Congress, the increased Republican membership enabled the conservative coalition in Congress to end such major New Deal programs as the WPA, CCC, and NYA.[122] Despite resistance from Congress, Roosevelt wanted to finance as much of the war expense as possible on a "pay as you go" basis, partially through high taxes on corporations and wealthy individuals. His request that Congress limit Americans' salaries during the war to $25,000 was easily defeated.[123] Besides wanting to minimize the post-war debt and control wartime consumer spending and inflation, Roosevelt also wanted to prevent big business interests from substantially increasing their economic and political power because of the war boom.[124]

Therefore, despite his Republican appointments and solicitation of business's cooperation for the sake of national unity behind the war effort, Roosevelt had not weakened or compromised his New Deal liberalism in domestic policy areas. On December 28, 1943, he stated at a press conference that the federal government must implement policies that would result "in more security, in more employment, in more recreation, in more health, in better housing for our citizens."[125] Two weeks later, he delivered his State of the Union address in which he proposed an "Economic Bill of Rights."[126] James MacGregor Burns referred to this address as "the most radical speech of his life."[127]

In this speech, he unequivocally claimed that there was a direct link between economic security and political democracy. Once the war ended, Roosevelt wanted the New Deal policy agenda expanded so that Americans would have their "rights" to adequate medical care, housing, education, full employment, and even recreation fulfilled.[128] Securing these economic "rights" would result in the attainment of "new goals of human happiness and well-being."[129]

Just as he became more combative from 1938–1940 due to intraparty conflicts and legislative defeats, Roosevelt asserted his liberalism on domestic policy issues during 1943 and 1944 as both Democrats and Republicans in Congress successfully overrode his vetoes of a tax relief bill, the anti-union Smith-Connally Act, and a bill increasing farm parity prices.[130] Even Senate majority leader Alben Barkley, usually a staunch Roosevelt ally, briefly vacated his leadership position in protest of the president's veto of the tax relief bill.[131]

Roosevelt, though, would be able to rely on the leadership of Barkley, Guffey, and other liberal Democrats in Congress in the prolonged struggle over extending to servicemen voting opportunities in the 1944 election.[132] Supporters of this suffrage extension argued that it would enable servicemen to participate in the democracy they were defending.[133] Opponents retorted that such a federal suffrage law represented excessive federal interference with the states' right to determine voter qualifications and administer elections.[134]

Northern Democrats in Congress such as Guffey and Wagner wanted a special federal ballot distributed to servicemen to expedite their voting and the tabulation of the results. Republicans and most southern Democrats wanted the states to print and distribute absentee ballots to retain control over their particular registration requirements.[135] Southerners in Congress feared that a federal ballot would enfranchise black servicemen from their states, which usually denied them the right to vote through poll taxes, literacy tests, and intimidation.[136] Southern segregationists were already concerned about the Supreme Court's 1944 decision in *Smith v. Allwright* striking down Texas's white-only primary.[137]

If a federal ballot were adopted, it would be administered by the Department of War. Even though the secretary of war was a Republican, leading Republicans in Congress suspected a partisan bias in this department.[138] Thus, many Republicans perceived a federal ballot as a devious ploy to assure Roosevelt's re-election by pressuring servicemen to vote for their commander in chief.[139]

The compromise bill that finally emerged from the conference committee was clearly favorable to the bipartisan states' rights coalition.[140] According to its provisions, the federal ballot could be obtained by a serviceman only if he had first requested an absentee ballot from his state and his state legislature had accepted the federal ballot.[141] Southern states that usually disfranchised blacks could prevent black servicemen from their states from voting, and only twenty states would accept these federal ballots.[142]

To express his opposition to the weaknesses of this suffrage bill while also allowing its enactment, Roosevelt refused to either veto it or sign it.[143] Instead, he delivered a carefully prepared speech criticizing the state-oriented provisions of this bill for complicating the voter registration process for servicemen, especially those overseas who were constantly moving. Such unnecessary red tape would discourage and even prevent voting by American citizens serving in the military. According to Roosevelt, the facilitation of voting opportunities for servicemen is a national obligation for those "who are at the front fighting with their lives to defend our rights and our freedoms."[144]

Encouraged by such legislative victories over Roosevelt and expecting a low voter turn-out among traditionally Democratic voters, Republican delegates convened in Chicago on June 26 to nominate a presidential candidate and wage a competitive campaign against Roosevelt.[145] Widely disdained within the Republican party for the rapport he had developed with Roosevelt since the 1940 election, Willkie was not a viable candidate for the nomination.[146] The best possi-

ble nominee would be a candidate who possessed a record and
rhetoric that would appeal to the more liberal, internationalist wing of the Republican party but who, unlike Willkie, was
clearly a party regular and proven vote-getter with years of
service to the party.

After easily defeating Willkie in several Republican primaries, it was evident as early as April that Governor Thomas
E. Dewey of New York would be nominated at the Republican
National Convention with only token opposition.[147] Elected
by a landslide as the first Republican governor of New York
since 1920, Dewey had distinguished himself as an efficient
administrator who championed tax reform, a streamlined
state bureaucracy, and an end to favoritism and featherbed-
ding in state employment.[148] The forty-two-year-old former
prosecutor projected the image of a competent, efficient public manager who readily accepted the need for social welfare
programs, labor reforms, and business regulations while de-
crying fiscal waste, bureaucratic incompetence, and excessive
federal control under the Roosevelt administration. In short,
the crusading young governor personified the "Me Too" philosophy and record of the moderate Republican politicians
who had emerged since 1936.[149]

Dewey, nevertheless, was careful not to repeat Willkie's
mistake of antagonizing the GOP's Old Guard. He chose as
his running mate Governor John Bricker of Ohio, a conservative isolationist favored by party regulars.[150] Dewey's decision was facilitated by Earl Warren's announcement that he
would not pursue the vice-presidential nomination. Warren,
the liberal Republican governor of California and the convention's keynote speaker, was broadly supported as Dewey's
running mate.[151]

As a further concession to the more conservative party
regulars, he generally allowed them to dominate the drafting
of the party's national platform. While agreeing with the
military strategy of Roosevelt, the party platform concentrated its attack on the New Deal's centralization of government and damage to economic growth and vowed to "avoid
federalization of government activities."[152] In more caustic
language, the Republican platform rebuked Roosevelt's labor

policies for representing "one of the New Deal's steps toward a totalitarian state."[153] One day after the convention, Dewey admitted to the press that his party's platform contained inconsistencies and that his own positions reflected only parts of it.[154]

Willkie's 1940 campaign had been plagued by frequent squabbles and lack of coordination between the Willkie clubs and regular party organizations, but Dewey, because of his compromises, enjoyed a degree of intraparty harmony behind his candidacy.[155] Consequently, Dewey was able to concentrate fully on his theme that the nation needed to change its presidential leadership and policy direction. Unlike Willkie, Dewey would challenge Roosevelt's foreign policy decisions, suggesting that Roosevelt and other New Deal Democrats were "afraid of peace" because of the depressing effect that the end of the war was expected to have on the economy.[156]

Despite several legislative defeats and Senator Harry F. Byrd's threat to establish an anti-Roosevelt third party, Roosevelt's renomination in 1944 was accepted by most Democrats.[157] The Texas delegation for the 1944 convention, however, was evenly divided between opponents and supporters of Roosevelt's renomination.[158] Roosevelt had again assured the selection of Chicago as the site of the Democratic national convention and assumed that Ed Kelly could skillfully manage another "controlled" convention. The only major source of contention within the Party was the choice of a running mate.

The diverse elements of the Democratic Party agreed on at least one matter—the need to replace Henry Wallace as vice-president. Southerners disliked his outspoken support of racial integration. The White House staff and top advisers, especially Harry Hopkins, regarded his eccentric personality and politically inept statements as embarrassing. Robert Sherwood suggests that Roosevelt had decided to dump Wallace as early as July 1943 after the vice-president had publicly and tactlessly criticized Secretary of Commerce Jesse Jones's policies with the Board of Economic Warfare.[159]

Busy with his military strategy and foreign affairs, Roosevelt did not want Wallace's renomination to threaten his re-election. He briefly suggested that Supreme Court justice William O. Douglas replace Wallace, but he realized that there was little support for Douglas from the Party leaders.[160] He readily accepted DNC chairman Bob Hannegan's suggestion that Senator Harry S. Truman of Missouri be given the nomination. Despite Jimmy Byrnes's vigorous lobbying for the vice-presidential nomination, Kelly and Hannegan dismissed his candidacy as being unacceptable to blacks, Catholics, and labor.[161]

Because he wanted to spend little time campaigning, Roosevelt tried to assure a consensual nomination process for a vice-presidential candidate. Truman would at least be grudgingly acceptable to all of the diverse elements of the party—blacks, southern whites, labor unions, and the machine bosses. Despite the general unity behind Roosevelt's renomination at the 1944 convention, Senator Harry F. Byrd's candidacy attracted the votes of 100 southern delegates.[162] Byrd's candidacy revealed the growing alienation of southern conservatives from the more liberal national Democratic party that had emerged under Roosevelt's leadership. It also served as a harbinger of the Deep South's noisy defection from Truman at the next national convention.

The greatest concern of Bob Hannegan, Ed Flynn, and other managers of Roosevelt's campaign was that voter apathy and the overconfidence of Democratic campaign workers would result in a low voter turn-out and an upset victory for Dewey. The youngest voters would be most likely to vote for Roosevelt.[163] However, military service or relocation because of defense plant employment meant that many of these Democratic voters would be unable to vote.[164] Because of the weak, heavily compromised provisions of the Servicemen's Voting Act, only about 85,000 servicemen would receive special federal ballots for the 1944 election.[165]

With the servicemen's vote expected to play such a minor role in the 1944 campaign, the DNC concentrated more on the micromanagement of voter mobilization efforts at the precinct level than it had in Roosevelt's three previous presidential campaigns.[166] The DNC sought to energize and coordinate the efforts of the approximately 125,000 Democratic precinct organizations throughout the United States. It provided detailed suggestions for registering and mobilizing voters and scheduled an October 5 nationwide radio broadcast by Roosevelt to all Democratic campaign workers.

The war effort and the anticipated low voter turn-out gave Democratic women a disproportionate degree of influence and responsibility in the 1944 campaign. In a memo to local Democratic committees, the DNC urged these committees not to segregate or subordinate female activists in assigning campaign responsibilities and tasks. Moreover, the memo urged local Democratic organizations to provide women with an equally important role and status in the voter mobilization drive. According to this memo, "Just as women are doing the work formerly performed by men in industries so we as a Democratic organization must realize that the women can go out and do the party job that in previous years has been done by men."[167]

As Republicans and southern conservatives frequently charged that Roosevelt was a political captive of the "Communist" CIO, Roosevelt became even more dependent on Sidney Hillman for the mobilization of labor's votes and campaign contributions in 1944 than he had been in 1940.[168] The Smith-Connally Act of 1943, which was passed over Roosevelt's veto, prohibited labor unions from contributing campaign funds to party committees, such as the DNC, once the presidential candidates were nominated.[169] The CIO circumvented this law by forming its own political action committee, CIO-PAC, in 1943 and collected approximately $647,000 from CIO unions before the national convention was held. Closely associated with the CIO-PAC was the National Citizens Political Action Committee (NC-PAC).[170]

After the Smith-Connally Act's prohibition of union contributions took effect, the CIO-PAC and the NC-PAC began a vigorous campaign to encourage CIO members to make individual contributions to the Roosevelt campaign.[171] The CIO-PAC and the NC-PAC raised approximately $470,000 and $378,000, respectively, in this manner. Besides financially contributing to Roosevelt's campaign outside of the DNC, the CIO provided essential campaign services, such as canvass-

ing voters and distributing leaflets.[172] The electoral support
of the CIO-dominated American Labor Party combined with
Democratic votes enabled Roosevelt to carry New York by a
narrow margin in the 1944 election.

The results of the 1944 election were similar to those of the
previous presidential election. Roosevelt won 53 percent of
the popular votes and 432 electoral college votes.[173] As in
1940, most of the twelve states that Roosevelt lost to the
Republican nominee were in the midwestern and western
farm belt.[174] As many non-southern rural WASPs continued
to reaffirm their Republican allegiance, Roosevelt became
increasingly dependent on urban voters for his margin of
victory.[175] Whereas only 25 percent of Roosevelt's plurality of
votes came from the nation's twelve largest cities in 1932, 65
percent of his margin of victory came from these cities in
1944.[176]

Despite his desire to achieve bipartisan support for his
foreign policy through Republican appointments, Roosevelt
did not weaken or compromise his liberal policy objectives
to achieve that support or the cooperation of conservatives
within his Party. Nor did the legislative defeats that he suffered in Congress in 1943 weaken his determination to represent the Party as a distinctly liberal one which would
advocate federal efforts to provide greater economic security
and better public services for average Americans. On the
contrary, his 1944 address outlining the "Economic Bill of
Rights" was the most comprehensive agenda of liberal policy
objectives he had ever announced. Although the southern
conservatives' support of Harry Byrd's candidacy at the 1944
convention indicated their willingness to oppose Roosevelt's
renomination openly, Roosevelt did not abandon his liberal
principles and policy objectives to appease them. By 1944, the
voting blocs and interest groups that favored the continuation
of New Deal liberalism as the Democratic party's ideology
and policy agenda were strong enough to defeat opposition by
conservatives within the Party.

EPILOGUE
FDR's Legacy in the Democratic Party

The Democratic party's electoral success and general direction on ideological and policy matters after Roosevelt's death in 1945 would reveal whether he had built an enduring electoral base and ideological-policy identity for the Party or if he had merely attracted a personal following that would disintegrate shortly after his death. Critics of Roosevelt's Party leadership, both Republicans and conservative Democrats, would dismiss his four elections to the presidency as merely being the result of the back-to-back crises of the Great Depression and World War II or the "purchase" of votes from economically desperate Americans through the "bribery" of New Deal welfare and subsidy programs.[1] Apparently, they assumed that Roosevelt's and his party's electoral success would evaporate shortly after these crises ended and the New Deal had lost its "vote-buying" appeal.[2] Such an assessment of Roosevelt's party leadership dismisses his political skills and the popularity of the New Deal's ideology.[3]

Roosevelt had consistently revealed his willingness to arouse intraparty opposition and threaten his own political position to maintain the clarity and consistency of his liberal principles as well as his determination to make the national Democratic party a distinctly liberal majority party.[4] Critics of his presidency appear to regard his liberal posture as an expedient adaptation to the political climate of the Depression, with its widespread economic discontent that produced leftist, populist movements.[5] They neglect the importance of the long-term strategy for expanding and liberalizing the Party that Roosevelt had developed during the 1920s.

At crucial times, therefore, Roosevelt's ideological commitment to the liberal transformation of the Democratic party as an enduring majority superseded expedient, momentary concerns for his own position in the Party. The ideological commitment also explains the qualified, conditional nature of his loyalty to an identification with the Party as a political institution.[6] His party loyalty had always been qualified according to the extent to which he could reform the principles and policy objectives of the Party.

Harry Truman's upset victory in 1948, despite intraparty discord resulting in the defections of the Progressives and the Dixiecrats, demonstrated the enduring quality of the accomplishments of Roosevelt's party-building efforts.[7] Truman's victory revealed that Roosevelt's personal leadership was not indispensable for maintaining a liberal Democratic party that could win a presidential election and regain control of both houses of Congress. What did appear to be crucial, though, for the continuation of Democratic hegemony was the maintenance and further enhancement of Roosevelt's ideological-policy legacy of New Deal liberalism.[8]

Despite the concern of some Roosevelt loyalists that Truman would prove to be a do-nothing moderate, the new president demonstrated his fidelity to New Deal liberalism by proposing what he called the Fair Deal.[9] Besides strengthening such existing New Deal policies as Social Security, public housing, and farm subsidies, the Fair Deal proposed to advance such unfulfilled liberal policy objectives as national health insurance, federal aid to education, and civil rights legislation for blacks. After Truman's presidency, these three major policy goals would be a focus of liberal Democrats in Congress and of the next two Democratic presidents.[10]

Like Roosevelt, Truman campaigned as a combative liberal instead of a cautious moderate. Despite criticism of Truman's civil rights plank among black leaders and some white liberals for being too mild and inadequate, it was strong enough to enrage the most committed white supremacists in the Deep South to support Strom Thurmond as the presidential nominee of the States' Rights party.[11] This intraparty rebellion by southern segregationists against Truman served to galvanize black support for the president. Because black electoral support of the Democratic party, especially among the middle class and intelligentsia, had declined somewhat during the 1940s because of military segregation during

World War II and the strong support of Willkie and Dewey for civil rights, the Dixiecrat revolt and Truman's civil rights plank helped to swing undecided black voters to Truman.[12]

Even though Truman consistently received low approval ratings in Gallup polls and experienced fierce intraparty opposition from both the left and the right as well as from Eleanor Roosevelt and her sons, he succeeded in winning an upset victory and assuring the continuation of the Democratic party as the majority party by constantly reminding voters of the New Deal's policy accomplishments and the Republicans' threat to their continuation.[13] In particular, Truman convinced labor unions and farm organizations that a Republican victory would threaten New Deal programs that had benefited their interests.[14] In short, Truman won the election and helped to regain Democratic control of Congress by making Democratic policy accomplishments under the New Deal—and not his own personal leadership—the dominant issue of the campaign.

Likewise, Roosevelt's policy legacy, presidential style, and liberal transformation of the Party proved to have an enduring impact on Truman's successors in the White House. To assure victory in the 1952 presidential election, Republicans realized they needed to nominate a candidate who basically accepted the New Deal policy foundation and who possessed an attractive suprapartisan image. Consequently, the Republican National Convention of 1952 nominated Dwight Eisenhower, who had been courted by Eleanor Roosevelt, Claude Pepper, and other liberal Democrats as their party's presidential nominee in 1948, instead of the staunchly conservative Robert A. Taft.[15]

John F. Kennedy and Lyndon B. Johnson realized the political importance of maintaining the New Deal coalition for electoral purposes as well as for eliciting public and congressional support for their domestic policy agenda. In preparing for and conducting their 1960 campaign, both Kennedy and Johnson found it necessary to assure the Party's liberal activists and interest groups that they were faithful to Roosevelt's ideology and policy objectives.[16] Under the pressures of current events and their party's expectations, Kennedy and

Johnson, especially the latter, proved to be more liberal in
their rhetoric and policy behavior than they had been in
Congress. Although generally regarded as a conservative
during his tenure in the Senate, Johnson began his presidency determined to equal and even surpass Roosevelt as
the liberal champion of the underprivileged in American
society.[17]

Toward the end of Johnson's administration, however, it
became apparent that the Party had reached the limits of
Roosevelt's legacy. Its ability to build coalitions, elect presidents, and dominate the domestic policy-making process had
clearly declined. The intensity of intraparty conflicts over
the civil rights movement and the Vietnam War badly fragmented the electoral coalition built by Roosevelt. Societal
changes and court decisions led to the emergence of such
politically divisive social issues as abortion, school prayer,
and forced busing to achieve racial integration in public
schools, which further weakened the party loyalty of Democratic voters.[18] Democratic candidates could no longer succeed by simply following Roosevelt's example of focusing on
economic issues while generally ignoring social issues like
race relations and the relationship between church and state.
The Republican landslides of 1972 and 1984, however, did not
effect the massive change in the party registration and identification of voters that Roosevelt's 1936 re-election had done
for the Democratic party.[19]

The fact that the liberal Democratic Party developed by
Roosevelt's party leadership could continue its electoral success and endure as the nation's majority, even when it was
led by a beleaguered, controversial successor like Truman,
widely perceived as being inferior to Roosevelt, revealed that
Roosevelt had not built a fragile, ephemeral personal following that would quickly disintegrate after his death.[20] Instead, his party leadership and party-building strategy
under the New Deal had transformed the Party into the
enduring majority party among the electorate at large, in
Congress, and, until 1968, in the presidency.[21] By instilling
New Deal liberalism in the Party as the essence of its ideology, domestic policy objectives, and the policy interests of its

major voting blocs and interest groups, Roosevelt provided liberal Democrats with a degree of clarity and cohesion that the Party had not enjoyed since the Age of Jackson.[22] He operated within the American federal system, whose structures and forces discourage and hamper strong party leadership by a president.[23] When Franklin D. Roosevelt's Party leadership and party-building efforts are assessed according to these criteria, he can be regarded as one of the most successful and effective party leaders in American history.

Notes

Abbreviations

DNC: Democratic National Committee
FDRL: Franklin D. Roosevelt Library, Hyde Park, New York
GPO: Government Printing Office
LOC: Library of Congress, Washington, D.C.
PL: Roosevelt, Elliott, ed., *F.D.R.: His Personal Letters*, 4 vols. (New York: Duell, Sloan and Pearce, 1947-50).
PPA: Rosenman, Samuel I., ed., *The Public Papers and Addresses of Franklin D. Roosevelt*, 13 vols. (New York: Random, 1938-50).
PPG: Roosevelt, Franklin D., *Public Papers of Governor Franklin D. Roosevelt*, 4 vols. (Albany: Lyon, 1930-39).
RNC: Republican National Committee

1 The Development of a Party-Building Strategy

1. Morton J. Frisch, "Franklin D. Roosevelt and the Problem of Democratic Liberty," *Ethics* 72 (Apr. 1962): 182; and Clinton Rossiter, "The Political Philosophy of F.D. Roosevelt," *Review of Politics* 2 (Jan. 1949): 89-91.   2. Robert Prescott to FDR, Jan. 29, 1925, FDR Papers: 1920-1928, FDRL; David Burner, *The Politics of Provincialism: The Democratic Party in Transition, 1918-1932* (Cambridge, Harvard Univ. Press, 1986), 150; and Robert S. Rankin, "The Future of the Democratic Party," *South Atlantic Quarterly* 28 (July 1929): 230-33.   3. Walter Lippmann, "The Reconstruction of the Democratic Party," *Yale Review* 18 (Sept. 1928): 21; Arthur M. Schlesinger, Jr., *The Crisis of the Old Order* (Boston: Houghton Mifflin, 1957), 98; and Paula Eldot, *Governor Alfred E. Smith: The Politician as Reformer* (New York: Garland, 1983), 343-44.
4. FDR to John K. Sague, Mar. 1, 1920, FDR Papers as Vice-Presidential Candidate 1920, FDRL.   5. FDR to William J. Bryan, June 20, 1923, FDR Papers: 1920-1928, FDRL.
6. Frank Freidel, *Franklin D. Roosevelt: The Ordeal*, (Boston: Little, Brown, 1954), 201-2.   7. FDR to Charles F. Murphy, Dec. 5, 1924, FDR Papers: 1920-1928, FDRL.   8. Cordell Hull, *The Memoirs of Cordell Hull*, 1 (New York: Macmillan, 1948): 116.
9. Burner, *Politics of Provincialism*, 146.   10. Marie Chatham, "The Role of the National Party Chairman from Hanna to Farley" (Ph.D. diss., Univ. of Maryland, 1953), 109.

11. Alfred E. Rollins, Jr., *Roosevelt and Howe* (New York: Knopf, 1962), 221.   12. Lee Allen, "The McAdoo Campaign for the Presi-

dential Nomination in 1924," *Journal of Southern History* 29 (May 1963): 211-28.   13. Richard T. Goldberg, *The Making of Franklin D. Roosevelt* (Cambridge: Abt, 1981), 70.   14. DNC, *The Campaign Book of the Democratic Party Candidates and Issues in 1928* (Albany: Lyon, 1928), 386; and Franklin D. Roosevelt, *The Happy Warrior: Alfred E. Smith* (New York: Houghton Mifflin, 1928).   15. Arthur Krock, "The Damn Fool Democrats," *American Mercury* 4 (Mar. 1925): 257; and Robert K. Murray, *The 103rd Ballot: Democrats and Disaster in Madison Square Garden* (New York: Harper & Row, 1976).   16. FDR to Eleanor Roosevelt, Oct. 1924, in *The Roosevelt Reader*, ed. Basil Rauch (New York: Holt, Rinehart and Winston, 1957), 43.   17. V.O. Key, *Politics, Parties, and Pressure Groups* (New York: Crowell, 1950), 263; and Arthur N. Holcombe, *The Political Parties of To-Day* (New York: Harper, 1925), 410.   18. Schlesinger, *Crisis of the Old Order*, 100-2; and Holcombe, 340-42.   19. FDR to Josephus Daniels, Dec. 5, 1924, in *Roosevelt and Daniels*, ed. Carroll Kilpatrick (Chapel Hill: Univ. of North Carolina Press, 1952), 82-83.   20. Schlesinger, *Crisis of the Old Order*, 103.

21. Ibid.   22. Richard O'Connor, *The First Hurrah* (New York: Putnam, 1970), 185.   23. Franklin D. Roosevelt, review of *Jefferson and Hamilton* by Claude Bowers, entitled "Is There a Jefferson on the Horizon?'" Dec. 3, 1925, in *Roosevelt Reader*, 43-47; and Wilson C. McWilliams, *The Idea of Fraternity in America* (Berkeley: Univ. of California Press, 1973), 209-33.   24. James A. Farley, *Behind the Ballots* (New York: Harcourt, Brace, 1938), 70-80.   25. Eleanor Roosevelt, *This I Remember* (New York: Harper, 1949), 45-46.

26. Rollins, *Roosevelt and Howe*, 235.   27. O'Connor, *First Hurrah*, 251.   28. Franklin D. Roosevelt, "The Problem of Water Power Sites" (Sept. 27, 1928), in *F.D.R., Columnist*, ed. Donald S. Carmichael (Chicago: Cuneo, 1947): 137-41.   29. Farley, *Behind the Ballots*, 53.   30. Eleanor Roosevelt, *This I Remember*, 346.

31. PPA, 1: 16-21.   32. Samuel B. Hand, "Al Smith, Franklin D. Roosevelt, and the New Deal: Some Comments on Perspective," *Historian* 27 (May 1965): 366; PPA, 1:38-44; and PPA, 1:54-59.   33. Harold F. Gosnell, *Champion Campaigner: Franklin D. Roosevelt* (New York: Macmillan, 1952), 226.   34. Bernard Bellush, *Franklin D. Roosevelt as Governor of New York* (New York: Columbia Univ. Press, 1955), 26.   35. Kenneth S. Davis, *FDR: The New York Years, 1928-1933* (New York: Random, 1985), 74.

36. Farley, *Behind the Ballots*, 55-57.   37. Max Lerner, "Jim Farley, Soldier and Artist," *New Republic* 97 (Dec. 28, 1939): 237; and Bernard Donahoe, *Private Plans and Public Dangers* (Notre Dame: Univ. of Notre Dame Press, 1965), 25-30.   38. Eleanor Roosevelt, *This I Remember*, 30-31.   39. Farley, *Behind the Ballots*, 55.   40. Susan Ware, *Beyond Suffrage: Women in the New Deal* (Cambridge: Harvard Univ. Press, 1981), 9.

41. Edward J. Flynn, *You're the Boss* (New York: Viking, 1947), 94.   42. Ibid., 92-93.   43. Gosnell, *Champion Campaigner,* 94.   44. Flynn, *You're the Boss,* 95.   45. Samuel Rosenman, *Working with Roosevelt* (New York: Harper, 1952), 29.
46. PPG, 1: 138, 153, 158, 161, 171.   47. James MacGregor Burns, *Roosevelt: The Lion and the Fox* (New York: Harcourt, Brace, Jovanovich, 1956), 114-15 (hereafter cited as *Lion and Fox*).
48. Rollins, *Roosevelt and Howe,* 233.   49. Earland I. Carlson, "Franklin D. Roosevelt's Post-Mortem of the 1928 Election," *Midwest Journal of Political Science* 8 (Aug. 1964): 298-308; and Rankin, "Future of the Party" 234.   50. Samuel Lubell, *The Future of American Politics* (New York: Harper, 1952), 28-41; and Kristi Andersen, *The Creation of a Democratic Majority, 1928-1936* (Chicago: Univ. of Chicago Press, 1979), 39-120.
51. Louis Howe, memo to FDR, "Summary of the Situation," 1930, Howe Papers, FDRL.   52. Ibid., 1.   53. Burns, *Lion and Fox,* 119.   54. Mrs. Merritt Van de Bogart to Louis Howe, Sept. 23, 1930, Howe Papers, FDRL.   55. Louis Howe to James J. Hoey, July 27, 1930, Howe Papers, FDRL.
56. Gosnell, *Champion Campaigner,* 226.   57. Warren Moscow, *Politics in the Empire State* (New York: Knopf, 1948), 168.
58. Earland I. Carlson, "Franklin Roosevelt's Fight for the Presidential Nomination, 1928-1932" (Ph.D. diss., Univ. of Illinois-Urbana, 1955), 77-93; and Farley, *Behind the Ballots,* 68-70.   59. Davis, *FDR: New York Years,* 164.   60. Frances Perkins, *The Roosevelt I Knew* (New York: Viking, 1946), 107.
61. PPG, 3: 173.   62. Carlson, "Franklin Roosevelt's Fight," 14.   63. Frank Freidel, *Franklin D. Roosevelt: The Triumph* (Boston: Little, Brown, 1956), 178 (hereafter cited as *Triumph*).
64. Farley, *Behind the Ballots,* 74.   65. Charles Michelson, *The Ghost Talks* (New York: Putnam's Sons, 1944), 4-5; and Thomas S. Barclay, "The Publicity Division of the Democratic Party, 1929-1930," *American Political Science Review* 25 (Fall 1931): 68-73.
66. Bancroft Henderson, "The Democratic National Committee" (Ph.D. diss., Univ. of Minnesota, 1958), 304.   67. James K. Pollock, "Campaign Funds in 1928," *American Political Science Review* 23 (Feb. 1929): 360-63.   68. Ibid., 66.   69. Wallace S. Sayre, "Personnel of the Republican and Democratic National Committees," *American Political Science Review* 26 (Apr. 1932): 360-63.
70. PL, 3: 228.
71. Chatham, "Role of National Party Chairman," 79.
72. Franklin D. Roosevelt, *Government—Not Politics* (New York: Stratford, 1932); and William E. Leuchtenberg, *Franklin D. Roosevelt and the New Deal, 1932-1940* (New York: Harper & Row, 1963), 9-12.   73. Walter Lippmann, Interpretations, 1931-1932 (New York: Macmillan, 1932), 262.   74. Rosenman, *Working with Roosevelt,* 30.

2 A Foundation for Party-Building

1. Paul Douglas, "The Prospects for a New Political Alignment," *American Political Science Review* 25 (Nov. 1931): 906-7.   2. Raymond Moley, *After Seven Years* (New York: Harper, 1939), 23.
3. Elliot Rosen, *Hoover, Roosevelt, and the Brains Trust: From Depression to New Deal* (New York: Columbia Univ. Press, 1977), 120.   4. John Franklin Carter, *The New Dealers* (New York: Simon & Schuster, 1934), 28-73; Donald R. Brand, *Corporatism and the Rule of the Law* (Ithaca: Cornell Univ. Press, 1988), 126.
5. Irving Bernstein, *The Turbulent Years: A History of the American Worker, 1933-1941* (Boston: Houghton Mifflin, 1970), 173-76.
6. Herbert Croly, *The Promise of American Life* (Cambridge: Belknap, 1965), 278-9.   7. Robert R. Brooks, *Unions of Their Own Choosing: An Account of National Labor Relations Board and Its Work* (New Haven: Yale Univ. Press, 1939), 39-40; and the United States Bureau of the Census, *Historical Statistics of the United States 1789-1945*, (Washington, D.C.: GPO, 1949), 72.   8. Brand, *Corporatism*, 231.   9. Robert Sherwood, *Roosevelt and Hopkins* (New York: Harper, 1948), 69.   10. Paul A. Kurzman, *Harry Hopkins and the New Deal* (Fair Lawn, N.J.: Burdick, 1974), 182-84.
11. Searle Charles, *Minister of Relief: Harry Hopkins and the Depression* (Syracuse: Syracuse Univ. Press, 1963), 179; Hopkins, form letter to WPA administrators, March 13, 1936; and FDR to Hopkins, July 18, 1936, both in Harry Hopkins Papers, FDRL; and *Congressional Record*, 74th Cong., 2d sess., 1936 pt. 4:3657.
12. James T. Patterson, *The New Deal and the States: Federalism in Transition* (Princeton: Princeton Univ. Press, 1969), 74-85.
13. Arthur W. MacMahon et al., *The Administration of Federal Work Relief* (Chicago: Public Administration, 1941), 269.   14. Charles, *Minister of Relief*, 182.   15. Kurzman, *Hopkins and the New Deal*, 183.
16. Herbert S. Hollander, *Spoils!* (Washington, D.C.: William Ullman, 1936), 116-7.   17. Paul P. Van Riper, *History of the United States Civil Service* (New York: Row, Peters, 1958), 320.
18. Ibid.   19. Morris Fiorina, "The Decline of Collective Responsibility in American Politics," *Daedalus* 109 (Summer 1980): 45.
20. U.S. Congress, Senate, *Positions Not Under the Civil Service: Senate Doc. 173*, 72d Cong., 2d sess., 1933.
21. Hollander, *Spoils!* 114.   22. Gloria W. Newquist, "James A. Farley and the Politics of Victory: 1928-1936" (Ph.D. diss., Univ. of Southern California, 1966), 282; Paul H. Appleby, *Big Democracy* (New York: Knopf, 1945), 144-55; Alfred J. Nock, "WPA, the Modern Tammany," *American Mercury* 45 (Oct. 1938), 215-19; Corrington Gill, "W.P.A.," *Current History* 48 (Jan. 1938), 40; and Carter, *New Dealers*, 244.   23. Lorena Hickok, memo to Hopkins, September 9, 1934, Harry Hopkins Papers, FDRL; Lillian Symes, "Politics vs.

Relief," *Survey Graphic* 24 (Jan. 1935): 8-10; and Farley, *Behind the Ballots*, 197-98.   24. James A. Farley to Louis M. Howe, September 27, 1933, Louis M. Howe Papers, FDRL; Duncan Aikman, "Big Jim Farley," *The American Politician*, ed. John T. Salter (Chapel Hill: Univ. of North Carolina Press, 1938): 223; and James A. Farley, "Passing Out the Patronage," *American Magazine* 116 (Aug. 1933), 77.   25. Henry F. Pringle, "Who's on the Payroll," *American Magazine* 117 (Nov. 1934): 19.
    26. Ibid.   27. Ibid.   28. Farley, "Passing Out the Patronage," 77.   29. Pringle, "Who's on the Payroll," 10.   30. William D. Reeves, "The Politics of Public Works, 1933-1935" (Ph.D. diss., Tulane Univ., 1968), 91; and Lawrence Sullivan, "Our New Spoils System," *Atlantic Monthly* 157 (Feb. 1936): 192-93.
    31. Farley, "Passing Out the Patronage," 22.   32. Sullivan, "Our New Spoils System," 191.   33. Van Riper, *History of Civil Service*, 320.   34. Farley, *Behind the Ballots*, 36.   35. Harold L. Ickes, *The Secret Diary of Harold L. Ickes*, 1 (New York: Simon and Schuster, 1954): 51-52; and Reeves, "Politics of Public Works," 49.
    36. "Political Notes, Peaceful Revolution," *Time* (Sept. 4, 1933): 13.   37. Farley to Howe, Sept. 27, 1933, Louis M. Howe Papers, FDRL.   38. Farley, *Behind the Ballots*, 234-35.   39. Richard S. Kirkendall, "Franklin D. Roosevelt and the Service Intellectual," *Mississippi Valley Historical Review* 49 (Dec. 1962): 456-71.
    40. Van Riper, *History of Civil Service*, 324.
    41. Ibid., 318.   42. Merle Curti, "Intellectuals and Other People," *American Historical Review* 60 (Jan. 1955): 279; and Lewis S. Feuer, John Dewey and the Back to the People Movement," *Journal of the History of Ideas* 20 (Oct.-Dec. 1959): 545-68.   43. Edward J. Flynn, *You're the Boss*, 161-68.   44. Joseph Alsop and Robert Kintner, *Men Around the President* (New York: Doubleday, 1939), 5-8.   45. Van Riper, *History of Civil Service*, 324.
    46. Rexford G. Tugwell, *The Brains Trust* (New York: Viking, 1968), 221-33; and Farley, *Behind the Ballots*, 212-21.   47. Henry A. Wallace, "Farm Economists and Agricultural Planning," *Journal of Farm Economics* 18 (Feb. 1936): 1-11.   48. Sherwood, *Roosevelt and Hopkins*, 84-85.   49. Rexford G. Tugwell, *The Democratic Roosevelt* (New York: Doubleday, 1957), 545-46; and James A. Farley, *Jim Farley's Story: The Roosevelt Years* (New York: Whittlesey, 1948), 147-50.   50. Patrick Anderson, *The President's Men* (New York: Doubleday, 1968), 41.
    51. Farley, *Jim Farley's Story* 150-53.   52. Tugwell, *Democratic Roosevelt*, 547-48.   53. Flynn, *You're the Boss*, 168-70; and Anderson, *President's Men*, 51.   54. Alsop and Kintner, *Men Around the President*, 197.   55. Arthur M. Schlesinger, Jr., *The Politics of Upheaval* (Boston: Houghton Mifflin, 1960), 272-73; and Van Riper, *History of Civil Service*, 328.
    56. Arthur M. Schlesinger, Jr., *The Crisis of the Old Order* (Bos-

ton: Houghton Mifflin, 1957), 93-145.   57. John C. O'Brien, "Robert F. Wagner: Pilot of the New Deal," *The American Politician,* ed. John T. Salter (Chapel Hill: Univ. of North Carolina Press, 1938): 111.   58. James E. Sargent, *Roosevelt and the Hundred Days: Struggle for the Early New Deal* (New York: Garland, 1981), 191. 59. Bernard Bellush, *The Failure of the NRA* (New York: Norton, 1976), 14-20; and Ellis W. Hawley, *The New Deal and the Problem of Monopoly* (Princeton: Princeton Univ. Press, 1966), 20. 60. Brand, *Corporatism,* 203.
      61. Burns, *Lion and Fox,* 41-43.   62. Arthur M. Schlesinger, Jr., *The Coming of the New Deal* (Boston: Houghton Mifflin, 1959), 402.   63. Lubell, *Future of American Politics,* 48-50; Carl N. Degler, "American Political Parties and the Rise of the City: An Introduction," *Journal of American History* 51 (June 1964): 41-59; and Andersen, *Creation of a Democratic Majority,* 30-38.   64. Samuel J. Eldersveld, "The Influence of Metropolitan Party Pluralities in Presidential Elections since 1920," *American Political Science Review* 43 (Dec. 1949): 1189-1206; and Norman A. Graebner, "Depression and Urban Votes," *Current History* 23 (Oct. 1952): 238. 65. J. Joseph Huthmacher, *Senator Robert F. Wagner and the Rise of Urban Liberalism* (New York: Atheneum, 1968), 118-19.
      66. James Sundquist, *Dynamics of the Party System* (Washington, D.C.: Brookings Institution, 1973), 212.   67. Sylvia Snowiss, "Presidential Leadership of Congress: An Analysis of Roosevelt's First Hundred Days," *Publius* 1 (1971): 59-87; Cortez A.M. Ewing, *Congressional Elections, 1896-1944* (Norman: Univ. of Oklahoma Press, 1947), 19; E. Pendleton Herring, "Second Session of the 73rd Congress," *American Political Science Review* 28 (Oct. 1934): 865; and *New York Times,* Mar. 3, 1933, 2.   68. James T. Patterson, *Congressional Conservatism and the New Deal* (Lexington: Univ. of Kentucky Press, 1967), 13.   69. Frank Freidel, *F.D.R. and the South* (Baton Rouge: Louisiana State Univ. Press, 1965), 34-35. 70. E. David Cronon, "A Southern Progressive Looks at the New Deal," *Journal of Southern History* 24 (May 1958), 151-76; and Dewey W. Grantham, Jr., *The Democratic South* (Athens: Univ. of Georgia Press, 1963), 69-75.
      71. V.O. Key, Jr., *Southern Politics in State and Nation* (Knoxville: Univ. of Tennessee Press, 1984), 6-8.   72. Grantham, *Democratic South,* 56.   73. Key, *Southern Politics,* 8-9, 63. 74. Eleanor Roosevelt to Steve Early, Aug. 8, 1935, FDR Papers, President's Personal File 1336, FDRL; Harvard Sitkoff, *A New Deal for Blacks* (New York: Oxford Univ. Press, 1978), 102; and Patterson, *Congressional Conservatism,* 145.   75. Ernest K. Lindley, "The New Congress," *Current History* 49 (Feb. 1939): 15-17; Milton Plesur, "The Republican Congressional Comeback of 1938," *Review of Politics* 24 (Oct. 1962): 525-62; and PL, 3: 827-28.
      76. Paul W. Ward, "Roosevelt Will Win," *Nation* 144 (Feb. 20,

1937): 202.   77. E. Kimbark MacColl, "The Supreme Court and Public Opinion: A Study of the Court Fight of 1937" (Ph.D. diss., Univ. of California, 1953), 223-25; and Joseph Alsop and Turner Catledge, *The 168 Days* (New York: Doubleday, 1938), 92-97. 78. Patterson, *Congressional Conservatism*, 88-90.   79. PL, 3: 657.   80. PPA, 6: 63-66.
     81. Ibid., 58, 123.   82. Jerry Voorhis, *Confessions of a Congressman* (Westport, Connecticut: Greenwood, 1970), 78. 83. Bernard F. Phelps, "A Rhetorical Analysis of the 1937 Addresses of Franklin D. Roosevelt in Support of Court Reform" (Ph.D. diss., Ohio State Univ., 1956), 20-134.   84. Alben W. Barkley, *That Reminds Me* (New York: Doubleday, 1954), 153.   85. Bascom N. Timmons, *Garner of Texas* (New York: Harper, 1948), 23; and Alfred Steinberg, *My Name Is Tom Connally* (New York: Hawthorne, 1954), 143.
     86. William Bankhead to FDR, Feb. 8, 1937, FDR Papers, President's Secretary's File 61, FDRL; and *Time* 29 (Feb. 22, 1937): 11. 87. Steinberg, *My Name Is Tom Connally*, 166.   88. Herbert Lehman to FDR, Feb. 26, 1937, FDR Papers, President's Personal File 93, FDRL.   89. Garner to FDR, June 20, 1937, FDR Papers, President's Personal File 1416, FDRL.   90. PL, 3: 692.
     91. Burton Wheeler to FDR, Oct. 24, 1936, and FDR to Wheeler, Oct. 23, 1936, both in FDR Papers, President's File 723, FDRL. 92. Patterson, *Congressional Conservatism*, 126-27.   93. Steinberg, *My Name Is Tom Connally*, 138-46.   94. Burton K. Wheeler, *Yankee from the West* (New York: Doubleday, 1962), 322-23. 95. *New York Times*, March 28, 1937, 21.
     96. Claude D. Pepper, *Pepper: Eyewitness to a Century* (New York: Harcourt, Brace, 1987), 56-57; and Alsop and Catledge, *168 Days*, 80-91.   97. Ibid., 208-24.   98. Alfred Steinberg, *Sam Rayburn: A Biography* (New York: Hawthorn, 1975), 146.   99. *Congressional Record*, 75th Cong., 1st sess., 1937, pt. 1: 6740-41. 100. Alva Johnston, "President Tamer," *Saturday Evening Post* 210 (Nov. 13, 1937): 9.
     101. Polly Ann Davis, *Alben W. Barkley: Senate Majority Leader and Vice President* (New York: Garland, 1979), 36.   102. O.R. Altman, "First Session of the Seventy-fifth Congress, Jan. 5, 1937, to Aug. 21, 1937," *American Political Science Review* 31 (1937): 1071-93.   103. United States Bureau of the Census, *The Statistical History of the United States from Colonial Times to the Present*, p. 691; Richard Polenberg, "The Decline of the New Deal, 1937-1940," *The New Deal*, ed. John Braeman, Robert H. Bremner, and David Brody (Columbus: Ohio State Univ. Press, 1975), 1: 249; and William E. Leuchtenberg, "Franklin D. Roosevelt's Supreme Court 'Packing' Plan," *Essays on the New Deal*, ed. Harold M. Hollingsworth and William F. Holmes (Austin: Univ. of Texas Press, 1969), 109-12. 104. Burns, *Lion and Fox*, 309; and Barkley, *That Reminds Me*,

153.   105. DNC, *Official Report of the Proceedings of the Democratic National Convention, 1932* (Washington, D.C.: DNC, 1932), 16-17, LOC.   106. James K. Libbey, *Dear Alben: Mr. Barkley of Kentucky* (Lexington: Univ. Press of Kentucky, 1979), 61-63.   107. Schlesinger, *Politics of Upheaval*, 580.   108. FDR, carbon copy of letter to Alben Barkley, Nov. 28, 1932, DNC Papers, FDRL.   109. Martha H. Swain, *Pat Harrison: The New Deal Years* (Jackson: Univ. Press of Mississippi, 1978), 33-57.   110. Ibid., 110-17.

111. *Congressional Record*, 74th Cong., 1st sess., 1935, 13210, 13213, 13254; and *New York Times*, Aug. 15, 1935, 1.   112. *New York Times*, July 17, 1937, 2; and FDR to Alben Barkley, July 16, 1937, FDR Papers, President's Personal File 3160, FDRL.

113. *Congressional Record*, 75th Cong., 1st sess., 1937, 1293, 1295, 1407-8; and *New York Times*, July 22, 1937, 3, July 23, 1937, 18.

114. Patterson, *Congressional Conservatism*, 148.   115. Farley, *Jim Farley's Story*, 92, 181; and Alva Johnston, "White House Tommy," *Saturday Evening Post* 210 (July 31, 1937).

116. Davis, *Alben W. Barkley*, 30-32.   117. Grace Tully, *F.D.R.: My Boss* (New York: Scribner, 1949), 225; and Ickes, *Secret Diary of Ickes* 2: 170-74.   118. *New York Times*, July 22, 1937, 1.

119. Michelson, *Ghost Talks*, 182; and Philip A. Grant, Jr., "Editorial Reaction to the Harrison-Barkley Senate Leadership Contest, 1937," *Journal of Mississippi History* 26 (May 1974): 140.

120. Farley, *Jim Farley's Story*, 68; and Tugwell, *Democratic Roosevelt*, 412-15.

121. William Smathers to FDR, June 21, 1937, FDR Papers, President's Personal File 4470, FDRL; and Stanley High, "Whose Party Is It?" *Saturday Evening Post* 209 (Feb. 6, 1937): 11, 45.

122. Schlesinger, *Politics of Upheaval*, 509-10.   123. Paul H. Douglas and Joseph Hackman, "The Fair Labor Standards Act of 1938," *Political Science Quarterly* 43 (1938): 491-515.   124. Richard B. Henderson, *Maury Maverick: A Political Biography* (Austin: Univ. of Texas Press, 1970), 173; and Pepper, *Pepper*, 102.

125. *Congressional Record*, 75th Cong., 1st sess., 1937, pt. 7872.

126. Steinberg, *Sam Rayburn: A Biography*, 150.   127. *Congressional Record*, 75th Cong., 2nd sess., 1937, 1835.   128. Polenberg, "Decline of the New Deal," 253.   129. Milton Derber and Edwin Young, *Labor and the New Deal* (Madison: Univ. of Wisconsin Press, 1956), 120.   130. Voorhis, *Confessions of a Congressman*, 86-95.

131. *New York Times*, Aug. 8, 1937, 4:3.   132. Stephen M. Shuff, "Partisan Realignment in the New Deal Era" (Ph.D. diss., Harvard Univ., 1983), 159, 175-76.   133. Patterson, *Congressional Conservatism*, 333-34.   134. Alan Brinkley, "The New Deal and Southern Politics," in *The New Deal and the South*, ed. James C. Cobb and Michael V. Namorato (Jackson: Univ. Press of Mississippi,

1984): 103-9.   135. Roland Young, *Congressional Politics in the Second World War* (New York: Columbia Univ. Press, 1956), 195-98. 136. Donald R. McCoy, *The Presidency of Harry S. Truman* (Lawrence: Univ. Press of Kansas, 1984), 163-90.   137. Morton J. Frisch, *Franklin D. Roosevelt: The Contribution of the New Deal to American Political Thought and Practice* (Boston: Wayne, 1975), 79-82 (hereafter cited as *Contribution of the New Deal*).   138. "A New Deal for the Negro," *Opportunity* 11 (May 1933): 135. 139. Richard Sterner, *The Negro's Share* (New York: Doubleday, 1943), 362-63.   140. Richard B. Sherman, *The Republican Party and Black America: From McKinley to Hoover, 1896-1933* (Charlottesville: Univ. of Virginia Press, 1973), 225-29; and Harold Gosnell, "The Negro Voter in Northern Cities," *National Municipal Review* 30 (May 1941): 264-67, 278.
      141. Julian D. Rainey to Louis M. Howe, Apr. 17, 1933; Rienzi Lemus to FDR, Oct. 28, 1933; and J. William Clifford to James A. Farley, Nov. 12, 1933, all in Official File 93, FDRL.   142. Ernest Collins, "Cincinnati Negroes and Presidential Politics," *Journal of Negro History* 41 (Apr. 1956): 133; Larry W. Dunn, "Knoxville Negro Voting and the Roosevelt Revolution," *East Tennessee Historical Society Publications* 43 (1971): 89; and John M. Allswang, "The Chicago Negro Voter and the Democratic Consensus: A Case Study, 1918-1936," *Illinois State Historical Society* 60 (Summer 1967): 168-74.   143. Larry H. Grothaus, "The Negro in Missouri Politics, 1890-1941" (Ph.D. diss., Univ. of Missouri 1970), 135; and "The National Election, 1932," *Opportunity* 10 (Nov. 1932): 336.
      144. Arthur Krock, "Did the Negro Revolt?" *Opportunity* 11 (Jan. 1933): 19; and Samuel Lubell, "The Negro and the Democratic Coalition," *Commentary* 38 (Aug. 1964): 20.   145. Leslie H. Fishel, Jr., "The Negro in the New Deal Era," *Wisconsin Magazine of History* 48 (Winter 1964): 113; and *Opportunity* 12 (Dec. 1934): 360.
      146. Marie W. Kruman, "Quotas for Blacks: The Public Works Administration and the Black Construction Worker," *Labor History* 16 (Winter 1975): 49; and Robert C. Weaver, "An Experiment in Negro Labor," *Opportunity* 14 (Oct. 1936): 295-98.   147. Dolores D. Lefall and Janet L. Sims, "Mary McLeod Bethune—The Educator," *Journal of Negro Education* 45 (Summer 1976): 342-59; and John Kirby, *New Deal Era and Blacks* (Urbana: Univ. of Illinois Press, 1971), 112.   148. William A.H. Birnie, "Black Brain Trust," *American Magazine* 135 (Jan. 1943): 37; and Alfred Edgar Smith, "Educational Programs for the Improvement of Race Relations: Government Agencies," *Journal of Negro Education* 13 (Summer 1944): 364.   149. B. Joyce Ross, "Mary McLeod Bethune and the National Youth Administration: A Case Study of Power Relationships in the Black Cabinet of Franklin D. Roosevelt," *Journal of Negro History* 60 (Jan. 1975): 1-28.   150. "Black Game," *Time* 38

(Aug. 17, 1936): 10-11; and "Wooing the Negro Vote," *Nation* 143 (Aug. 1, 1936): 119. 151. DNC Colored Division, Report, "Has the Roosevelt New Deal Helped the Colored Citizen?" Aug. 24, 1936, Official File 93, FDRL. 152. *New York Times,* June 26, 1936, 15. 153. Everett C. Ladd and Charles D. Hadley, *Transformations of the American Party System* (New York: Norton, 1975), 59; Earl Brown, "How the Negro Voted in the Presidential Election," *Opportunity* 14 (Dec. 1936): 359; and Gosnell, "The Negro Voter in Northern Cities," 267. 154. Walter White to Eleanor Roosevelt, June 24, 1938, Eleanor Roosevelt Papers, FDRL. 155. FDR to Bishop R.R. Wright, Jr., Nov. 14, 1936, President's Personal File 4120, FDRL; and *Nation* 146 (Feb. 26, 1938): 258.

156. Jimmy Byrnes to FDR, Apr. 27, 1937, Official File 79, FDRL; and Farley, *Jim Farley's Story,* 85. 157. Edwin L. Best to FDR, Oct. 31, 1933; and Chicago NAACP to FDR, June 2, 1933, Official File 93, FDRL. 158. "Lynching No Crime," *Crisis* 43 (June 1936): 179; and Ralph Bunche, "A Critique of New Deal Social Planning as It Affects Negroes," *Journal of Negro Education* 5 (Jan. 1936): 59-65. 159. Ladd and Hadley, *Transformations,* 60. 160. DNC Colored Division, Pamphlet, "Why the Colored Citizen Should Help Re-elect President Roosevelt," 1940, Official File 93, FDRL. 161. Ladd and Hadley, *Transformations,* 62.; and Lawrence H. Fuchs, "American Jews and the Presidential Vote," *American Political Science Review* 49 (June 1955): 385-86. 162. Walter White to FDR, Nov. 4, 1940, President's Personal File 1336, FDRL. 163. Ladd and Hadley, *Transformations,* 112; and "The Election," clipping from *Life,* (Nov. 20, 1944): 24, DNC Papers, FDRL. 164. Theodore H. White, *America in Search of Itself: The Making of the President, 1956-1980* (New York: Warner, 1982), 333-35. 165. Lawrence Grossman, *The Democratic Party and the Northern Negro, Northern and National Politics, 1868-92* (Urbana: Univ. of Illinois Press, 1976), 170-71; Ernest Collins, "Cincinnati Negroes and Presidential Politics," *Journal of Negro Politics* 41 (Apr. 1956): 131-32; and C. Vann Woodward, *The Strange Career of Jim Crow* (New York: Oxford Univ. Press, 1966), 82-93.

166. Freidel, *F.D.R. and the South,* 119-20. 167. PL 2: 566; and Burner, *Politics of Provincialism,* 150. 168. Joe Starnes and Marvin McIntyre, Dec. 1, 1935, Official File, FDRL. 169. Patterson, *Congressional Conservatism,* 5-7; and Freidel, *F.D.R. and the South,* 43-47. 170. Ralph M. Goldman, *Search for Consensus: The Story of the Democratic Party* (Philadelphia: Temple Univ. Press, 1979), 173.

171. Alexander Heard, *A Two-Party South* (Chapel Hill: Univ. of North Carolina Press, 1952), 117. 172. Allswang, *The New Deal and American Politics,* 48-52. 173. Zane L. Miller, *Urbanization*

of Modern America (New York: Harcourt, Brace, Jovanovich, 1973), 153-63; and Hutchmacher, Senator Wagner and Urban Liberalism, 34-36.   174. Sitkoff, New Deal for Blacks, 332.   175. PPA 7: 167-68.   176. Patterson, Congressional Conservatism, 133-34. 177. Samuel H. Beer, "Liberalism and the National Idea," Public Interest (Fall 1966): 75-76.   178. Ibid.   179. Lubell, Future of American Politics, 21.

3 Roosevelt and the Machine Bosses

1. Tugwell, Democratic Roosevelt, 69.   2. Oscar Handlin, Al Smith and His America (Boston: Little, Brown, 1958), 90-111. 3. Frank R. Kent, The Great Game of Politics (New York: Doubleday, 1936), 19-24.   4. Ladd and Hadley, Transformations, 54-57, 70-71.   5. Frank Kingdon, Architects of the Republic (New York: Alliance, 1947), 224-25.
6. Charles Van Devander, The Big Bosses (New York: Howell Soskin, 1944), 316-17.   7. Broadus Mitchell, Depression Decade (New York: Rinehart, 1947), 105; and Irving Bernstein, The Lean Years: History of the American Worker, 1920-1933 (Boston: Houghton Mifflin, 1960), 297-98.   8. Barbara Blumberg, The New Deal and the Unemployed: The View from New York City (Lewisburg, Pa.: Bucknell Univ. Press, 1979), 27.   9. Leonard Chalmers, "The Crucial Test of La Guardia's First Hundred Days: The Emergency Economy," New York Historical Society Quarterly 57 (July 1973): 237-53; Steven P. Erie, Rainbow's End: Irish-Americans and the Dilemmas of Urban Machine Politics, 1840-1985 (Berkeley: Univ. of California Press, 1988), 108-11; and Charles Garrett, The La Guardia Years: Machine and Reform Politics in New York City (New Brunswick, N.J.: Rutgers Univ. Press, 1961), 104.   10. Morton Grodzins, The American System: A New View of Government in the United States (Chicago: Univ. of Chicago Press, 1966), 41-57; and Daniel J. Elazar, "The Shaping of Intergovernmental Relations in the Twentieth Century," The Annals of the American Academy of Political and Social Science 359 (May 1965): 10-22; and C.C. Ludwig, "Cities and the National Government under the New Deal," American Political Science Review 29 (Aug. 1935): 640-48.
11. Rosalie Genevro, "Site Selection and the New York City Housing Authority, 1934-1939," Journal of Urban History 12 (Aug. 1986): 334-52; and Roger Biles, Big City Boss in Depression and War: Mayor Edward J. Kelly of Chicago (DeKalb, Ill.: Northern Illinois Univ. Press, 1984), 74-80.   12. Miller, Urbanization of Modern America, 161.   13. Mark I. Gelfand, A Nation of Cities: The Federal Government and Urban America, 1933-1965 (New York: Oxford Univ. Press, 1975), 385; Charles E. Merriam, "Observations on Cen-

tralization and Decentralization: The Federal System in Wartime," *State Government* 15 (Jan. 1943): 15; and Seward H. Mott, "Urban Redevelopment Legislation Analyzed," *American City* 60 (Aug. 1945): 83-84.   14. Erie, *Rainbow's End*, 129-31; and John J. Harrigan, *Political Change in the Metropolis* (Glenview, Ill.: Scott, Foresman, 1989), 161-9.   15. Philip J. Funigiello, *The Challenge to Urban Liberalism: Federal-City Relations during World War II* (Knoxville: Univ. of Tennessee Press, 1978), 14-30; and Donoh W. Hanks, Jr., "Neglected Cities Turn to U.S.," *National Municipal Review* 35 (Apr. 1946): 173.

16. George E. Mowry, *The Urban Nation, 1920-1960* (New York: Hill and Wang, 1965), 88; and Gene D. Jones, "The Origins of the Alliance between the New Deal and the Chicago Machine," *Journal of the Illinois State Historical Society* 67 (June 1974), 253-274. 17. Flynn, *You're the Boss*, 94-95; and Davis, *New York Years*, 130-67.   18. Tugwell, *The Democratic Roosevelt*, 228-29; and Frank Freidel, *Franklin D. Roosevelt Launching the New Deal* (Boston: Little, Brown, 1973), 79-82; and PPA 1: 669-701. 19. Daniel R. Fusfeld, *The Economic Thought of Franklin D. Roosevelt and the Origins of the New Deal* (New York: AMS, 1970), 84; and Howard S. Zavin, "Forward to the Land: Franklin D. Roosevelt and the City, 1882-1933" (Ph.D. diss., New York Univ., 1972). 20. Hull, *Memoirs of Cordell Hull* 1: 141; Freidel, *F.D.R. and the South*, 30-32; and Gloria W. Newquist, "Farley and the Politics of Victory" (Ph.D. diss., Univ. of Southern Calif., 1966), 121.

21. Davis, *The New York Years*, 253.   22. Freidel, *Triumph*, 257-58.   23. Flynn, *You're the Boss*, 105-6.   24. William M. Reddig, *Tom's Town: Kansas City and the Pendergast Legend* (Columbia: Univ. of Missouri Press, 1986), 203-5.   25. Freidel, *Triumph*, 239-40.

26. Biles, *Big City Boss* 74-80; and Alex Gottfried, *Boss Cermak of Chicago: A Study of Political Leadership* (Seattle: Univ. of Washington Press, 1962), 171-75.   27. Farley, *Jim Farley's Story*, 21.   28. Dayton D. McKean, *The Boss: The Hague Machine in Action* (Boston: Houghton Mifflin, 1940) (hereafter cited as *Hague Machine*), 95-96; Farley, *Behind the Ballots*, 115.   29. Edward Kelleher to Howard Bible, June 1, 1933, Official File 300, FDRL; and Frank Hague to FDR, Nov. 24, 1933, President's Personal File 1013, FDRL.   30. Thomas J. Fleming, "I Am the Law," *American Heritage* 20 (June 1969): 33-48.

31. Frank Hague to FDR, July 3, 1943, Official File 300, FDRL.   32. Flynn, *You're the Boss*, 161.   33. Irwin Ross, "Big City Machines and Liberal Voters," *Commentary* 10 (Oct. 1950): 306-7.   34. Burns, *Lion and Fox*, 41.   35. J.F. O'Donnell to James A. Farley, Sept. 10, 1936, DNC Papers, FDRL.

36. PL, 3: 1328.   37. Frank Hague to FDR, Oct. 29, 1942, Official File 300, FDRL.   38. Thelma Parkinson to James A.

Farley, Sept. 14, 1936, DNC Papers, FDRL.   39. McKean, *Hague Machine*, 73-76; and Alfred Steinberg, *The Bosses* (New York: Macmillan, 1972), 59.   40. Fleming, "I Am the Law," 39.
41. Richard J. Connors, *A Cycle of Power: The Career of Jersey City Mayor Frank Hague* (Metuchen, N.J.: Scarecrow, 1971), 130.
42. McKean, *Hague Machine*, 104.   43. Connors, *Cycle of Power*, 88.   44. PPA, 5: 410.   45. Bruce Bliven, Jr., "Will the Witness Step Down?" *New Republic* 95 (June 29, 1938): 11-12; McAlister Coleman, "Hague's Army Falls Back," *Nation* 147 (Nov. 26, 1938): 557-60; Heywood Broun, "Shoot the Works," *New Republic* 93 (Jan. 19, 1938): 7-9; and Jack Alexander, "King Hanky-Panky of Jersey City," *Saturday Evening Post* 213 (Oct. 26, 1940): 9.
46. Ickes, *Secret Diary of Ickes*, 2: 414, 417; and J. Owen Grundy to FDR, Dec. 17, 1938; and James F. Murray to James A. Farley, Jan. 28, 1938, both in Official File 300, FDRL.   47. "Boss," *Time* 35 (May 20, 1940): 20; and "Hague-Washington Axis?" *Time* 36 (Oct. 7, 1940): 18-19.   48. Donahoe, *Private Plans*, 5-6; and Parmet and Hecht, *Never Again*, 30.   49. Thomas J. Fleming, "City in the Shadow," *Saturday Evening Post* 225 (Jan. 6, 1962): 82; and John Kincaid, "Political Success and Policy Failure: The Persistence of Machine Politics in Jersey City" (Ph.D. diss., Temple Univ., 1981), 477.   50. Fleming, "I Am the Law," 44.
51. Connors, *Cycle of Power*, 142-43.   52. Steinberg, *Bosses*, 67-71.   53. Dianne M. Pinderhughes, *Race and Ethnicity in Chicago Politics* (Urbana: Univ. of Illinois Press, 1987), 39-65; and Paul M. Green, "Anton J. Cermak: The Man and His Machine," in *The Mayors: The Chicago Political Tradition*, ed. Paul M. Green and Melvin G. Holli (Carbondale, Ill.: Southern Illinois Univ. Press, 1987), 107-10.   54. Charles E. Merriam, Chicago: *A More Intimate View of Urban Politics* (New York: Macmillan, 1929), 134-36.   55. Green, "Anton J. Cermak," 105; and Biles, *Big City Boss*, 13.
56. Edward R. Kantowicz, *Polish-American Politics in Chicago, 1888-1940* (Chicago: Univ. of Chicago Press, 1975), 209; and John M. Allswang, *A House for All Peoples: Ethnic Politics in Chicago, 1890-1936* (Lexington: Univ. Press of Kentucky, 1971), 156-60.
57. Paul M. Green, "Irish Chicago: The Multi-Ethnic Road to Machine Success," in *Ethnic Chicago*, ed. Melvin G. Holli and Peter A. Jones (Grand Rapids, Mich.: Eerdman's, 1984), 434-39.
58. "Chicago Swaps Bosses," *New Republic* 66 (Apr. 22, 1931): 260-62.   59. "Old Pat," *Newsweek* 22 (Oct. 18, 1943): 62; Lester Freeman, "Tony Cermak, the Political Attila—None Ever Wielded Such Power—None Misused Power More," *Real America* 2 (Oct. 2, 1933): 46-49; and Gottfried, *Boss Cermak*, 184.   60. Green, "Anton J. Cermak," 109.
61. Ibid., 109-10.   62. Harold F. Gosnell and Norman Gill, "An Analysis of the 1932 Presidential Vote in Chicago," *American Politi-*

cal Science Review 29 (Dec. 1935): 967-84; and Duncan MacRae, Jr., and James A. Meldrum, "Critical Elections in Illinois, 1888-1958," *American Political Science Review* 54 (Sept. 1960): 669-83. 63. Ed Kelly to FDR, postmarked Aug. 30, 1932, President's Personal File 1366, FDRL.   64. Gottfried, *Boss Cermak*, 316-21. 65. Thomas Littlewood, *Horner of Illinois* (Evanston, Ill.: Northwestern Univ. Press, 1969), 67-69.

66. Victor Rubin, "You've Gotta Be a Boss," *Collier's* 116 (Sept. 25, 1945): 20, 32-33, 36.   67. Lyman B. Burbank, "Chicago Public Schools and the Depression Years, 1928-1937," *Journal of the Illinois State Historical Society* 64 (Winter 1971): 376.   68. Gene D. Jones, "The Local Political Significance of New Deal Relief Legislation in Chicago, 1933-1940" (Ph.D. diss., Northwestern Univ., 1970), 48-52.   69. Howard O. Hunter, memo to Harry Hopkins, Apr. 5, 1935, Harry Hopkins Papers, FDRL.   70. Gene D. Jones, "Origin of the Alliance," 253-54.

71. Jones, "Local Political Significance," 13.   72. Harry Hopkins, memo to Robert Dunham, Dec. 9, 1936, Harry Hopkins Papers, FDRL.   73. James A. Farley to Ed Kelly, Sept. 17, 1936, DNC Papers, FDRL.   74. St. Clare Drake and Horace R. Clayton, *Black Metropolis: A Study of Negro Life in a Northern City* (New York: Harcourt, Brace, 1945), 353.   75. Nancy J. Weiss, *Farewell to the Party of Lincoln* (Princeton: Princeton Univ. Press, 1983), 206-7.

76. Biles, *Big City Boss*, 92-94.   77. Roger Biles, "'Big Red in Bronzeville': Mayor Ed Kelly Reels in the Black Vote," *Chicago History* 10 (Summer 1981): 99-111.   78. Biles, *Big City Boss*, 186; Rita W. Gordon, "The Change in the Political Alignment of Chicago's Negroes during the New Deal," *Journal of American History*, 56 (Dec. 1969): 598; and Weiss, *Farewell to the Party of Lincoln*, 206-7, 287.   79. Harry Hopkins to FDR, July 11, 1938, Harry Hopkins Papers, FDRL.   80. Carl W. Condit, *Chicago, 1930-1970: Building, Planning, and Urban Technology* (Chicago: Univ. of Chicago Press, 1974), 34; "New Chicago Subway Opens," *Life* 14 (Apr. 19, 1943): 32-33; and Arthur W. MacMahon, *Administration of Federal Work Relief* (Chicago: Public Administration Review, 1941), 199.

81. Biles, *Big City Boss*, 78-79.   82. Jones, "Local Political Significance," 182-90.   83. Ickes, *Secret Diary of Ickes*, 1: 463. 84. Howard O. Hunter to Harry Hopkins, Nov. 21, 1938, Harry Hopkins Papers, FDRL.   85. Ed Kelly to FDR, Apr. 1, 1940, President's Personal File 3166, FDRL; Raymond Clapper, "Third Term for Roosevelt?" *Current History* 50 (Aug. 1939): 13-16; and Frank R. Kent, "Great Corcoran Drive for the Third Term Idea," *Current History* 50 (July 1939): 40.

86. FDR to Ed Kelly, July 31, 1940, President's Personal File 3166, FDRL; and PL, 3: 1045.   87. Arnold R. Hirsch, "Martin H. Kennelly: The Mugwump and the Machine," in *The Mayors: Chi-*

cago Political Tradition (Carbondale: Southern Illinois Univ. Press, 1987), 126. ed. Paul M. Green and Melvin G. Holli.   88. Milton Rakove, *Don't Make No Waves—Don't Back No Losers: An Insider's Analysis of the Daley Machine* (Bloomington: Indiana Univ. Press, 1975), 7-35.   89. John M. Allswang, *Bosses, Machines, and Urban Voters: An American Symbiosis* (New York: Kennikat, 1977), 134-38.   90. Biles, *Big City Boss*, 75-79.

91. Allswang, *Bosses, Machines, and Urban Voters*, 152.
92. Jones, "Local Political Significance," 245. Biles, *Big City Boss*, 88.   93. Lyle W. Dorsett, *The Pendergast Machine* (New York: Oxford Univ. Press, 1968), 103-4.   94. Arthur M. Curtis to Harry Hopkins, May 21, 1936, Harry Hopkins Papers, FDRL.   95. Steinberg, 263.

96. Gene Schmidtlein, "Harry S. Truman and the Pendergast Machine," *Midcontinent American Studies Journal* 7 (Fall 1966): 30; and Franklin D. Mitchell, *Embattled Democracy: Missouri Democratic Politics, 1919-1932* (Columbia: Univ. of Missouri Press, 1968), 254.   97. Marvin H. McIntyre, memo to Harry Hopkins, July 7, 1938; and Lloyd Stark, telegram to FDR, July 13, both in Official File 300, FDRL.   98. Farley, *Behind the Ballots*, 86.   99. Steinberg, *Bosses*, p. 336.   100. Lyle W. Dorsett, "Kansas City and the New Deal," in *The New Deal: The State and Local Levels*, ed. John Braeman, Robert H. Bremner, and David Brody (Columbus: Ohio State Univ. Press, 1975), 411.

101. Ike Dunlap to FDR, July 9, 1931, DNC Papers, FDRL.
102. Erving Young Mitchell, telegram to FDR, Mar. 30, 1932; and Ike Dunlap to FDR, Apr. 2, 1932, both in DNC Papers, FDRL.
103. Ike Dunlap to FDR, May 26, 1932, DNC Papers, FDRL.
104. Harry B. Hawes to FDR, Mar. 29, 1932, DNC Papers, FDRL; and Freidel, *Triumph*, 277.   105. Farley, *Behind the Ballots*, 142-43.

106. Mitchell, *Embattled Democracy*, 156-157.   107. Dorsett, *Pendergast Machine*, 107-8.   108. Richard L. Miller, *Truman: The Rise to Power,* (New York: McGraw-Hill, 1986), 241-42.   109. MacMahon, *Administration of Federal Work Relief,* 199.   110. Timothy K. Evans, "'This Certainly Is Relief!': Matthew S. Murray and Missouri Politics during the Depression," *Bulletin of the Missouri Historical Society* 28 (July 1972): 219-33.

111. Dorsett, *Pendergast Machine*, 110-11.   112. T.J. Edmonds to Harry Hopkins, Feb. 6, 1934, Harry Hopkins Papers, FDRL.
113. Ibid.   114. Dorsett, *Pendergast Machine*, 119-21.
115. Ibid., 310.

116. Ibid.   117. Harry Hopkins, memo to Marvin McIntyre, July 7, 1938; and Lloyd Stark, telegram to FDR, July 13, 1938, both in Official File 300, FDRL.   118. Lloyd Stark to FDR, Aug. 3, 1938, Official File 300, FDRL.   119. Morgenthau Diaries, entry for Apr. 6, 1939, 182-86, FDRL.   120. Steinberg, *Bosses*, 359-60.

121. Thomas H. Greer, *What Roosevelt Thought* (East Lansing: Michigan State Univ. Press, 1958), 117-22.   122. Raymond Moley, "Boss Flynn Can't Lose," *Saturday Evening Post* 213 (Oct. 5, 1940): 111.   123. Roosevelt, *This I Remember,* 66.   124. Erie, *Rainbow's End,* 175; and Roy Peel, *The Political Clubs of New York City* (New York: Putnam 1935), 65.   125. Flynn, *You're the Boss,* 95.
      126. Alfred Connable and Edward Silberfarb, *Tigers of Tammany: Nine Men Who Ran New York* (New York: Holt, Rinehart and Winston, 1967), 268-69.   127. "Al Smith and Tammany Hall," *New Republic* 90 (Oct. 10, 1928): 188-91.   128. Bernard R. Gifford, "New York City and Cosmopolitan Liberalism," *Political Science Quarterly* 93 (1978): 559-84.   129. "The Rise of Tammany," *Colliers* 98 (Dec. 5, 1925): 221; and Joseph McGoldrick, "The New Tammany," *American Mercury* 15 (Sept. 1928): 1-12.
130. Amos Pinchot, "Walter Lippmann II. 'The New Tammany,'" *Nation* 150 (July 12, 1933): 36-37.
      131. William H. Allen, *Al Smith's Tammany Hall: Champion Political Vampire,* (New York: Institute for Public Service, 1928) 334.   132. "Tammany from Smith to Walker," *New Republic* 91 (May 8, 1929): 321.   133. Wallace S. Sayre and Herbert Kaufman, *Governing New York City Politics in the Metropolis* (New York: Sage, 1960), 18; and Jonathan Reider, *Canarsie: The Jews and Italians of Brooklyn against Liberalism* (Cambridge: Harvard Univ. Press, 1985), 51-54.   134. James E. Finegan, *Tammany at Bay* (New York: Dodd, 1933), 122.   135. Allan Nevins, *Herbert H. Lehman and His Era* (New York: Scribner, 1963), 123-132.
      136. Louis Eisenstein and Elliot Rosenberg, *A Stripe of Tammany's Tiger* (New York: Speller, 1966), 76.   137. Ibid., 80.
138. "Hands Off, Mr. Farley!," *Nation* 137 (Oct. 4, 1933): 367.
139. Richard Rovere, "Profile: Ed Flynn," *New Yorker* 21 (Sept. 8, 1945): 30.   140. "Joseph McKee, Reformer?" *Nation* 135 (Dec. 21, 1932): 605.
      141. Theodore J. Lowi, *At the Pleasure of the Mayor: Patronage and Power in New York City, 1898-1958* (New York: Free Press, 1964), 29-46; and Thomas M. Henderson, *Tammany Hall and the New Immigrants: The Progressive Years* (New York: Arno, 1976), 83-87.   142. Ronald H. Bayor, *Neighbors in Conflict: The Irish, Germans, Jews, and Italians of New York City, 1929-1941* (Baltimore: Johns Hopkins Univ. Press, 1978), 127; and Arthur Mann, *La Guardia Comes to Power, 1933* (New York: Lippincott, 1965), 124, 138-46.   143. Erie, *Rainbow's End,* 120.   144. Paul Blanshard, "La Guardia Versus McKee," *Nation* 135 (Oct. 25, 1933): 476; and "Fusion Baits the Tammany Tiger in New York," *Literary Digest* 117 (Sept. 2, 1933): 7.   145. Mann, *La Guardia Comes to Power,* 138-46.
      146. Flynn, *You're the Boss,* 139.   146. Warren Moscow, *Politics in the Empire State,* 254.   148. Van Devander, *Big Bosses,*

313.   149. Charles Garrett, *La Guardia Years*, 255.   150. Edward L. Schapsmeier and Frederick H. Schapsmeier, *Political Parties and Civic Action Groups* (Westport, Conn.: Greenwood, 1981), 38-39.
151. Matthew Josephson, *Sidney Hillman: Statesman of American Labor* (New York: Doubleday, 1952), 394-401; and Max D. Danish, *The World of David Dubinsky* (New York: World, 1957), 97.   152. Schlesinger, *Politics of Upheaval*, 593-95.   153. Moscow, *Politics in the Empire State*, 105.   154. Ibid., 106-7; and Alan Shaffer, *Vito Marcantonio, Radical in Congress* (Syracuse: Syracuse Univ. Press, 1966), 41-97.   155. Hugh A. Bone, "Political Parties in New York City," *American Political Science Review*, 40 (Apr. 1946): 272-82.
156. George Britt, "La Guardia Will Win," *New Republic* 104 (Oct. 20, 1941): 499; and "New York May Ring Own Curfew on La Guardia in November Vote," *Newsweek* 25 (Apr. 2, 1945): 44.
157. Will Chasan, "Can Tammany Come Back?" *Nation* 153 (Apr. 19, 1941): 465-66; and Garrett, *La Guardia Years*, 390.   158. August Heckscher, *When La Guardia Was Mayor* (New York: Norton, 1978), 398; and Robert G. Spivack, "New York's Mayoralty Race," *New Republic* 118 (July 9, 1945): 43.   159. "New York's Revolt against the Tammany Old Guard," *Literary Digest* 117 (Sept. 30, 1938): 8.   160. Flynn, *You're the Boss*, 166-68.
161. Ibid., 164; and Farley, *Farley's Story*, 182-83.   162. Flynn, *You're the Boss*, 165-70.   163. Ibid., 175-76.   164. Dan Tobin to Edward J. Flynn, Nov. 11, 1940, President's Personal File 1180, FDRL; and Hugh A. Bone, *Party Committees and National Politics* (Seattle: Univ. of Washington Press, 1958), 38.   165. Flynn, *You're the Boss*, 177-91.
166. Ickes, *Secret Diary of Ickes* 3: 278-79.   167. Donahoe, *Private Plans*, 185.   168. Ibid., 193-94.   169. Rosenman, *Working with Roosevelt*, 444-51.   170. Fiorello H. La Guardia, "Bosses Are Bunk: A Reply to Ed Flynn," *Atlantic Monthly* 158 (July 1947): 21-24.
171. Samuel J. Eldersveld, "Metropolitan Party Pluralities" 1189-1202.   172. Ladd and Hadley, *Transformations*, 71.
173. Sundquist, *Dynamics of the Party System*, 200-9.   174. Harold F. Gosnell, "The Political Party Versus the Machine," *Annals of the American Academy of Political and Social Science* 169 (Sept. 1933): 26.   175. Gelfand, *Nation of Cities*, 24.
176. Biles, *Big City Boss*, 78-79.   177. Paul B. Beers, *Pennsylvania Politics, Today and Yesterday* (University Park: Pennsylvania State Univ. Press, 1980), 239-66.   178. Funigiello, *Challenge to Urban Liberalism*, 250-57.   179. Harrigan, *Political Change in the Metropolis*, 98-101.   180. Lyle W. Dorsett, "The City Boss and the Reformer: A Reappraisal," *Pacific Northwest Quarterly* 63 (Oct. 1972): 150-54.

181. Van Devander, *Big Bosses*, 313-18.   182. E.E. Schatt-schneider, *Party Government* (New York: Holt, Rinehart and Winston, 1942), 180.   183. John F. Martin, *Civil Rights and the Crisis of Liberalism: The Democratic Party, 1945-1976* (Boulder, Colo.: Westview, 1979), 84-85; and Eric L. McKitrick, "The Study of Corruption," *Political Science Quarterly* 72 (Dec. 1957): 509.
184. Alsop and Kintner, *Men Around the President*, 181.
185. Lyle W. Dorsett, *Franklin D. Roosevelt and the City Bosses* (New York: Kennikat, 1977), 114.
186. Sundquist, *Dynamics of the Party System*, 200-17; and Martin, *Civil Rights*, 47-61.   187. Ross, "Big City Machines and Liberal Voters," 301-2.   188. Ibid., 307.

4 Roosevelt and the Democratic National Committee

1. James A. Farley to FDR, Jan. 30, 1937, James A. Farley Papers, LOC.   2. Mary Dewson to Eleanor Roosevelt, Feb. 23, 1934, DNC Papers, Women's Division; and Daniel J. Tobin, circular letter, Aug. 31, 1932, DNC Papers, FDRL.   3. Howard R. Penniman, *Sait's American Parties and Elections* (New York: Appleton-Century-Crofts, 1948), 330.   4. Chatham, "Role of National Party Chairman," 87.   5. Farley, *Behind the Ballots*, 159-60.
6. Farley, "Passing Out the Patronage," 20-22.   7. Newquist, "Farley and the Politics of Victory," 289.   8. James A. Farley to Louis M. Howe, Sept. 27, 1933, Louis M. Howe Papers, FDRL.
9. Farley to FDR, Jan. 30, 1937, James A. Farley Papers, LOC.
10. Thomas Barclay, "Publicity Division," 68.
11. Michelson, *Ghost Talks*, 16-17.   12. "The Democratic Party," *Fortune* 11 (April 1935): 66-67; and Charles P. Stewart, "Raskob's Management of Democratic Party Viewed as Brilliant," *Democratic Bulletin* (June 1932): 14, 28, LOC.   13. DNC, *Official Report of the Proceedings of the Democratic National Convention, 1936* (Washington, D.C.: DNC 1936), 438, LOC.   14. Dean Kohlkoff, "Frank Comerford Walker," *Franklin D. Roosevelt: His Life and Times*, ed. Otis L. Graham, Jr. (Boston: Hall, 1985), 440.   15. U.S. 77th Cong., 1st sess., Senate, *Hearings of the Special Committee Investigating Campaign Expenditures, 1940*, 8: 692-721.
16. Louise Overacker, *Presidential Campaign Funds* (Boston: Boston Univ. Press, 1946), 15, 32.   17. *Politics, Parties, and Pressure Groups*, 464.   18. Louise Overacker, "Trends in Party Campaign Funds," in *The Future of Government in the United States*, ed. Leonard D. White (Chicago: Univ. of Chicago Press, 1942), 128.
19. Ibid.   20. Freidel, *Ordeal*, 210-211.
21. W. Forbes Morgan to George B. Hills, Aug. 27, 1936, Official File 300, FDRL.   22. Louise Overacker, "Campaign Funds in the Presidential Election of 1936," *American Political Science Review* 31

(1937): 473.   23. Louise Overacker, "Campaign Finance in the
Presidential Election of 1940," *American Political Science Review* 35
(1941): 701.   24. Theodore Cousens, *Politics and Political Organizations in America* (New York: Macmillan, 1942), 440-41.
25. U.S. Statutes, 54, Sec.(13), 608(b).
    26. Overacker, "Trends in Party Campaign Funds," 127-28.
27. Chatham, "Role of National Party Chairman," 131.   28. Ronald Stinnett, *Democrats, Dinners, and Dollars* (Ames, Iowa: Iowa
State Univ. Press, 1967), 134-35.   29. Key, *Politics, Parties, and
Pressure Groups,* 466.   30. DNC, *Official Report of the Proceedings of the Democratic National Convention, 1940* (Washington,
D.C.: DNC, 1940), 282, LOC.
    31. PPA, 6: 121.   32. Ibid., 8: 167.   33. Overacker, *Presiden-
tial Campaign Funds,* 59.   34. Louise Overacker, "Labor's Political Contributions," *Political Science Quarterly* 54 (1939): 59.
35. Douglas and Hackman, "Fair Labor Standards Act," 491-515.
    36. White House press release, Aug. 26, 1940, President's Per-
sonal File 1898, FDRL.   37. Fay Calkin, *The CIO and the Democratic Party* (Chicago: Univ. of Chicago Press, 1952), 1-11; and
Josephson, *Sidney Hillman,* 394-452.   38. Henderson, "The Democratic National Committee," 267-73.   39. Daniel J. Tobin circular letter, Aug. 31, 1932, DNC Papers, FDRL.   40. Bone, *Party
Committees and National Politics,* 54.
    41. Joseph L. Johnson to Louis M. Howe, July 6, 1933, Official
File 93, FDRL; and Weiss, *Farewell to the Party of Lincoln,* 14.
42. White House press release, Aug. 26, 1940, Official File 300,
FDRL.   43. "The Favored Party Set Up," memo, Jan. 7, 1939,
Mary Dewson Papers, FDRL.   44. Paul C. Taylor, "Mary Williams
Dewson," in *Notable American Women: The Modern Period,* ed.
Barbara Sicherman and Carol Hurd Green (Cambridge: Harvard
Univ. Press, 1980), 188-89.   45. Mary Dewson to FDR, May 29,
1935, Official File 300, FDRL.
    46. Ware, *Beyond Suffrage,* 70.   47. Mary Dewson to Demo-
cratic committeemen, Feb. 3, 1934, Official File 300, FDRL.
48. "What the Women Could and Should Do for the Democratic
Party," pamphlet, Jan. 1, 1935, DNC Papers, Women's Division,
FDRL.   49. "Suggested Programs for Democratic Women's Organizations," chart, 1936, Mary Dewson Papers, FDRL.   50. Susan Ware, *Partner and I* (New Haven: Yale Univ. Press, 1987), 221.
    51. Mary Dewson to Charles Michelson, July 17, 1936, Official
File 300, FDRL.   52. Mary Dewson to Charles Michelson, July 7,
1936, DNC Papers, Women's Division, FDRL.   53. Dorothy McAlister to Bernard Baruch, Dec. 16, 1938, Eleanor Roosevelt Papers,
FDRL.   54. Ware, *Partner and I,* 199.   55. Taylor, "Dewson,"
190.
    56. Mary Dewson to Caroline O'Day, Mar. 15, 1934, DNC Papers,
Women's Division, FDRL.   57. Taylor, "Dewson," 190.

58. "The Favored State Party Set Up for Democratic Women," chart, 1938, President's Personal File 603, FDRL. 59. Mary Dewson to Caroline O'Day, Mar. 15, 1934, DNC Papers, Women's Division, FDRL. 60. Ware, *Partner and I*, 204.
61. *New York Times*, June 25, 1936, 1. 62. Ware, *Beyond Suffrage*, 81. 63. Taylor, "Dewson," 190. 64. Mary Dewson to FDR, Apr. 18, 1936, Official File 300, FDRL. 65. Sitkoff, *New Deal for Blacks*, 84-99.
66. Walter White to Jacob Billikopf, Oct. 9, 1940, Official File 2538, FDRL; and George Gallup, *The Gallup Poll: Public Opinion, 1935-1971* 1 (New York: Random, 1972), 207. 67. Robert B. Ennis to James A. Farley, Sept. 30, 1936, Official File 300; and FDR, memo to James A. Farley, March 2, 1936, President's Personal File 6714; both in FDRL. 68. Joseph L. Johnson to Louis M. Howe, July 6, 1933, Official File 93, FDRL. 69. Key, *Politics, Parties and Pressure Groups*, 137. 70. Donald R. McCoy, "The Good Neighbor League and the Presidential Campaign," *Western Political Quarterly* 13 (Dec. 1960): 1011; and Emmett Cunningham to Robert E. Hannegan, Dec. 13, 1944, DNC Papers, FDRL.
71. Daniel J. Tobin, circular letter, Aug. 31, 1932, DNC Papers, FDRL. 72. Labor's Non-Partisan League, "He Fights for Labor: The Position of Franklin D. Roosevelt on Labor Problems," booklet, 1936, FDRL. 73. Newquist, "Farley and the Politics of Victory," 651. 74. Clipping, "Hillman Assails Record Dewey," *New York Times*, Sept. 10, 1944, Mary Dewson Pamphlet Collection, FDRL. 75. White House press release, Aug. 26, 1940, President's Personal File 1898, FDRL.
76. Richard Roper, form letter to political science professors, Oct. 5, 1932, DNC Papers, FDRL. 77. Richard Roper to Marvin McIntyre, Oct. 17, 1933, President's Personal File 236, FDRL.
78. Richard Roper, speech to Young People's Democratic League of Illinois, Mar. 3, 1934, President's Personal File 236, FDRL.
79. FDR to Pitt Tyson Maner, Aug. 8, 1939, President's Personal File 236, FDRL. 80. PPA, 8: 437.
81. Joseph J. Yosko to Dorothy Vredenburg, Sept. 8, 1944, Official File 300, FDRL. 82. Jesse Macy, *Party Organizations and Machinery* (London: T. Fisher Unwin, 1905), 80. 83. Farley, radio address, Nov. 2, 1936, James A. Farley Papers, FDRL.
84. Mary Dewson to John T. Casey, Jan. 15, 1938, Mary Dewson Papers, FDRL. 85. John Syrett, "Jim Farley and Carter Glass: Allies against a Third Term," *Prologue* 15 (Summer 1983): 91.
86. James A. Farley, speech to American Political Science Association, "History and Function of the Democratic National Committee," Dec. 29, 1933, Official File 300, FDRL. 87. Farley, *Jim Farley's Story*, 146-47. 88. James A. Farley, "The Big Build-Up 'Why I Broke with Roosevelt,' III," *Collier's* 120 (July 5, 1947):

16.   89. Moley, "Boss Flynn Can't Lose," 27, 111-18.   90. Davis, *New York Years*, 201-2.
91. Henry F. Pringle, "Roosevelt's Flynn," *Collier's* 111 (Oct. 12, 1940): 46.   92. Eisenstein and Rosenberg, *A Stripe of Tammany's Tiger*, 76-80.   93. Schapsmeier and Schapsmeier, *Political Parties and Civic Action Groups*, 38-39.   94. Roosevelt, *This I Remember*, 66.   95. Moley, "Boss Flynn Can't Lose," 117; and Flynn, *You're the Boss*, 164-68.
96. Pringle, "Roosevelt's Flynn," 46.   97. Flynn, *You're the Boss*, 175-76.   98. Moley, "Boss Flynn Can't Lose," 117.
99. Flynn, *You're the Boss*, 176-79.   100. David Berenstein to Edward J. Flynn, Feb. 4, 1941, DNC Papers, FDRL.
101. Dorsett, *Roosevelt and the City Bosses*, 67-68.   102. Rosenman, *Working with Roosevelt*, 444-51.   103. Robert Vexler, *Vice-Presidents and Cabinet Members* 2 (New York: Oceana, 1975), 600.   104. "Analysis of Letters from County Chairmen in Answer to Form Letter," booklet, Jan. 15, 1944, DNC Papers, FDRL.
105. Oscar R. Erving, telegram to FDR, Apr. 16, 1944, Official File 299, FDRL.
106. Robert E. Hannegan to Democratic state chairman, Nov. 20, 1944, DNC Papers, FDRL.   107. Henderson, "Democratic National Committee," 266; and Newquist, "Farley and the Politics of Victory," 439.   108. James Irwin to Robert E. Hannegan, Nov. 27, 1944; and Emmett Cunningham to Hannegan, Dec. 13, 1944, both in DNC Papers, FDRL.

5 The Formation of an Electoral Coalition: 1932-1936

1. John K. Galbraith, *The Great Crash, 1929* (Boston: Houghton Mifflin, 1961), 112; and Rollins, *Roosevelt and Howe*, 233.   2. Rollins, *Roosevelt and Howe*, 311-15.   3. Geoffrey C. Ward, *A First-Class Temperament: The Emergence of Franklin Roosevelt* (New York: Harper & Row, 1989), 786-89; and Freidel, *F.D.R. and the South*, 32.   4. James H. Farley, "Selling Roosevelt to the Party," *American Magazine* 111 (Aug. 1938): 9-11.   5. Joseph Guffey to Louis Howe, Dec. 3, 1931; and James M. Curley to FDR, Sept. 11, 1931, FDR Papers: 1929-1932, both in FDRL.
6. Farley, *Behind the Ballots*, 69-72.   7. PL, 3: 151-52.
8. Carlson, "Franklin Roosevelt's Fight," 71-93.   9. Farley, "Selling Roosevelt to the Party," 94-96; and L.A. Manning, Jr., to FDR, Jan. 18, 1930; W.H. Kittrell, Jr., to FDR, Jan. 4, 1930; and Anne L. Madden to FDR, Jan. 14, 1930, all in Louis M. Howe Papers, FDRL.   10. Louis M. Howe to Cordell Hull, Dec. 1, 1931, DNC Papers, FDRL.
11. PL, 3: 109.   12. Farley, *Behind the Ballots*, 106, 181-82.
13. Bellush, *Roosevelt as Governor of New York*, 50-112; and PPA, 1:

135-43.   14. PPA, 1: 693-711, 812-19.   15. Patterson, *Congressional Conservatism*, 6.
16. Wheeler, *Yankee from the West*, 250-51.   17. James T. Patterson, "The New Deal in the West," *Pacific Historical Review* 38 (1969): 327; and Brinkley, "New Deal and Southern Politics," 110-11.   18. Roy V. Peel and Thomas C. Donnelly, *The 1932 Campaign: An Analysis* (New York: Farrar & Rinehart, 1935), 60-61.
19. Franklin D. Roosevelt, *Government—Not Politics* (New York: Stratford, 1932), 20-79.   20. Lippmann, *Interpretations*, 262; and Leuchtenburg, *Roosevelt and the New Deal*, 9-12.
21. Kristi Andersen, *Creation of a Democratic Majority*, 72.
22. United States Bureau of the Census, *Historical Statistics of the United States, 1789-1945*, 293.   23. DNC, *The Democratic Bulletin* (June 1932), 16, LOC; and Burner, *Politics of Provincialism*, 248.   24. George Q. Flynn, *American Catholics and the Roosevelt Presidency, 1932-1936* (Lexington: Univ. Press of Kentucky, 1968), 4-12; and Hand, "Smith, Roosevelt, and the New Deal," 361-72.
25. PL, 3: 248-49.
26. Ibid, 227-33; George Wolfskill, *The Revolt of the Conservatives: A History of the American Liberty League, 1934-1940* (Boston: Houghton Mifflin, 1962), 7-10.   27. Davis, *New York Years*, 244-45.   28. Burner, *Politics of Provincialism*, 187; and Overacker, *Presidential Campaign Funds*, 15.   29. Lubell, *Future of American Politics*, 49.   30. FDR to James M. Curley, Apr. 28, 1932, President's Personal File 1154, FDRL; and Peel and Donnelly, *1932 Campaign*, 75.
31. Ted Morgan, *FDR: A Biography* (New York: Simon & Schuster, 1985), 328.   32. DNC, *Official Report, 1932*, 10-11, LOC.
33. Wheeler, *Yankee from the West*, 302-4; Betty Glad, *Key Pittman: The Tragedy of a Senate Insider* (New York: Columbia Univ. Press, 1986), 210-11; and Josephine G. O'Keane, *Thomas J. Walsh: A Senator from Montana* (Francestown, N.H.: Marshall Jones, 1955), 212.   34. Farley, *Behind the Ballots*, 103-6.   35. DNC, *Official Report, 1932*, 16-17, LOC.
36. Flynn, *American Catholics*, 109.   37. Peel and Donnelly, *1932 Campaign*, 32-40.   38. Oswald G. Vallard, editorial, *Nation* 34 (Apr. 1932), 414.   39. Frank Freidel, "Election of 1932," in *History of American Presidential Elections: 1789-1968* 3, ed. Arthur M. Schlesinger, Jr. (New York: Chelsea House Publishers, 1971), 2724.   40. Peel and Donnelly, *1932 Campaign*, 101-103.
41. *New York Times*, June 18, 26, 27, 29, 1932.   42. Farley, *Behind the Ballots*, 116-19.   43. Key, *Politics, Parties, and Pressure Groups*, 412-413.   44. DNC, *Official Report, 1932*, 315-20.   45. Farley, *Behind the Ballots*, 147-51.
46. DNC, *Official Report of the Proceedings of the Democratic National Convention, 1932*, 324-25; and *New York Times*, July 2, 1932.   47. Kirk H. Porter and Donald B. Johnson, *National Party*

Platforms, 1840-1964 (Urbana: Univ. of Illinois Press), 331.
48. E. Francis Brown, "The Presidential Campaign," *Current History* 37 (Nov. 1932): 197-98; Ernest K. Lindley, *The Roosevelt Revolution: First Phase* (New York: Viking Press, 1933), 7; and PPA, 1: 693-741.   49. Moley, *After Seven Years,* 16-48; and PPA, 1: 684-710, 727-94.   50. PPA, 1: 648.
51. Ibid., 648-49.   52. Ibid, 649.   53. Paul Y. Anderson, "Roosevelt Woos the Progressives: Insurgency Goes Democratic," *Nation* 135 (Oct. 12, 1932): 331; Marty Hamilton, "Bull Moose Plays an Encore: Hiram Johnson and the Presidential Campaign of 1932," *California Historical Society Quarterly* 10 (Sept. 1962): 211-21; and *New York Times,* Sept. 24, 1932, 1.   54. Richard Lowitt, *George W. Norris: The Triumph of a Progressive, 1933-1944* (Urbana: Univ. of Illinois Press, 1978), 4-5.   55. PPA, 1: 171-79.
56. David Fellman, "The Liberalism of Senator Norris," *American Political Science Review* 40 (Feb. 1946), 27-51; and Alfred Lief, *Democracy's Norris* (New York: Stackpole, 1939), 388-94.
57. Brown, "Presidential Campaign," 197; and Freidel, "Election of 1932," 2734.   58. PPA, 1: 639; and John K. Galbraith, "On the Economics of F.D.R.; What a President Ought to Know," *Commentary* 22 (Aug. 1956): 174.   59. Elliot A. Rosen, "Intranationalism vs. Internationalism: The Interregnum Struggle for the Sanctity of the New Deal," *Political Science Quarterly* 81 (June 1966), 274-97; and Rosen, *Hoover, Roosevelt, Brains Trust,* 275-303.   60. PPA, 1: 643; and Moley, *After Seven Years,* 23-24.
61. PPA, 1: 742-756.   62. Ibid., 755.   63. Brown, "Presidential Campaign," 197.   64. Gosnell, *Champion Campaigner,* 132.   65. Thomas Finn to National Progressive League for Franklin D. Roosevelt, Oct. 14, 1932, DNC Papers, FDRL; Peel and Donnelly, *1932 Campaign,* 217-22; and Andersen, *Creation of a Democratic Majority,* 28.
66. Shuff, "Partisan Realignment," 167; and Weiss, *Farewell to the Party of Lincoln,* 29-33.   67. William F. Ogburn and Estelle Hill, "Income Classes and the Roosevelt Vote in 1932," *Political Science Quarterly* 50 (June 1935): 186-93.   68. Peel and Donnelly, *1932 Campaign,* 220.   69. Rosen, *Hoover, Roosevelt, Brains Trust,* 120-40; and Newquist, "Farley and the Politics of Victory," 39-40.
70. Lindley, *Roosevelt Revolution,* 10.
71. FDR to Edward House, Mar. 10, 1934, President's Personal File 222; and Emily Newell Blair to Democratic Women's Clubs, Sept. 12, 1932, DNC Papers, both in FDRL.   72. Rosen, *Hoover, Roosevelt, Brains Trust,* 303-4.   73. Newquist, "Farley and the Politics of Victory," 305-8.   74. PPA, 1: 859; and PL, 3: 309-10.
75. FDR to J. Francis McDermott, Dec. 24, 1934, President's Personal File 2123, FDRL.
76. William E. Leuchtenburg, "Franklin D. Roosevelt: The First Modern President," in *Leadership in the Modern Presidency,* ed.

Fred Greenstein (Cambridge: Harvard Univ. Press, 1988), 16-21.
77. Leo Rosten, *The Washington Correspondents* (New York: Harcourt, Brace, 1937), 70; and Frisch, *Contribution of the New Deal,* 49.   78. Basil Rauch, *History of the New Deal, 1933-1938* (New York: Creative Age, 1944), 7-80.   79. Pete Daniel, "The New Deal, Southern Agriculture, and Economic Change," in *The New Deal and the South,* ed. James C. Cobb and Michael V. Namurato (Jackson: Univ. Press of Mississippi, 1984), 40-55; Leonard Arrington, "The New Deal in the West: A Preliminary Statistical Inquiry," *Pacific Historical Review* 38 (1969): 311-16; and Donald C. Swain, "The National Park Service and the New Deal, 1933-1940," *Pacific Historical Review* 41 (1972): 312-32.   80. John M. Allswang, *The New Deal and American Politics: A Study in Political Change* (New York: Wiley & Sons, 1978), 48-52.
81. Sundquist, *Dynamics of the Party System,* 112-13.
82. Ronald A. Mulder, *The Insurgent Progressives in the United States Senate and the New Deal, 1933-1939* (New York: Garland, 1979), 1-34.   83. Patterson, "New Deal in the West," 324-27.
84. *History of American Presidential Elections* 3: 2242, 2581.
85. Michael P. Malone, "The Montana New Dealers," in *The New Deal: The State and Local Levels,* ed. John Braeman, Robert H. Bremner, and David Brody (Columbus: Ohio State Univ. Press, 1975), 249-51; Royce D. Delmatier, "The Rebirth of the Democratic Party in California, 1928-1938" (Ph.D. diss., Univ. of California at Berkeley, 1955), 235-40; and Alan Brinkley, *Voices of Protest* (New York: Vintage, 1982), 226-30.
86. Reeves, "Politics of Public Works," 88-89; and Steve Early, memo to FDR, July 18, 1936, President's Personal File, FDRL.
87. James A. Farley to FDR, Nov. 3, 1933, President's Personal File 289; William Hynes to James A. Farley, Sept. 8, 1936, DNC Papers; and James J. Law to Farley, Sept. 15, 1936, DNC Papers, all in FDRL.   88. Fred Schilpin to Marvin McIntyre, Oct. 6, 1936, Official File 300, FDRL; and Schlesinger, *Politics of Upheaval,* 102-8.
89. Mrs. Henry B. Wiesner to James A. Farley, Oct. 16, 1934, Official File 300, FDRL.   90. Schapsmeier and Schapsmeier, *Political Parties and Civic Action Groups,* 38-39; and PPA, 5: 357.
91. Frisch, *Contribution of the New Deal,* 74.   92. Samuel J. Astorino, "The Decline of the Republican Dynasty in Pennsylvania, 1929-34" (Ph.D. diss., Univ. of Pittsburgh, 1963), 309.   93. Joseph F. Guffey, *Seventy Years on the Red-Fire Wagon* (Pittsburgh: privately printed, 1952), 65-75; Thomas J. Donaghy, *Keystone Democrat: David Lawrence Remembered* (New York: Vantage Press, 1986), 37-50; and *New York Times,* Apr. 6, 1936, 2, and June 22, 1936, 3.   94. Edward F. Cooke and Edward G. Janosik, *Pennsylvania Politics,* rev. ed. (New York: Holt, Rinehart, Winston, 1965), 10-11.   95. Guffey, *Seventy Years on the Red-Fire Wagon,* Guffey, 80.

96. Richard C. Keller, *Pennsylvania's Little New Deal* (New York: Garland, 1982), 157-201.   97. Cooke and Janosik, *Pennsylvania Politics*, 13.   98. Delmatier, "Rebirth of Democratic Party," 235-40; and Robert E. Burke, *Olson's New Deal for California* (Berkeley: Univ. of California Press, 1953), 4-5.   99. Andersen, *Creation of a Democratic Majority*, 33-38.   100. Gosnell, *Champion Campaigner*, 150.

101. Wolfskill, *Revolt of Conservatives*, 11-97; and Wallace S. Sayre, "Political Ground-Swell," *Current History* 44 (June 1936): 59.   102. Brinkley, *Voices of Protest*, 243-61; and "Doctor Townsend," *Current History* 45 (Oct. 1936): 86-89; and Sayre, "Political Ground-Swell," 53-60.   103. Michelson, *The Ghost Talks*, 44-45; Gallup, *Gallup Poll* 1, 10-15; and William E. Leuchtenburg, "Election of 1936," *History of American Presidential Elections, 1789-1968*, 3: 2809-10.   104. Rosenman, *Working with Roosevelt*, 98-99.

105. Good Neighbor League booklet, Dr. Charles Stezle, 1936, Mary Dewson Pamphlet Collection, FDRL; Stanley High, *Roosevelt—and Then?* (New York: Harper & Brothers, 1937); and PL, 3: 574-75.

106. Labor's Non-Partisan League, Aug. 1, 1936, Official File 407, FDRL.   107. David J. Stern to FDR, Jan. 11, 1936, President's Personal File 1039, FDRL.   108. PPA, 5: 230-36, 534-36, 540-44.   109. Greer, *What Roosevelt Thought*, 208.   110. PPA, 5: 390.

111. Ibid., 504.   112. Ibid., 211-12.   113. Ibid., 557-58. 114. Ibid., 240-43, 486, and 557.   115. Ibid., 5: 233.

116. Ibid, 236.   117. Sidney M. Milkis, "The New Deal, Administrative Reform, and the Transcendence of Partisan Politics," *Administration & Society* 18 (Feb. 1987): 460.   118. Leuchtenburg, "Election of 1936," 2834.   119. Sitkoff, *New Deal for Blacks*, 93.   120. "Has the Roosevelt New Deal Helped the Negro Citizen?" Aug. 24, 1936, report, Official File 93, FDRL.

121. Paul T. David, Ralph M. Goldman, and Richard C. Bain, *The Politics of National Party Conventions* (Washington, D.C.: Brookings Institution, 1960), 209-12.   122. David et al., *Politics of Conventions*, 211.   123. Harold F. Bass, Jr., "Presidential Party Leadership and Party Reform: Franklin D. Roosevelt and the Abrogation of the Two-Thirds Rule," paper delivered at Annual Meeting of Southern Political Science Association, Nov. 7-9, 1985, Nashville, Tennessee, 18.   124. Patterson, *Congressional Conservatism and the New Deal*, p. 257.   125. Bass, "Party Leadership and Party Reform," 21.

126. Ibid.   127. Schlesinger, *Politics of Upheaval*, 581. 128. Leuchtenburg, "Election of 1936," 2829-30.   129. Key, *Politics, Parties, and Pressure Groups*, 413.   130. Schlesinger, *Politics of Upheaval*, 581.

131. Bass, "Party Leadership and Party Reform," 23. 132. Richard C. Bain and Judith H. Parris, *Convention Decisions*

and Voting Records (Washington, D.C.: Brookings Institution, 1973), 249; and Heard, Two-Party South, 117.   133. Samuel H. Beer, "In Search of a New Public Philosophy," The New American Political System, ed. Anthony King (Washington, D.C.: American Enterprise Institute, 1980), 10.   134. Ibid., 11.   135. Beer, "Liberalism and the National Idea," Public Interest, no. 5 (Fall 1966): 70-74.

136. Beer, "In Search of a New Public Philosophy," 10-13; and Beer, "Liberalism and the National Idea," 75-77.   137. Edward G. Benson and Paul Perry, "Analysis of Democratic-Republican Strength by Population Groups," Public Opinion Quarterly 4 (Sept. 1940): 464-73; and William F. Ogburn and Lolagene C. Coombs, "The Economic Factor in the Roosevelt Elections," American Political Science Review 34 (Aug. 1940): 719.   138. RNC, Official Proceedings of the Twenty-first Republican National Convention (New York: Tenny, 1936), 137, LOC; and New York Times, Feb. 6, 1936, 2, Mar. 6, 1936, 15.   139. Leuchtenburg, "Election of 1936," 2811-12.   140. RNC, Official Proceedings of Twenty-first Convention, 141-48.

141. Ibid., 146.   142. Leuchtenburg, "Election of 1936," 2812.   143. Donald R. McCoy, Landon of Kansas (Lincoln: Univ. of Nebraska Press, 1966), 14-17, 32.   144. Mulder, Insurgent Progressives in the Senate, 141-42.   145. Leo T. Crowley to Marvin H. McIntyre, Sept. 8, 1936, President's Personal File 6659, FDRL; and New York Times, Sept. 28, 1936, FDRL.

146. Leuchtenburg, "Election of 1936," 2813.   147. Sundquist, Dynamics of the Party System, 198.   148. Gosnell, Champion Campaigner, 157-58.   149. Leuchtenburg, Roosevelt and the New Deal, 190.   150. Shuff, "Partisan Realignment," 175; and Edgar E. Robinson, They Voted for Roosevelt: The Presidential Vote, 1932-1944 (Stanford: Stanford Univ. Press, 1947), 22, 56.

151.   Andersen, Creation of a Democratic Majority, 172. 152. Ladd and Hadley, Transformations, 51-53.   153. Ibid., 71.   154. Ibid.   155. Weiss, Farewell to the Party of Lincoln, 204-7; and Fuchs, "American Jews," 386.

156. Lubell, Future of American Politics, 49.   157. Goldman, Search for Consensus, 117.

6 The Purge Campaigns of 1938

1. Altman, "First Session of the Seventy-fifth Congress," 1071-93; and David L. Porter, Congress and the Waning of the New Deal (New York: Kennikat, 1980), 136.   2. J. Frederick Essary, "The Split in the Democratic Party," Atlantic Monthly 160 (Dec. 1937): 752-55.   3. "G.O.P. Picnic," Newsweek 12 (Sept. 5, 1938): 9-10. 4. PPA, 7: 37-44, and 512-20.   5. Ibid., xxx.

6. Ibid., xxxi.   7. Ibid., 8: 437.   8. FDR to Eleanor Roose-

214

Notes to Pages 130-136

velt, July 19, 1936, President's Personal File 3; and FDR to Key Pittman, Aug. 25, 1934, President's Personal File 745, both in FDRL. 9. Gosnell, *Champion Campaigner,* 224-25. 10. John E. Hopper, "The Purge, Franklin D. Roosevelt and the 1938 Democratic Nomination" (Ph.D. diss., Univ. of Chicago 1966), 43; and James Roosevelt to FDR, Dec. 27, 1937, President's Personal File 1820, FDRL. 11. Alva Johnston, "Jimmy's Got It," *Saturday Evening Post,* 111 (July 2, 1938): 8-9; "Hopkins' Intervention in Iowa Sets Off Washington Explosion," *Newsweek* 11 (June 6, 1938): 9-10; "Roosevelt Applying Pressure on Farley to Join in Purge," *Newsweek* 12 (Sept. 5, 1938): 7-8; and Walter Davenport, "It Seems There Were Two Irishmen," *Collier's* 102, (Sept. 10, 1938): 76-79. 12. Alsop and Kintner, *Men Around the President,* 8. 13. J.B. Shannon, "Presidential Politics in the South—1938, I," *Journal of Politics* 1 (Apr. 1939): 150-51. 14. Patterson, *Congressional Conservatism,* 266. 15. Max Lerner, "Mr. Roosevelt: Ringmaster," *Nation* 146 (Jan. 15, 1938): 63-64.

16. Ickes, *Secret Diary of Ickes,* 2: 262. 17. Bibb Graves to FDR, Jan. 4, 1938, Official File 300, FDRL. 18. Shannon, "Presidential Politics in the South," 150. 19. Alexander Heard and Donald S. Strong, *Southern Primaries and Elections, 1920-1949* (New York: Books for Libraries, 1950), 17. 20. Ibid.

21. Pepper, *Pepper,* 69-72. 22. *New York Times,* May 8, 1938, 8; and Ickes, *Secret Diary of Ickes,* 2: 342. 23. Pepper, *Pepper,* 68. 24. Mark Wilcox to FDR, Jan. 4, 1938, Official File 300, FDRL. 25. *Time* 32 (May 2, 1938), 9.

26. Ibid. 27. Pepper, *Pepper,* 69. 28. Merlin G. Cox, "David Sholtz: New Deal Governor of Florida," *Florida Historical Quarterly* 43 (Oct. 1964): 142-52. 29. Brinkley, "New Deal and Southern Politics," 104. 30. *Time* 32 (May 2, 1938): 10.

31. Pepper, *Pepper,* 73. 32. *New York Times,* Feb. 11, 1938, 5. 33. James Roosevelt to FDR, Dec. 27, 1937, President's Personal File 1820, FDRL. 34. Pepper, *Pepper,* 52-59. 35. *Time* 32 (May 2, 1938): 12.

36. Heard and Strong, *Southern Primaries,* 47. 37. *Newsweek* 11 (Mar. 16, 1938): 9; and *Time* 32 (May 16, 1938): 14. 38. Shannon, "Presidential Politics in the South, I," 152. 39. Ickes *Secret Diary of Ickes,* 2: 493-94. 40. *New York Times,* Jan. 23, 1938, 4, 10. 41. Ibid., Mar. 2, 1938, 6, Mar. 10, 1938, 6. 42. *Time* 32 (May 30, 1938): 13. 43. *New York Times,* Jan. 23, 1938, 10, Mar. 13, 1938, 13. 44. *New York Times,* May 20, 1938, 4; Charles H. Martin to James A. Farley, Jan. 3, 1938; and Ray L. Jenkins to Farley, Dec. 19, 1938, both in DNC Papers, FDRL. 45. Lowitt, *George W. Norris,* 203; and *New York Times,* May 16, 1938, 2, May 17, 1938, 18.

46. *Time* 32 (Mar. 30, 1938): 13. 47. Ickes *Secret Diary of Ickes,* 2: 500. 48. Roosevelt, *Complete Presidential Press Con-*

ferences, 11: 323, 425, 430.   49. Hopper, "Purge, Roosevelt and 1938 Nomination," 10-11.   50. *New York Times,* May 26, 1938, 5.   51. *Time* 32 (June 13, 1938): 16.   52. Patterson, *Congressional Conservatism,* 272.   53. Paul Y. Anderson, "Congressional Fade-out," *Nation* 146 (June 18, 1938): 690-91.   54. *New York Times,* June 1, 1938, 1, June 3, 1938, 2.   55. *Time* 32 (June 13, 1938): 16.   56. *New York Times,* June 8, 1938, 1.   57. Ferner Nuhn, "Iowa Speaks Up," *New Republic* 85 (July 6, 1938): 252-53; *New York Times,* June 4, 1938, 1; and FDR to Harold Ickes, Aug. 17, 1938, President's Personal File 3650, FDRL.   58. *New York Times,* June 1, 1938, 4, June 3, 1938, 20.   59. Raymond Clapper, "Roosevelt Tries the Primaries," *Current History* 49 (Oct. 1938): 18-19.   60. PPA, 7: 391.   61. Ibid., 399.   62. PPA, 7: 438.   63. PL, 3: 765; and Davis, *Alben W. Barkley: Majority Leader,* 54-55.   64. *New York Times,* Feb. 13, 1938, 4, 3.   65. Davis, *Alben W. Barkley,* 36.   66. *New York Times,* July 22, 1937, 3.   67. *New York Times,* July 22, 1937, 3.   68. Libbey, *Dear Alben,* 9-16.   69. FDR, memo to Steve Early, Apr. 6, 1938, President's Personal File 3458, FDRL; and Davis, *Alben W. Barkley,* 58.   70. *New York Times,* May 26, 1938, 4.

71. J.M. McIntire to Marvin McIntyre, Feb. 21, 1938; and Charles R. Mills to Marvin McIntyre, Jan. 30, 1938, both in Official File 300, FDRL.   72. J.B. Shannon, "'Happy' Chandler: A Kentucky Epic," *The American Politician,* ed. John T. Salter (Chapel Hill: Univ. of North Carolina Press, 1938), 188-89.   73. George T. Blakey, *Hard Times and New Deal in Kentucky, 1929-1939* (Lexington: Univ. Press of Kentucky, 1986), 176-77.   74. Robert J. Leupold, "The Kentucky WPA: Relief and Politics, May-November 1935," *Filson Club History Quarterly* 149 (Apr. 1975): 160-61.   75. James C. Klotter and John W. Muir, "Boss Ben Johnson, the Highway Commission, and Kentucky Politics, 1927-1937," *Register of the Kentucky Historical Society* 84 (Winter 1986): 45.

76. Barkley, *That Reminds Me,* 163-64.   77. Blakey, *Hard Times and New Deal,* 179.   78. Barkley, *That Reminds Me,* 164.   79. Ibid., 165; and *Time* 32 (July 18, 1938): 7.   80. Walter Davenport, "Happy Couldn't Wait," *Collier's* 102 (July 16, 1938): 12-13, 49-51; and *Time* 32 (Aug. 1, 1938): 12.

81. Patterson, *New Deal and the States,* 150.   82. Blakey, *Hard Times and New Deal,* 180-81.   83. *Time* 32 (Aug. 1, 1938): 11.   84. Ickes *Secret Diary of Ickes,* 2: 342.   85. Shannon, "Presidential Politics in the South, I," 161.

86. *Congressional Record,* 75th Cong., 1st sess., 1937, 8694.   87. Charles R. Mills to Marvin McIntyre, Jan. 30, 1938, Official File 300, FDRL.   88. Barkley, *That Reminds Me,* 162.   89. Marvin McIntyre to FDR, Mar. 8, 1938, President's Personal File 6222, FDRL; and Hopper, "Purge, Roosevelt and 1938 Nomination,"

101-4.   90. Ickes *Secret Diary of Ickes,* 2: 328; and *New York Times,* Feb. 13, 1938, 4, 3.
91. Weiss, *Farewell to the Party of Lincoln,* 44; and William J. Thompkins to Marvin H. McIntyre, July 23, 1938, Official File 54, FDRL.   92. Libbey, *Dear Alben,* 67, 76-80.   93. *New York Times,* May 26, 1938, 4.   94. Ibid., May 27, 1938, 6.   95. Thomas L. Stokes, *Chip off My Shoulder* (Princeton, N.J.: Princeton Univ. Press, 1940), 534-36.
96. *New York Times,* July 1, 1938, 6; Davis, *Alben W. Barkley,* 62; and Sherwood, *Roosevelt and Hopkins,* 98.   97. *Congressional Record,* 75th Cong., 3rd sess., 1938, 7996.   98. *New York Times,* July 16, 1938, 12.   99. J.M. McIntire to Marvin McIntyre, Feb. 21, 1938, Official 300, FDRL.   100. *New York Times,* Aug. 1, 1938, FDRL.
101. PPA, 7: 438.   102. *Time* 32 (Aug. 8, 1938): 11.
103. *New York Times,* July 27, 1938, 1.   104. *Time* 32 (Aug. 8, 1938): 11.   105. Shannon, "Presidential Politics in the South, I," 168-69.
106. Barkley, *That Reminds Me,* 162; and Malcolm E. Jewell, *Kentucky Votes: Presidential Elections, 1952-1960; U.S. Senate Primary and General, 1920-1960* 1 (Lexington: Univ. of Kentucky Press, 1963): 30-31.   107. *New York Times,* Aug. 1, 1938, 2.
108. John H. Hatcher, "Alben Barkley, Politics in Relief and the Hatch Act," *Filson Club Historical Quarterly* 40 (July 1966): 249-63; Stokes, *Chip off My Shoulder,* 534-39; and U.S. Senate, *Report of the Special Committee to Investigate Senatorial Campaign Expenditures and Use of Government Funds in 1938,* 76th Cong., 1st sess., 1939, Senate Report No. 1, pt. 1, 11-19.   109. Heard and Strong, *Southern Primaries,* 47.   110. Patterson, *Congressional Conservatism,* 348; and Alan A. Michie and Frank Ryhlick, *Dixie Demagogues* (New York: Vanguard, 1939), 166.
111. Holmes Alexander, "Millard E. Tydings: The Man from Maryland," *The American Politician,* ed. John T. Salter (Chapel Hill: Univ. of North Carolina Press, 1938), 124-37.   112. Farley, *Jim Farley's Story,* 144-45.   113. *Time* 32 (Sept. 19, 1938): 27.
114. *New York Times,* July 29, 1938, 3.   115. "The New Deal Round-Up," *Nation* 147 (Aug. 13, 1938): 140; and *New York Times,* July 3, 1938, 2.
116. Shannon, "Presidential Politics in the South, II," 293.
117. Gallup, *Gallup Poll,* 1: 116; and *New York Times,* Aug. 22, 1938, 1.   118. Farley, *Jim Farley's Story,* 122; and *New York Times,* Apr. 26, 1938, 4.   119. "The President and the Primaries," *New Republic* 95 (June 29, 1938): 202; and *Time* 32 (Sept. 12, 1938): 21.
120. *New York Times,* Aug. 30, 1938, 1.
121.   Hopper, "Purge, Roosevelt and 1938 Nomination," 204-7; Roosevelt, *Complete Presidential Press Conferences,* 12: 24-25; and PPA, 7: 512-15.   122. PPA, 7: 518.   123. Ibid., 520.

124. *New York Times,* Sept. 7, 1938, 2.   125. U.S. Senate, *Report of the Special Committee,* 134-37.
126. Shannon, "Presidential Politics in the South, II," 295.
127. "Purge Will Rise Again," *New Republic* 96 (Sept. 28, 1938): 212; *New York Times,* Aug. 24, 1938, 10; and Hopper, "Purge, Roosevelt and 1938 Nomination," 200.   128. Shannon, "Presidential Politics in the South, II," 299.   129. *Congressional Digest,* 17 (Oct. 1938): 254; and *New York Times,* June 2, 1938, 1.   130. Luther H. Zeigler, Jr., "Senator Walter George's 1938 Campaign," *Georgia Historical Quarterly* 43 (Dec. 1959): 334.
131. Patterson, *Congressional Conservatism,* 45.   132. James C. Cobb, "Not Gone, But Forgotten: Eugene Talmadge and the 1938 Purge Campaign," *Georgia Historical Quarterly* 59 (Summer 1975): 201.   133. *New York Times,* Aug. 11, 1938, 1.   134. Ibid.
135. Cobb, "Not Gone, But Forgotten," 199-204.
136. *New York Times,* June 5, 1938, 41.   137. PPA, 7: 463-64.   138. Ibid., 465.   139. Ibid., 468.   140. *New York Times,* Aug. 11, 1938, 1, Aug. 12, 1938, 1.
141. PPA, 7: 470.   142. Cobb, "Not Gone, But Forgotten," 201.   143. *New York Times,* July 24, 1938, 1.   144. Zeigler, "Senator Walter George's 1938 Campaign," 337.   145. Hopper, "Purge, Roosevelt and 1938 Nomination," 169.
146. *New York Times,* Aug. 9, 1938, 2.   147. Cobb, "Not Gone, But Forgotten," 207.   148. Zeigler, "Senator Walter George's 1938 Campaign," 343-44; *Time* 32 (Aug. 22, 1938): 26; and "The President and the Primaries," *New Republic* 95 (June 29, 1938): 203.
149. Roy E. Fossett, "The Impact of the New Deal on Georgia Politics, 1933-1941" (Ph.D. diss., Univ. of Florida, 1960), 295-306; and *New York Times,* Aug. 16, 1938, 1.   150. *New York Times,* Aug. 16, 1938, 3.
151. Ibid., Aug. 21, 1938, 3.   152. Cobb, "Not Gone, But Forgotten," 284; and *New York Times,* Sept. 5, 1938, 4.   153. *New York Times,* Aug. 20, 1938, 4.   154. Zeigler, "Senator Walter George's 1938 Campaign," 350.   155. Shannon, "Presidential Politics in the South," 285.
156. Gallup, *Gallup Poll,* 1: 118.   157. American Institute of Public Opinion, poll, Sept. 4, 1938, Emil Hurja Papers, FDRL; and Heard and Strong, *Southern Primaries,* 64.   158. Shannon, "Presidential Politics in the South, II," 285.   159. *Southern Politics in State and Nation,* 242-43.   160. *New York Times,* May 17, 1938, 2.
161. Marvin Cann, "Burnet Maybank and Charleston Politics in the New Deal Era," *Proceedings of the South Carolina Historical Association,* 1970, 47-48; and *New York Times,* Aug. 14, 1938, 1.
162. *Time,* 32 (Aug. 29, 1938): 11.   163. *New York Times,* Aug. 12, 1938, 4.   164. PPA, 7: 476-77.   165. *Nation* 147 (Sept. 17, 1938): 234.

166. George B. Tindall, *The Emergence of the New South, 1913-1945* (Baton Rouge: Louisiana State Univ. Press, 1967), 629.
167. Shannon, "Presidential Politics in the South II," 288.
168. *New York Times*, Aug. 28, 1938, 5, Aug. 29, 1938, 5.
169. Hopper, "Purge, Roosevelt and 1938 Nomination," 190-195.
170. *New York Times*, Aug. 28, 1938, 5, Aug. 29, 1938, 2.
171. Byrnes, *All in One Lifetime*, 102.   172. Heard and Strong, *Southern Primaries*, 110.   173. Charles M. Price and Joseph Boskin, "The Roosevelt 'Purge': A Reappraisal," *Journal of Politics* 28 (Aug. 1966): 665.   174. Patterson, *Congressional Conservatism*, 53, 176-177.   175. Richard Polenberg, "Franklin Roosevelt and the Purge of John O'Connor: The Impact of Urban Change on Political Change," *New York History* 49 (July 1968): 306-326.
176. Flynn, *You're the Boss*, 164-65; and *New York Times*, Sept. 15, 1938, 3.   177. Lindley, "New Congress," 15-17; and Sidney M. Milkis, "Presidents and Party Purges: With Special Emphasis on the Lessons of 1938," in *Presidents and Their Parties: Leadership or Neglect?*, ed. Robert Harmel (New York: Praeger, 1984), 168.
178. Stokes, *Chip off My Shoulder*, 502.   179. Charles M. Price and Joseph Boskin, "The Roosevelt 'Purge': A Reappraisal," *Journal of Politics* 28 (August 1966): 661-62.   180. E. Pendleton Herring, *The Politics of Democracy* (New York: Norton, 1940), 222; and William H. Riker, *Democracy in the United States* (New York: Macmillan, 1965), 276.
181. Farley, *Jim Farley's Story*, 147.   182. James T. Patterson, "The Failure of Party Realignment in the South, 1937-1939," *Journal of Politics* 27 (Aug. 1965): 617.   183. Brinkley, "New Deal and Southern Politics," 108-9.   184. Clapper, "Roosevelt Tries the Primaries," 18.   185. Shannon, "Presidential Politics in the South," 296-97.
186. Ibid.   187. Price and Boskin, 669-70.   188. Hopper, "Purge, Roosevelt and 1938 Nomination," 220.   189. Ibid., p. 221.   190. Milkis, "Presidents and Party Purges, 168.
191. Ibid., 170.   192. Milkis, "New Deal, Administrative Reform," 434.   193. Milkis, "Presidents and Party Purges," 168.
194. Beer, "Liberalism and the National Idea," 74-76.   195. Donahoe, *Private Plans*, 178.
196. Schattschneider, *Party Government*, 165-66.   197. PL, 3: 805.   198. Tugwell, 461-78; and Rosenman, *Working with Roosevelt*, 176-180.   199. Stokes, *Chip off My Shoulder*, 505.
200. Frisch, *Contribution of the New Deal*, 82.
201. Ibid.   202. Brinkley, "New Deal and Southern Politics," 112-15.   203. Donahoe, *Private Plans*, 178-79.

7 The Struggle to Maintain a Liberal Party: 1940-1944

1. Milton Plesur, "Republican Congressional Comeback," 525-62; and Lindley, "New Congress," 15-17.   2. Ladd and Hadley, *Transformations*, 55.   3. Donald B. Johnson, *The Republican Party and Wendell Willkie* (Urbana: Univ. of Illinois Press, 1960), 108; and Leslie H. Southwick, *Presidential Also-Rans and Running Mates, 1788-1980* (Jefferson, N.C.: McFarland, 1984), 540-41.   4. *New York Times*, Oct. 23, 1938, 38.   5. Gallup, *Gallup Poll*, 1: 116.   6. Alsop and Kinter, *Men Around the President*, 139-40.   7. *Time* 32 (Nov. 21, 1938): 14.   8. Gallup, *Gallup Poll*, 1: 23, 28, 40.   9. Ibid., 122.   10. Plesur, "Republican Congressional Comeback," 529-31; and *Congressional Record*, 75th Cong., 1st sess., 1937, 1832, 75th Cong., 2nd sess., 1937, 301-2.

11. *New York Times*, Aug. 7, 1938, 2, Sept. 5, 1938, 2, Oct. 23, 1938, 33.   12. *Time* 32 (Nov. 7, 1938): 10.   13. Farley to James Roosevelt, Oct. 19, 1938, James A. Farley Papers, LOC; FDR to John G. Saxon, Oct. 11, 1938, President's Personal File 1763, FDRL; and *New York Times*, Nov. 10, 1938, 1, 5, 24.   14. John J. McDevitt to Marvin McIntyre, Dec. 7, 1938, Official File 300, FDRL; and *New York Times*, Nov. 10, 1938, 24.   15. Robert A. Taft, "A Republican Program," speech at Republican Party Convention of Ohio, Sept. 4, 1938, Robert A. Taft Papers, LOC.

16. Lindley, "New Congress," 15.   17. *Time* 32 (Nov. 21, 1938): 12.   18. Ibid.   19. "The Republican Party; Up from the Grave," *Fortune* 20 (Aug. 1939): 33-36; *Congressional Record*, 76th Cong., 1st sess., 1939, 3093; and *New York Times*, Mar. 22, 1939, 1.   20. James A. Farley to Worth Allen, Nov. 17, 1938, DNC Papers, FDRL.

21. Excerpts of reports from Rhode Island, South Dakota, and Wisconsin, Nov. 17, 1938, DNC Papers, FDRL.   22. C.A. Painter to Marvin McIntyre, Oct. 29, 1938; Louis J. Fruchter, telegram to FDR, Nov. 11, 1938; and J.E. Alschuler to Farley, December 15, 1938, all in Official File 300, FDRL.   23. W.W. Jones to Farley, Jan. 7, 1939; and Leo M. Mitchell to Farley, Dec. 12, 1938; both in Official File 300, FDRL.   24. Excerpts of reports from Rhode Island, South Dakota, Wisconsin, and Pennsylvania, Nov. 17, 1938; Charles R. Eckert to James A. Farley, Feb. 2, 1939, DNC Papers; and Hubert Utterback to FDR, July 24, 1939, Official File 2360; all in FDRL.   25. Harry Wirin to Hopkins, Dec. 29, 1938; Howard Hunter, press release, Sept. 21, 1938; and Bob Brackin to Hopkins, Aug. 23, 1938, Harry Hopkins Papers, FDRL.

26. James A. Farley, "Why I Broke with Roosevelt," *Collier's* 120 (July 12, 1947): 24-25, 83-85.   27. Farley, *Jim Farley's Story*, 147.   28. Frisch, *Contribution of the New Deal*, 79.   29. FDR to George L. Berry, Aug. 3, 1936, Official File 407; and FDR to Pitt Tyson Maner, Aug. 8, 1939, Official File 236; both in FDRL.   30. PPA, 8: 62.

31. Ibid., 437.   32. Ickes, *Secret Diary of Ickes*, 2: 526.
33. Ed Kelly to FDR, Apr. 1, 1940, President's Personal File 3166, FDRL; Raymond Clapper, "Return of the Two-Party System," *Current History* 49 (Dec. 1938): 14-16; and Guffey, *Seventy Years on the Red-Fire Wagon*, 114.   34. Ed Kelly to FDR, Apr. 1, 1940, President's Personal File 3166, FDRL; Raymond Clapper, "Third Term for Roosevelt?" *Current History* 50 (Aug. 1939): 13-16; and Frank R. Kent, "Great Corcoran Drive for the Third Term Idea," *Current History* 50 (July 1939): 40.   35. Roosevelt, *Complete Presidential Press Conferences*, 15: 5-6, 25-26.
36. Ickes, *Secret Diary of Ickes*, 2: 706.   37. Parmet and Hecht, *Never Again*, 10; and Frank Freidel, *Franklin Roosevelt: A Rendezous with Destiny* (Boston: Little, Brown, 1990), 343.
38. Charles, *Minister of Relief*, 214-16.   39. "McNutt for '40?" *Current History* 51 (Aug. 1939): 7; and Farley, *Jim Farley's Story*, 153.   40. Marvin McIntyre, memo to Aubrey Williams, Apr. 22, 1938, Official File 300; and William Hynes to James A. Farley, Sept. 8, 1936, DNC Papers; both in FDRL.
41. Morgan, *FDR: A Biography*, 490; and Sherwood, *Roosevelt and Hopkins*, 740-46.   42. Gallup, *Gallup Poll*, 1: 127.
43. Ibid.   44. Davenport, "It Seems There Were Two Irishmen," 76-79; and Syrett, "Farley and Glass," 89-102.   45. Ickes, *Secret Diary of Ickes*, 2: 708-9; and Farley, *Behind the Ballots*, 20-22.
46. "Washington Notes," *New Republic* 99 (June 21, 1939): 187; and Marquis James, "Poker-Playing, Whiskey-Drinking, Evil Old Man!" *Saturday Evening Post* 212 (Sept. 9, 1939): 25.   47. Donahoe, *Private Plans*, 97.   48. Tom Miller to A.J. Wirtz, Apr. 11, 1940; A.J. Wirtz to Ray Brooks, Apr. 12, 1940; both in Harry Hopkins Papers, FDRL; Ickes, *Secret Diary of Ickes*, 3: 155; and *New York Times*, May 8, 1940, 1, May 9, 1940, 12.   49. PPA, 8: 483.
50. Ickes, *Secret Diary of Ickes*, 3: 43-45.
51. Francis O. Wilcox, "The Neutrality Fight in Congress: 1939," *American Political Science Review* 33 (Oct. 1939): 811-25.
52. Patterson, *Congressional Conservatism*, 337; and Roosevelt, *Complete Presidental Press Conferences*, 16: 82.   53. Michelson, *Ghost Talks*, 198-202.   54. Donahoe, *Private Plans*, 154; Gallup, *Gallup Poll*, 1: 227; and Ross, "Roosevelt's Third Term Nomination," 80-85.   55. Porter and Johnson, *National Party Platforms*, 382-83.
56. *New York Times*, June 19, 1940, 1.   57. *Time* 34 (July 8, 1940): 12; and Johnson, *Republican Party and Wendell Willkie*, 86.   58. Porter and Johnson, *National Party Platforms*, 389-90.   59. Ibid., 390.   60. RNC, *Official Report of the Proceedings of the Twenty-Second Republican National Convention* (Washington, D.C.: Judd and Detweiler, 1940), 152-53.
61. *Newsweek* 16 (July 8, 1940): 11-18.   62. Ibid., 16.
63. *New York Times*, July 26, 1940, 1.   64. Joseph Barnes, *Willkie*

(New York: Simon & Schuster, 1952), 155.   65. *New York Times,* Jan. 17, 1940, 39, Mar. 27, 1940, 20; Wendell L. Willkie, "We, the People," *Fortune* 21 (Apr. 1940): 64-65; and Wendell L. Willkie, "The Faith That Is America," *Reader's Digest* 36 (Dec. 1939): 1-4.
66. Robert E. Burke, "Election of 1940," in *History of American Presidential Elections,* 4, (New York: Chelsea House Publishers, 1971), 2928; *New York Times,* Apr. 5, 1940, 1; and Dorothy D. Bromley, "The Education of Wendell Willkie," *Harper's* 181 (Oct. 1940): 447-85.   67. Henry O. Evjen, "The Willkie Campaign: An Unfortunate Chapter in Republican Leadership," *Journal of Politics* 14 (May 1952): 247; and *New York Times,* May 19, 1940, 2.   68. James A. Farley to FDR, Feb. 2, 1940, DNC Papers, FDRL; and Russell Kirk and James McClellan, *The Political Principles of Robert A. Taft* (New York: Fleet, 1967), 37-38.   69. *Newsweek* 16 (July 8, 1940): 13.
70. *New York Times,* June 29, 1940, 1.
71. Warren Moscow, *Roosevelt and Willkie* (Englewood Cliffs, N.J.: Prentice-Hall, 1968), 137-40.   72. *New York Times,* Sept. 24, 1940, 1, Sept. 26, 1940, 12, and Oct. 9, 1940, 1; and Wendell Willkie, "I Challenge Roosevelt," *Look* 4 (Sept. 10, 1940): 10-12.
73. Fiorello La Guardia, memo to Edward J. Flynn, Oct. 25, 1940, President's Personal File 1376, FDRL.   74. "Mister Farley's Succession," *New Republic* 102 (Apr. 8, 1940): 471; and Ed Kelly to FDR, Apr. 1, 1940, President's Personal File 3166, FDRL.   75. Ickes, *Secret Diary of Ickes,* 3: 122.
76. Ickes, *Secret Diary of Ickes,* 3: 122.   77. Farley, *Jim Farley's Story,* 268.   78. Hull, *Memoirs of Hull,* 1: 856; Tugwell, *Democratic Roosevelt,* 530-33; and Sherwood, *Roosevelt and Hopkins,* 171, 945.   79. Farley, *Behind the Ballots,* 259-62.   80. John Morton Blum, *From the Morgenthau Diaries: Years of Crisis, 1928-1938* (Boston: Houghton Mifflin, 1959), 327.
81. DNC, *Democratic Convention Manual 1940* (Washington, D.C.: DNC, 1940), 29-31, LOC; and Parmet and Hecht, *Never Again,* 38-39.   82. Louis M. Jiggits to FDR, Nov. 15, 1939, President's Personal File 2405, FDRL.   83. Donahoe, *Private Plans,* 139, 155.   84. James A. Farley, "The Parting of the Ways," *Collier's* 120 (July 19, 1947): 28, 52, 55, 57.   85. Howard Hunter to Harry Hopkins, Dec. 6, 1938; and Willis Mahoney to Hopkins, Jan. 1939, Harry Hopkins Papers, FDRL.
86. Sherwood, *Roosevelt and Hopkins,* 173-79.   87. Robert Sherwood, *Roosevelt and Hopkins,* 173-79.   88. Rosenman, *Working with Roosevelt,* 206, 210.   89. Ross, "Roosevelt's Third Term Nomination," 80-95; and DNC, *Official Report of the Proceedings of the Democratic National Convention, 1940* (Washington, D.C.: DNC, 1940), 167, LOC.   90. Carleton, "Revolution in the Nominating Convention," 224-40; and MacNeil, "How to Rig a Convention," 29.
91. FDR to Ed Kelly, July 31, 1940, President's Personal File 3166, FDRL; and PL, 3: 1045.   92. Hull, *Memoirs of Hull,* 2:

860-61.   93. Rosenman, *Working with Roosevelt*, 202.
94. "Who Willed the Third Term?," *New Republic* 53 (July 29, 1940):
135; and *Newsweek* 16 (July 29, 1940): 16.   95. Morgan, *FDR: A
Biography*, 531-34.
      96. DNC, *Convention, 1940*, 240-241, LOC.   97. Reports from
South Dakota and Wisconsin to Farley, Nov. 17, 1938, DNC Papers,
FDRL.   98. Moscow, *Roosevelt and Willkie*, 196-97; PL, 3: 1072;
and Burke, "Election of 1940," 2946.   99. Hugh A. Bone, *Smear
Politics: An Analysis of 1940 Campaign Literature* (Washington,
D.C.: American Council on Public Affairs, 1941), 8; and Theodore M.
Black, *Democratic Party Publicity in the 1940 Campaign* (New York:
Plymouth, 1941), 54-60.   100. Henry O. Evjen, "Analysis of Some
of the Propaganda Features of the Campaign of 1940," *Southwest
Social Science Quarterly* 27 (Dec. 1946): 254; and Bone, *Smear
Politics*, 9.
      101. Evjen, "Willkie Campaign," 241-256.   102. Edward C.
Johnston to Emil Hurja, Nov. 1, 1940, Emil Hurja Papers, FDRL;
and Moscow, *Roosevelt and Willkie*, 133.   103. Key, *Politics, Parties, and Pressure Groups*, 598.   104. Irving Bernstein, "John L.
Lewis and the Voting Behavior of the C.I.O.," *Public Opinion Quarterly* 50 (June 1941): 234; and Edwin Watson, memo to FDR, Oct. 17,
1940, Official File 300, FDRL.   105. Gosnell, *Champaign Campaigner* 187.
      106. Burke, "Election of 1940," 2946; and *New York Times*,
Nov. 6, 1940, 1-2, 4, 9, 18.   107. Moscow, *Roosevelt and Willkie*,
188-89.   108. Tugwell, *Democratic Roosevelt*, 412.   109. Donahoe, *Private Plans*, 178.   110. Leon Friedman, "Election of 1944,"
in *History of American Presidential Elections, 1789-1968*, ed. Arthur
M. Schlesinger, Jr., (New York: McGraw-Hill, 1971), 3: 3010; and
Time 40 (Nov. 16, 1942): 16.
      111. Morgan, *FDR: A Biography*, 528; and James McGregor
Burns, *Roosevelt: Soldier of Freedom* (New York: Harcourt, Brace,
Jovanovich, 1970), 274 (hereafter cited as *Soldier of Freedom*).
112. FDR to James Cox, Apr. 10, 1943, President's Personal File 53,
FDRL.   113. Hull, *Memoir of Hull*, 2: 1154; Edward L. Schapsmeier and Frederick H. Schapsmeier, *Prophet in Politics: Henry A.
Wallace and the War Years, 1940-1965* (Ames: Iowa State Univ.
Press, 1970), 14-21; and Young, *Congressional Politics*, 22-24.
114. *Newsweek* 20 (Nov. 12, 1942): 43-54; and Gallup, *Gallup Poll*, 1:
348-49.   115. PL, 4: 1355; and Sherwood, *Roosevelt and Hopkins*,
658.
      116. Friedman, "Election of 1944," 3010-11.   117. *Newsweek*
20 (Nov. 16, 1942): 46.   118. Ladd and Hadley, *Transformations*,
98-99.   119. *Newsweek* 20 (Nov. 16, 1942): 46.   120. Clarence
A. Berdahl, "Political Parties and Elections," *American Political
Science Review* 37 (Feb. 1943): 68-81.
      121. *New York Times*, Feb. 1, 1944, 13, Feb. 11, 1944, 18.

122. Young, *Congressional Politics*, 119.   123. PPA, 12: 33-34.
124. Ibid., 41-42.   125. PPA, 12: 574.
  126. Ibid. 13: 32-44.   127. Burns, *Soldier of Freedom*, 424.
128. PPA, 13: 41.   129. Ibid.   130. Friedman, "Election of
1944," 3010-14; and "President Roosevelt's Message on Servicemen's
Vote Bill," newspaper clipping, *Philadelphia Record*, Apr. 1, 1944,
DNC Papers, FDRL.
  131. Libbey, *Dear Alben*, 85.   132. PPA, 13: 53-60.
133. Guffey, *Seventy Years on the Red-Fire Wagon*, 150-51; and Allen
Drury, *A Senate Journal, 1943-1945* (New York: McGraw-Hill,
1963), 45, 60-61.   134. *Congressional Record*, 77th Cong., 2nd
sess., 1942, 7065; and *New York Times*, Mar. 4, 1944, 1.
135. Young, *Congressional Politics*, 83; and *New York Times*, Jan.
27, 1944, 18.
  136. *Time*, 44 (Feb. 7, 1944): 3.   137. Stanley H. Lowell, "Votes
for Negroes?" *Nation* 158 (Apr. 22, 1944): 470-72.   138. *Congressional Record*, 78th Cong., 2nd sess., 1944, 6937; and *New York
Times*, Aug. 12, 1944, 1.   139. *New York Times*, Mar. 5, 1944,
26.   140. Ibid., Mar. 9, 1944, 26.
  141. Young, *Congressional Politics*, 87-88.   142. *New York
Times*, Mar. 20, 1944, 1.   143. Ibid., Apr. 1, 1944, 1.   144. PPA,
13: 114.   145. RNC, *Official Report of Twenty-Third National
Convention* 7.
  146. Johnson, *Republican Party and Wendell Willkie*, 298-99.
147. Gallup, *Gallup Poll*, 1: 435; *New York Times*, Apr. 6, 1944, 1;
and *Time* 44 (July 10, 1944): 17-26.   148. Richard N. Smith,
Thomas E. Dewey and His Times, (New York: Simon and Schuster,
1982) 352-92.   149. Frank Kingdon, *The Inside Story of the Coming Election* (New York: Arco, 1944), 2-4.   150. RNC, *Official
Report of Twenty-Third National Convention*, 216-17.
  151. *New York Times*, June 27, 1944, 1; and *Time* 44 (July 10,
1944): 20.   152. Porter and Johnson, *National Party Platforms*,
407-8; and RNC *Official Report of Twenty-Third National Convention*, 138.   153. Ibid., 140.   154. *New Republic* 111 (July 10,
1944): 33-34.   155. Evjen, "Willkie Campaign," 241-56.
  156. *Time* 44 (Sept. 18, 1944): 222; Smith, *Thomas E. Dewey*, 412;
and *New York Times*, Sept. 8, 1944, 12.   157. Guffey, *Seventy
Years on the Red-Fire Wagon*, 151-52.   158. Key, *Politics, Parties,
and Pressure Groups*, 401.   159. Sherwood, *Roosevelt and Hopkins*, 740-41.   160. Rosenman, *Working with Roosevelt*, 444-45.
  161. James F. Byrnes, *All in One Lifetime* (New York: Harper,
Row, 1958), 227-28.   162. Kingdon, *Inside Story*, 5.   163. Ladd
and Hadley, *Transformations*, 80.   164. Shuff, "Partisan Realignment," 216.   165. Friedman, "Election of 1944," 3014.
  166. "Complete National Plan for the Precinct Victory Drive,"
pamphlet, Oct. 5, 1944; and Mrs. Charles W. Tillett, memo to Bob
Hannegan, Aug. 22, 1944, both in DNC Papers, FDRL.

167. "Organization—County and Precinct Party Officials," undated memo, 1944 election, DNC Papers, FDRL.   168. Smith, *Thomas E. Dewey,* 433.; and Calkin, *CIO and Democratic Party,* 1-11. 169. *Congressional Record,* 78th Cong., 1st sess., vol. 89, 1943, 6487-88.   170. Overacker, *Presidential Campaign Funds,* 58-63. 171. "Hillman Assails Record of Dewey," clipping, *New York Times,* Sept. 10, 1944, Official File 407, FDRL.   172. Joseph Rosenbarb, "Labor's Role in the Election," *Public Opinion Quarterly* 8 (Fall 1944): 376-90; and Louis Waldman, "Will the CIO Capture the Democratic Party?" *Saturday Evening Post* 217 (Aug. 26, 1944): 22.   173. Clipping, *Life* 17 (Nov. 20, 1944): 24, DNC Papers, FDRL.   174. Ibid.   175. Ladd and Hadley, *Transformations,* 71.

176. Eldersveld, "The Influence of Metropolitan Party Pluralities," 1198-1206.

Epilogue: FDR's Legacy in the Democratic Party

1. Gosnell, *Champion Campaigner,* 219-20; Nock, "WPA, the Modern Tammany," 215-19; and Smith, *Thomas E. Dewey,* 423-25.   2. Edgar E. Robinson, "The Roosevelt Leadership," in *The New Deal: What Was It?* ed. Morton Keller (New York: Holt, Rinehart and Winston, 1963), 46; and H.L. Mencken, "Three Years of Dr. Roosevelt," *American Mercury* 37 (Oct. 1936): 257-65.   3. V.O. Key, Jr., *The Responsible Electorate* (New York: Vintage, 1966), 56.   4. Frisch, *Contribution of the New Deal,* 74-75; and Donahoe, *Private Plans,* 178.   5. Burns, 206-8; and Floyd B. Olson, "My Political Creed," *Common Sense* 4 (Apr. 1935): 6-7.

6. Arthur M. Schlesinger, Jr., *The Cycles of American History* (Boston: Houghton Mifflin, 1986), 266-67.   7. William E. Leuchtenburg, *In the Shadow of FDR: From Harry Truman to Ronald Reagan* (Ithaca: Cornell Univ. Press, 1985), 28-31; Irwin Ross, *The Loneliest Campaign: The Truman Victory of 1948* (New York: New American Library, 1968), 263; and Allen Yarnell, *Democrats and Progressives: The 1948 Presidential Election as a Test of Postwar Liberalism* (Berkeley: Univ. of California Press, 1974), 62-86. 8. Sundquist, *Dynamics of the Party System,* 216.   9. Herbert S. Parmet, *The Democrats: The Years after FDR* (New York: Macmillan, 1976), 65.   10. Ross, *Loneliest Campaign,* 265; and Leuchtenburg, *In the Shadow of FDR,* 121-42.

11. Monroe Billington, "Civil Rights, President Truman, and the South," *Journal of Negro History* 58 (Apr. 1973): 127-39; Key, *Southern Politics in State and Nation,* 332-35; and *Congressional Record,* 80th Cong., 2nd sess., 1948, 928-29.   12. Weiss, *Party of Lincoln,* 274-80; and Harvard Sitkoff, "Harry Truman and the Election of 1948: The Coming of Age of Civil Rights in American Politics,"

Journal of Southern History 37 (Nov. 1971): 597-616.   13. Gallup, *Gallup Poll*, 1: 739, 745, 749; Clifton Brock, *Americans for Democratic Action: Its Role in National Politics* (Washington, D.C.: Public Affairs Press, 1962), 100-103; and Alonzo L. Hamby, *Beyond the New Deal: Harry S. Truman and American Liberalism* (New York: Columbia Univ. Press, 1973): 250-51.   14. Alonzo L. Hamby, *Liberalism and Its Challengers: FDR to Reagan* (New York: Oxford Univ. Press, 1985), 69-70.   15. Pepper, *Pepper*, 158-68; and Kirk and McClellan, *Political Principles of Taft*, 174.

16. JFK to William Loeb, July 10, 1957, Theodore Sorenson Papers, John F. Kennedy Library; and Larry German, "Lyndon B. Johnson: Paths Chosen and Opportunities Lost," *Leadership in the Modern Presidency*, ed. Fred Greenstein (Cambridge, Mass.: Harvard University Press, 1988), 134-35.   17. Robert A. Caro, *The Years of Lyndon Johnson: Means of Ascent* (New York: Knopf, 1990), xix-xxxiv; and Leuchtenburg, *In the Shadow of FDR*, 121-60.
18. Jonathan Rieder, "The Rise of the 'Silent Majority,'" in *The Rise and Fall of the New Deal Order, 1930-1980*, ed. Steve Fraser and Gary Gerstle (Princeton, N.J.: Princeton Univ. Press, 1989), 24-68.   19. Ladd and Hadley, *Transformations*, 266; Thomas B. Edsall, "The Changing Shape of Power," *The Rise and Fall of the New Deal Order, 1930-1980*, ed. by Steve Fraser and Gary Gerstle, 285; and Sundquist, *Dynamics of the Party System*, 183-217.
20. Leuchtenburg, *In the Shadow of FDR*, ix-x; Richard S. Kirkendall, "The Election of 1948," *History of American Presidential Elections*, 4, (New York: Chelsea House, 1971), 3144-45.
21. Morris Fiorina, *Retrospective Voting in American National Elections* (New Haven: Yale Univ. Press, 1981), 202; David F. Prindle, "Voter Turnout, Critical Elections, and the New Deal Realignment," *Social Science History* 3 (Winter 1979): 144-70; and Barbara Sinclair, *Congressional Realignment, 1925-1978* (Austin: University of Texas Press, 1982), 83-105.   22. Hugh A. Bone, *American Politics and the Party System* (New York: McGraw-Hill, 1949), 87; Clinton Rossiter, *Parties and Politics in America* (Ithaca: Cornell Univ. Press, 1960), 74-75, 122-23; and Everett C. Ladd, Jr., *American Political Parties: Social Change and Political Change* (New York: Norton, 1970), 208-18.   23. Hamby, *Liberalism and Its Challengers*, 50-51; Otis L. Graham, Jr., "The Democratic Party, 1932-1945," *History of U.S. Political Parties* 3, ed. Arthur M. Schlesinger, Jr. (New York: Chelsea House, 1973), 1962; and Vladimir O. Pechatnov, "Franklin D. Roosevelt and the Democratic Party," in *Franklin D. Roosevelt: The Man, the Myth, the Era, 1882-1945*, ed. Herbert D. Rosenbaum and Elizabeth Bartelme (Westport, Conn.: Greenwood, 1987), 56-57.

Index

CPSIA information can be obtained at www.ICGtesting.com
Printed in the USA
LVOW11*0719120815

449726LV00002B/25/P